"The American Negro has been fashioned, body, mind, and spirit, in the New World."

In this remarkably objective and informed report the award-winning author and journalist Louis E. Lomax takes a searching new look at American history——from the early seventeenth century up to the present——as he traces some three hundred years of struggle, during which the American Negro has sought to attain full freedom.

He clarifies the current racial movement and explains that it is directed not only against the prevailing white power-structure, but also against the old guard, ultra-conservative Negro organizations. Here you will learn about the dedicated groups of people, both white and Negro, who guide the revolt, about where they get their support and what their problems and goals are. Here is the inside story of Washington and Dixie, North and South . . . the unflinching truth about the subjugated Americans who are testing the conscience of democracy and the validity of the Constitution as they militantly demand their American rights in THE NEGRO REVOLT.

"He has written what is far and away the best book on the Negro of the present that I have read. He is honest, realistic, forthright, moving and, at times, profound."—Washington (D. C.) Sunday Star

"Read Louis Lomax's new book seriously and you're going to have trouble getting to sleep tonight—or any night."—Newark News

Signet and Mentor Books
of Related Interest

Louis E. Lomax

THE
NEGRO
REVOLT

A SIGNET BOOK
Published by The New American Library

32869

SIGNET TRADEMARK REG. U.S. PAT. OFF. AND FOREIGN COUNTRIES
REGISTERED TRADEMARK—MARCA REGISTRADA
HECHO EN CHICAGO, U.S.A.

SIGNET BOOKS are published by The New American Library, Inc., 1301 Avenue of the Americas, New York, New York 10019

PRINTED IN THE UNITED STATES OF AMERICA

To Hugh, my ten-year-old son, in the faith that his will be a better nation, and in the hope that his color will never be a curse or a blessing. For if the Negro revolt succeeds, he will have to take his stand as a man. And that, with God's help, is what I am rearing him to be.

CONTENTS

ACKNOWLEDGMENTS

Such a book as this is born in debt. The debt can never be paid; I can only pause to mention some of the writers and reporters whose materials I have drawn upon for my presentation.

Dr. E. Franklin Frazier's *Black Bourgeoisie,* Dr. John Hope Franklin's *From Slavery to Freedom* and Lerone Bennett, Jr.'s excellent series on Negro history in *Ebony* magazine were my Bibles. Both of James Baldwin's books, *Notes of a Native Son* and *Nobody Knows My Name,* were invaluable. Equally helpful were the various house organs and research papers printed by the NAACP, the Urban League, the Southern Christian Leadership Conference, the Southern Regional Council and the Student Non Violent Coordinating Committee. The several reports of the President's Commission on Civil Rights provided much of the data cited in this book and I wish to thank my friend Otto McLaurin, a member of the staff of the Commission, for sending these reports to me as fast as they came off the press.

Several persons read and gave valuable criticisms of the manuscript. Among them are Dr. John Hope Franklin, the Reverend James Robinson, Dr. Kenneth Clark, Judge Thurgood Marshall, and Mrs. Nancy Wechsler. Henry Moon, publicist for the NAACP, Guichard Paris, publicist for the Urban League, Maggie Long of the Southern Regional Council and the Reverend Wyatt Tee Walker of the Southern Christian Leadership Conference provided me with many time-saving suggestions and pointers as I went about studying their respective organizations. I wish to thank all of them for their efforts.

I also wish to thank William Dabney, Jr. and Ann Brown for their help as readers of the final draft, during the late hours of the night when my eyes were so tired I could only read what I had intended to write rather than what, indeed, I had written.

A special thanks to my editor, Genevieve Young, who worked even on her days off to give this book organizational soundness and impartial criticism.

Most of all I wish to express my thanks to my wife, Betty, who resigned herself to the role of a writer's widow, although I was only a few feet away, through the long days and nights of my research and writing.

"Greater than the tread of mighty armies is the idea whose time has arrived."
　　　　　　　　　　—Victor Hugo

The Britannica World Language Dictionary defines a revolt, among other things, as an extensive or drastic change in a condition, method or idea. And it is in this precise sense that I contend that the American Negro has been in a state of revolt for more than five years.

The Negro revolt involves a drastic change in our methods and ideas concerning segregation and established Negro leadership organizations.

Concerning segregation, the revolt lies in the fact that we not only have decided that the last vestige of that evil must be eliminated, but have embraced a new methodology, and armed ourselves with new weapons in our war against segregation and all of its concomitants.

And the revolt against the established Negro leadership organizations has come about because these organizations are wed to weapons which, though they accomplished some gains, have proved incapable of dealing segregation a final death blow.

To say that we have revolted against certain methods and the civil rights organizations that sponsored them is not to say that we have completely abandoned or turned against them; rather, it means that we Negroes have demanded tactical changes, that our traditional leadership organizations have debated, rather than acted upon, our demands, and that while the established Negro leaders were still locked in the methodological debate, rank-and-file Negroes have moved on their own, employed new tactics and achieved incomparable results. As a result, established Negro leadership is in the position of the oddly dressed man who said to a bystander, "Please tell me which way the parade went; after all, I'm leading it."

To understand the Negro revolt one must stay his anxiety about Albany, Georgia; Little Rock, Arkansas; McComb, Mississippi; and the growing cleavage between the several Negro leadership organizations long enough to recall the basic elements of Negro history. For it is only after one remembers this history that he can understand the Negro present; and until both the Negro past and present are clarified it is utter nonsense to offer suggestions about the Negro's future.

The American Negro revolt is one of the nonwhite uprisings now sweeping the world. In every single case, the black man has a grievance against the white man; these grievances are already couched in bitterness, and many serious thinkers, Negro and white, believe they could one day soon burst into open and bloody conflict. In a very real sense, the American Negro holds the key to the rise of nonwhite peoples all over the world. And to the degree that the question of the American Negro is admitted and resolved, the probability of a world free from racial strife is increased.

It is in this spirit and in this hope that this book has been written.

LOUIS E. LOMAX

Jamaica, New York
January, 1962

PART I

A Negro View of American History

1.

BACKGROUND OF THE REVOLT

DAY WAS DONE, and Mrs. Rosa Parks was tired. Her job as a seamstress in the Montgomery Fair, a department store, was demanding; and what with fitting after fitting, customer after customer, garment after garment, Mrs. Parks welcomed approaching nightfall with its promise of home and rest.

"Home" and "rest"—these were meaningful words to Rosa Parks. A widow in her early fifties, Mrs. Parks had been forced to spend all too many days and nights away from home at work. Working tirelessly—sometimes at two jobs—she had educated three children. Yet Mrs. Parks was well preserved: an olive-skinned, freckle-faced woman, her attractiveness had been ripened, rather than destroyed, by the years. Soft-spoken, diminutive but plump, Mrs. Parks could easily have been mistaken for a schoolteacher. As a matter of fact, had you seen her as she walked out of the Montgomery Fair late on the afternoon of December 1, 1955, chances are that you would have thought Rosa Parks was a customer. She wore a tailored, two-piece blue suit, and her long black hair was parted in the center and combed to the sides, flowing down over her ears and covering the hooks in the rims of her glasses. As she walked toward the bus stop a slight limp became evident, a favoring of her left foot; Rosa Parks it seems to me, to isolate and understand the forces that have shaped the Negro into what he is today. Until we do this, we are dealing in nothing but comfortable presumptions.

The American Negro is a man—not God—made race. We are the result of alliances between slave masters and their female slaves. (There were liaisons between Negro men and white women of the pre-Civil War era but all scholars agree that the white man-Negro woman relationship was, by far, the more frequent.) This indisputable historical and biological fact has caused Southern states to spend thousands of dollars and millions of man-hours trying to determine just who among them are Negroes. Prior to 1910, the state of Virginia decreed that a Negro was anyone with one-fourth or more Negro blood in him. By 1910 the burgeoning number of non-negroid Negroes caused the keepers of white purity to revise their thinking and declare that one was Negro if he had as much as one-sixteenth Negro blood in his veins. By 1930 this definition was not sufficient to maintain the bastions of white supremacy and it was enacted into Virginia law that anyone having "any quantum of Negro blood whatsoever" was a Negro.

Blood sampling aside, the fact remains that few of today's Negroes are of pure African descent. Biologically, then, we were fashioned in the New World; every conceivable blood flows in our veins. We speak an Anglo-Saxon tongue, worship the Christian God, and our political ideals are identical with those of this nation's founding fathers.

Thus the American Negro does not have a culture in the precise and classic sense of that word. Although we are socially and economically segregated from the American mainstream, we are culturally integrated with it. We speak the language of the majority and, when allowed to, we participate in majority institutions. When not allowed, we form our own institutions and pattern them after those of the majority. Thus the only difference between the Negro Baptist Church and the Baptist Church proper is that Negroes attend the former and white people attend the latter.

This, of course, is a sore point with Negroes as well as white people. Since the general histories of this nation omit the deeds and contributions of the Negro, there is a tendency on the part of many Negroes to isolate their contribution to the nation and cite it as a culture. Only in the loosest sense can it be called that. Rather the Negro, like America itself, is a participant in and contributor to what the late Professor Solomon Bloom of Brooklyn College called "Atlantic Civilization." We are a product of the hammering out of a way of life that has been going on in "Atlantic" countries—in the Old World and the New —for centuries.

The American Negro has been fashioned, body, mind and spirit, in the New World. Unlike other "minorities" in American society, we Negroes do not share a positive sense of identity. Alas, the only thing one Negro has exclusively in common with another Negro is the animus of the white man.

There is no denying that, historically, the white majority is the founder of Atlantic Civilization, nor can it be questioned that our African ancestors were introduced into this culture as handymen. Once here, however, the Negro not only absorbed the culture but made remarkable contributions to its evolution. We have remained marginal members of this civilization because only doors on the periphery have been opened to us. We cannot change our color; instead, our efforts have been directed toward achieving what must be called "cultural whiteness," although we and our ancestors made substantial contributions to that culture. We sought this cultural whiteness in the now apparently ill-fated hope that acquiring the manners and value system of the majority would merit us the rights and the freedoms enjoyed by white people.

This cultural confusion has everything to do with the current Negro revolt. It explains the deep schism within the Negro race and it accounts for the fact that the Negro individual has no hope of final and secure identification except with the general American social structure. And so it is that the American Negro is the only American who, as an individual, must reach beyond his own group for absolute identification; therefore we Negroes are the only Americans unwilling to make even the slightest compromise with the American creed as stated by the founding fathers. We have an ultimate and final stake in the triumph of Atlantic Civilization, intact, without reservations and with all the chaotic possibilities involved in the proposition that the voice of the people, rightly heard, is the voice of God and that, indeed, all men are created free and, in that sense, equal.

To understand the Negro one must reread *The Federalist,* come to grips anew with the basic assumptions about man, God and government that guided Hamilton, Madison and Jay. These are the political ideals that drive the Negro as he seeks integration or "cultural whiteness," and Negro history is but our continuing efforts to escape the boundaries placed upon us by the white majority and to find identification in the American main-stream. We have made some progress, but, on the whole, our every effort toward majority identification, regardless of the tool we employed, has been thwarted. Now we are employing a new weapon, or at least an old weapon with a new militancy in our hearts. This, in essence, is what the Negro revolt is about.

2.

THE AMERICAN REVOLUTION
AND ITS AFTERMATH

THE GENERAL TENDENCY is to think of the Negro as a slave, first introduced to this country in 1619. Nothing could be further from the truth.[1] Negroes—in large numbers, as explorers and as servants—came with the first Europeans as they set out to exploit the resources of the New World. Thirty Negroes, including Nuflo de Olano, were with Balboa when he discovered the Pacific. Cortez carried Negroes with him into Mexico and one of them is recorded as having reaped the first wheat crop of the New World. Several Negroes were with Narváez on his expedition of 1527, and many more were with Cabeza de Vaca in the exploration of the Southwestern part of the United States. Not only were Negroes with the French during the conquest of the Mississippi Valley in the seventeenth century, but they were among the first pioneers to settle there.

The Negro was involved from the very beginning in the problems of America, first as a group of colonies, then as a nation. It is estimated that some ten thousand free Negroes and indentured servants were in the United States

[1]Much of the material in this section is drawn from John Hope Franklin's *From Slavery to Freedom* (Knopf) and Lerone Bennett, Jr.'s excellent magazine series on the history of the American Negro.

by the first quarter of the seventeenth century, the period during which slavery became widespread. In fact, slaves were introduced to America after, and only because, efforts to make slaves of Indians and white indentured servants failed. The Indians proved totally unsuitable for arduous labor beneath the scorching Southern sun, and white indentured servants, though somewhat more effective, were too hard to keep track of. They refused to renew their terms of indenture, and when forced into it ran away and became indistinguishable from the general white populace. Africans, on the other hand, were easily recoverable if they ran away and were a good deal less informed as to their rights and privileges than were their fellow white servants. Thus, starting in 1619, Negroes were imported in large numbers and with time they passed from indentured servitude into slavery.

Despite the rise of the institution of slavery the Negro never wavered in his loyalty to the American dream. Indeed, free Negroes played a major role in the colonial agitation that preceded the American Revolution. Negroes were not only among the mob that rushed into the streets of Boston on Friday, March 2, 1770, but a Negro was in the lead.

"You black rascal," a white loyalist called out, "what have you to do with white people's quarrels?"

"I suppose I may look on!" the Negro leader of the mob shouted back. But the Negro did more than look on; he knocked the white man down and that was the signal for full-scale bedlam. Boston boiled Saturday and Sunday, and late Monday afternoon eight British soldiers emerged from their barracks armed with cudgels and tongs and marched on the Boston Patriots. The Patriots were led by Crispus Attucks, a Negro and runaway slave. Moving among his fellow Patriots, Attucks exhorted them to stand firm. Insults were exchanged, fights broke out, somebody ran to the old brick Meeting House and rang the fire bell. The people poured into the streets shouting for independence and the Boston Massacre was under way. The British fired; the first man to fall, dead, was Attucks.

A monument to him now stands in Boston's Common.

"From that moment on," Daniel Webster wrote later, "we may date the severance of the British Empire." John Adams was even more specific: "Not the Battle of Lexington or Bunker Hill, not the surrender of Burgoyne or Cornwallis were more important events in American history than the Battle of King Street on the 5th of March, 1770."

Attucks and his fellow Negroes who died in the Revolutionary War—there were over five thousand of them—epitomized the Negro's involvement with America. Slavery was then one hundred and fifty years old, free Negroes had been in the nation for over two hundred years and it was clear that by historical fate they had no alternative but to identify with the American dream. Then, as now, Negroes used their participation in the war as a basis for demanding a better role in the American mainstream. And, as they do now, they had their supporters. Abigail Adams once said to her husband, John, "It always appeared a most iniquitous scheme to me to fight ourselves daily for that which we are robbing and plundering from those who had as good a right to freedom as we have."

Thomas Jefferson, himself a slaveholder, was troubled by the same thing; he made an attempt to include a section in the Declaration of Independence that would have condemned the King of England for allowing the slave trade, and he then went on to advocate the abolition of slavery. Both of Jefferson's attempts failed; the compromises that went into the Constitution and the Declaration of Independence indicated that the new nation was to be ruled by a coalition of power forces which was unwilling to take the economic and social risks involved in the abolition of slavery.

Jefferson's concern was prophetic, and his brooding about the Negro sums up the gnawing doubt that was to plague good men, Negro and white, about the future of an America in which the two races, both free, would try and live side by side, in peace and harmony.

"Nothing is more certainly written in the book of fate,"

Jefferson said, "than that these people [Negroes] are to be free; nor is it less certain that the two races, equally free, cannot live in the same government. Nature, habit, opinion, have drawn indelible lines of distinction between them. It is still in our power to direct the process of emancipation and deportation, peaceably, and in such slow degree, as the evil will wear off insensibly, and their place be filled up by white laborers."

But deportation of America's Negroes was as impractical as emancipation, and for the same reasons. That was the economics of the issue; the moral question was even more troubling for a new nation that had shed blood in the name of freedom, independence and individual dignity.

The slaves realized this and they sounded a note disturbingly similar to that struck by today's Negro rebels as this nation struggles with the Communist threat. Petitioning the Massachusetts Assembly of 1777 for their freedom, the slaves wrote: "That every principle from which America has acted in the course of her difficulties with Great Britain, bears stronger than a thousand arguments in favor of your humble petitioners."

This is a classic example of the Negro's jargon when he talks to the white man. In plain, liberated English the slaves were saying that it was incongruous that a nation that fought for freedom and independence allowed slavery and discrimination within its own borders.

Many right-thinking white people realized that racialism was a social cancer, and records of the post-Revolutionary era show they attempted to do something about it. At least two prominent Negro ministers were called to pastor "white" churches. But this era was short-lived. The Haitian Revolt of 1791 and the Virginia slave uprising of 1800 cost the Negro many supporters, but the main reason for the retrogression was the impact of the Industrial Revolution upon the New World. By 1783 the economy of the South was in danger; the nation was in a depression, soil erosion and a gutted market had all but killed the tobacco trade, and it appeared that Southern plantation owners would have no alternative but to release their slaves. But they refused to do so, feeling certain that a better day would come. The invention of the cotton gin proved to be that day. The gin made the handling of cotton faster and cheaper, and thus even more slaves were needed to till the field and ready King Cotton for the whirling machines of the South. As a result slavery increased. In 1803, for example, over twenty thousand additional slaves were imported into Georgia and South Carolina.

Thus it was that the power forces controlling the new nation allowed the Negro to be sucked into a situation as bad as, if not worse than, he had endured before the Revolution.

The Negro soon realized this. There is no more troubling cry in American history than that emitted by Prince Hall as he addressed the Negro Masons in Philadelphia in 1787:

". . . Patience, I say; for were we not possessed of a great measure of it, we could not bear up under the daily insults we meet with on the streets of Boston, much more on the public days of recreation. How, at such times, are we shamefully abused, and that to such a degree, that we may truly be said to carry our lives in our hands, and the arrows of death are flying about our heads."

With free Negroes living in terror and the remainder groveling in the shackles of slavery, Negroes continued their involvement with America by adopting the precise values and manners of the white population. Austin Stewart, an ex-slave who wrote his autobiography in 1857, gives this account of social life on the slave plantation:

House servants were, of course, the stars of the party; all eyes were turned on them to see how they conducted themselves, for they, among the slaves, are what military men call "fugle men." The field hands and such others of them as have been generally excluded from the dwellings of their owners, look to the house servants as patterns of politeness and gentility. And, indeed, it was often the only method of gaining any knowledge of the manners of what is called "genteel society"; hence, they are ever regarded as a privileged class; and are sometimes greatly envied, while others are bitterly hated.

Free Negroes divided along similar lines. By 1848 there were upwards of 488,000 free Negroes in the United States. The ownership of land was the principle source of wealth open to them and they took advantage of it. In 1830 free Negroes in Virginia owned 32,000 acres of land valued at $185,000. North Carolina records show that, as of 1860, slightly more than 10 percent, or 3,659 of the 30,463 free Negroes in the state, owned land having a total value of half a million dollars. The situation in Louisiana was even more impressive. A class of mulattoes or *gens de couleur* had gained considerable status. Surviving records show they owned plantations ranging in value from forty thousand to two hundred thousand dollars. Dr. John Hope Franklin suggests that at least four thousand Negroes owned slaves as of 1860 and that, with the exception of those living in Louisiana, most of them were urban dwellers. It is impossible to say how many Negroes bought slaves for humanitarian reasons, but it is clear that the bulk of the Negro slaveowners were motivated by the same factor that impelled white slaveowners: profit. Thus there was in the nineteenth century a substantial moneyed class of free Negroes, some of whom owned slaves. The social and personal lives of these free Negroes were limited, to be sure, but, all things considered, they were comfortable. They set themselves apart from the masses of free Negroes as well as from the slaves. Thus, by a curious contortion of American values, these free and moneyed Negroes developed a vested interest in the *status quo,* that is to say, slavery.

These peculiarly isolated free Negroes dug in and produced an impressive class of artisans. Among the 700 employed free Negroes in Charleston as of 1850, for example, were 122 carpenters, 87 tailors, 30 shoemakers, 18 bricklayers, 23 butchers, 10 bootmakers and 11 painters. Other records show that Southern free Negroes were cigar makers, brokers, clerks, teachers and capitalists. It is estimated that free Negroes accumulated over fifty million dollars in real and personal wealth by the Civil War.

The compelling thing about this is the spirit and alacrity with which free Negroes went about the business of money-making. Dr. E. Franklin Frazier of Howard University makes this incisive observation:

"The savings and business undertakings of the Negro reflected the spirit and values of their environment. Through thrift and savings, white American artisans hoped to accumulate wealth and get ahead. This spirit was encouraged among free Negroes by their leaders, one of whom was described as 'the black Benjamin Franklin.' In fact, these free Negroes were trained in the 'old style' bourgeois spirit represented by Benjamin Franklin."

But not all free Negroes of the pre-Civil War era were preoccupied with the Puritan values of thrift and saving. The Revolution unleashed a bevy of Black Abolitionists upon the Republic. By 1830 there were at least fifty Negro organizations demanding the end of slavery; by 1844 their patience had worn thin, and they were advocating violence as a means of overthrowing slavery. At the Buffalo Convention of Colored Citizens in 1842, Henry Highland Garnet delivered a speech that shocked even the white abolitionists. Said Garnet:

"Brethren, arise, arise! Strike for your lives and liberty. Now is the day and the hour. Let every slave throughout the land do this and the days of slavery are numbered. No oppressed people have secured their liberty without resistance."

The Black Abolitionists were joined by such white liberals as William Lloyd Garrison, James G. Birney and Prudence Crandall, to say nothing of John Brown and John Fairfield. Thus encouraged, slaves escaped en masse and made their way to the Northern states and Canada via the famous Underground Railroad. Governor Quitman of Mississippi declared that in the five decades between 1810 and 1860 the South lost more than one hundred thousand slaves valued at more than thirty million dollars. Current scholars have concluded that the Governor was fairly accurate. Available records show that more than forty thousand slaves passed through Ohio alone en route to freedom.

One of the great sins of general American history is that it omits the heroic deeds of the white and Negro "officials" of the Underground Railroad. As certainly as Washington and Jefferson and Adams were the fathers of our country, these abolitionists were the saviors of our ethical and political heritage. They realized that the real enemy of freedom is within, not without, our country. And they scorched that enemy with the searchlight of world opinion. The white child never reads of these patriots, and their contribution to our tradition of freedom is omitted. As a result the Negro sit-ins and freedom riders look like Topsy; it is as if they "jest growed," whereas they are but another in the long line of courageous Americans who clanged freedom's bells while others would mute them:

Jane Lewis, a slight but strong woman from New Lebanon, Ohio, who moved by night, rowing fugitive slaves across the Ohio River.

John Parker, who purchased his freedom for two thousand dollars (only God knows how he did it) and then joined up with John Rankin, a white abolitionist, in the Underground Railroad.

Josiah Henderson, born a slave, who escaped with his wife and children to Canada, where he learned to read and write. Once he was literate, Henderson made frequent trips back into the South and aided other slaves in their escape to freedom.

Then there was Harriet Tubman, easily the best known of the Underground Railroad officials. Miss Tubman was sickly, suffering from frequent dizzy spells, but she not only escaped from slavery herself but returned to the South at least nine times and conducted more than three hundred slaves to freedom. Completely illiterate, she handled her slave caravans with the iron fist of a Western wagon master. She started her runaway caravans on Saturday night and was well on her way by the time the slaveowners got around to reporting their missing property on Monday morning. She was equally resolute with the slaves once they were aboard her caravan. She threatened to kill all slaves who expressed a desire to turn back. Prior to 1850, Miss Tubman delivered her slaves to freedom in Philadelphia, Boston or New York. But once the Fugitive Slave Act was passed, giving owners the right to recover their slaves from free states, she delivered her charges into Canada.

✓The arresting thing about the Negro abolitionists— other than their deeds, that is—is the language of their preachments. It was—as the language of the current revolt now is—the text of the Declaration of Independence and the United States Constitution. When Henry Highland Garnet brought the Buffalo Convention of Colored Citizens screaming to its feet by shouting, "No oppressed people have secured their liberty without resistance," he was talking about the Boston Tea Party. And when that convention voted a resolution calling for the slaves to strike for "liberty or death" they pilfered a line from Patrick Henry's ultimate defiance of the English.

Allied and deeply dedicated, the white abolitionists— men of great courage, women of unyielding zeal—carried the Negro plea to the inner circles of the white power structure. These white liberals—as do their modern counterparts—soon abandoned gradualism and moderation. Said William Lloyd Garrison: "I will be as harsh as truth, and as uncompromising as justice. On this subject [slavery] I do not wish to think, to speak, or to write with moderation. I am in earnest—I will not equivocate—I will not excuse—I will not retreat a single inch—AND I WILL BE HEARD!" (Style and capitalization his.)

And the white clergymen and rabbis who take freedom rides today had their counterpart in the abolitionist movement. In 1834 James G. Birney published his *Letter to the Ministers and Elders,* which contained the staggering simplicity that slavery was contrary to Christianity since Jesus taught the doctrine of universal brotherhood, and one of the cardinal principles of Christianity was that all men are created in the image of God.

✓Under bitter attack, the South became defiant. Southern

clergymen and scholars defended slavery—as they now do segregation—as morally right and intellectually sound. Southern intellectuals summoned a body of spurious scientific opinion to show that the Negro was incapable of learning. Apparently nobody realized the contradiction on the face of this proslavery logic. While intellectuals were approving slavery on the grounds that Negroes could not learn, clergymen were approving it on the grounds that this was the only way to teach them Christ.

But the South was not content to let the argument remain academic. The peculiar institution on which its whole economy rested threatened, its way of life in deep peril, the South resorted to violence just as it does today. In October of 1831 the state of Georgia offered four thousand dollars for the arrest of William Lloyd Garrison. The head of the white abolitionist, Arthur Tappan, was worth twelve thousand dollars in Macon, Georgia, and twenty thousand in New Orleans. Southerners broke into the post offices and burned copies of the abolitionist paper, *The Liberator*. When federal post office officials failed to take action, local postmasters took up the practice of burning abolitionists' newspapers themselves. White people who spoke kindly of Negroes were flogged and driven out of town. Hundreds of Negroes were killed by roaming white bands, and all Northerners became suspect. The bad blood spread into every social institution. Not even the gospel of Christ was able to heal the breach. Thus, fifteen years before the Civil War, the Baptist, Methodist and Presbyterian churches split into two groups, North and South, over the question of the Negro.

3.

THE CIVIL WAR

THE CIVIL WAR with its confused motivations is not under discussion here. The end result of that conflict, however, is of cardinal importance: some four million slaves, practically all of them illiterate, were set free. They were homeless, landless, skill-less and—through no fault of their own—competely unprepared to accept the responsibilities of an economically complex society.

The abolitionists had argued in the name of the American founding documents and Christian ethics that slavery was wrong. They won the war but they lost the peace; they freed the Negro but—during the chaotic years from 1865 to 1877—through opportunism, the greed of others and their own lack of planning, they set the stage for the institution of segregation that plagues us until now.

The debate on the future of the Negro after the Civil War began before the war was over, with only a small minority of white opinion suggesting that, once free, the Negro should become an integral and equal member of American society. The Negro question became submerged in the struggle to save the Union. From the onset Abraham Lincoln had viewed the war as a rebellion of Southern citizens, not of Southern states, and once the war was over Lincoln was of a mind to let the several Southern states work out the Negro problem as they saw fit. Lincoln proposed that each state be readmitted to the Union when one-tenth of the 1860 voting population complied with the Emancipation Proclamation. Abolitionists in Congress distrusted the proposal and attempted to thwart it. Their effort—the Wade-Davis bill, which would have imposed harsher penalties on the South—was vetoed by Lincoln, and the President's proposal went into effect.

The suspicions of the abolitionists proved correct. Andrew Johnson, Lincoln's successor, proved even more lenient toward the South. By 1866 the South was well on its way to self-rule, with Negroes under control. Negroes were intimidated on the streets, forced to work under threat of penalties and fines; they were arrested for such crimes as "seditious speeches" and "uppity behavior"; thousands were jailed for violating the curfew and possessing firearms. There was total denial of Negro suffrage in the South, and many Negroes felt they were drifting back into slavery.

Friends of the Negro struck back with fury. The Republican-controlled Congress of 1865, with encouragement from the Abolitionists, decided to make Southern reconstruction a legislative rather than an administrative function. With Thaddeus Stevens taking the lead, Congress passed two major "Negro" bills. One bill made the Freedmen's Bureau—a federal organization that had been giving aid to Negroes before the close of the Civil War—a permanent fixture. The second gave the Negro full civil rights. President Johnson vetoed both bills and expressed objections to the proposed Fourteenth Amendment, which would abolish slavery. Congress overrode the veto and passed the Fourteenth Amendment. The South, with Johnson's help, rejected the constitutional amendment and enforced the infamous Black Codes—a series of laws which reduced the Negro to a free slave—and signified their intransigence by public disorder. Congress struck back by enacting the laws that undergirded what historians now call "Radical Reconstruction."

The South was divided into five military districts and placed under martial law. Negroes were enfranchised,

and the former white rebels were disfranchised. It was
further decreed that each state would call a constitutional
convention based upon universal suffrage and that the
individual states would be received back into the Union
when the convention of a state completed a constitution
that was acceptable to Congress. No state was to be readmitted until it accepted the Fourteenth Amendment.

Although the plight of the Negro was relieved to an
extent by this action, he was caught in a struggle between
the die-hard South and what Professor Franklin calls "a
coalition of interests—crusaders, politicians and industrialists—all of whom hoped to gain something substantial
through Congressional Reconstruction."

Here, in the crucible of Reconstruction, is the beginning
of the modern Negro's problem. Radical Reconstruction
was a fight between white people about the Negro, but the
Negro was by no means all they were fighting about.

The crusaders not only felt strongly about freedom, but
they were convinced that only a proper education stood
between the Negro and a separate but equal place in
American society. Thus the Freedmen's Bureau, a federal
agency with representatives throughout the South, gave
aid to Negroes by furnishing medical supplies, establishing
schools and mediating disputes between Negro workers
and white employers. On many occasions the Bureau felt
Negroes couldn't get a fair hearing in local courts and
organized freedmen's courts and arbitration boards. But
the Bureau's greatest thrust was in the field of education.
Several Negro colleges now caught up in freedom rides
and sit-ins were founded during this era with help from
the Bureau. Howard University, Hampton Institute, Fisk
University and Johnson C. Smith University are but a few
of the schools which were founded then and which have
produced today's rebels.

While working for the Negro in the South, the Bureau
also advanced the cause of the Republican party. With
the help of the Union League, the Republicans, with the
agents of the Bureau taking great part, recruited thousands
of Negroes—then the major voting stock of the South—

to the GOP banner. The Northern industrialists gained control of the Republican party and were itching to exploit Southern resources and markets. Dr. Horace Mann Bond of Atlanta University has published material showing that iron and railroad interests were so anxious to capture the cheap labor resources of Alabama, for example, that they forced a hasty, and highly suspect, reconstruction of that state. By 1871 the South had a whopping reconstruction debt of some $300 million, one-third of which had been incurred by the issue of railroad bonds by Northern industrialists.

Against this backdrop the conventions of the several states met to hammer out constitutions that would be acceptable to Congress. Negroes were members of all the conventions.

The Charleston, South Carolina, *Daily News* of 1867 called the Negro members of that state's convention "beyond all question the best men in the convention. They have assembled neither to pull wires, like some, nor to make money, like others; but to legislate for the welfare of the race to which they belong."

This statement by Beverly Nash, a Negro member of the South Carolina Convention, reflects the burden borne by sincere men of that time:

"I believe, my friends and fellow citizens, we are not prepared for this suffrage. But we can learn. Give a man tools and let him commence to use them, and in time he will learn a trade. So it is with voting. We may not understand it at the start, but in time we shall learn to do our duty. We recognize the Southern white man as our true friend. In these public affairs we must unite with our white fellow citizens. They tell us that they have been disfranchised, yet we shall tell the North we will not let the halls of Congress be silent until we remove that disability."

Negroes went on to play important roles in state and the national legislatures but at no time did any state fall under Negro rule. Some Negro legislators served with distinction —particularly in the United States Senate—while others joined with white legislators and wallowed in graft.

Despite the presence of federal troops and the humanitarian laws passed by the several state conventions, the hard-core South never gave up. Bands of hooded white men—Jayhawkers, Black Horse Cavalrymen, the Ku-Klux Klan—roamed the South at night terrorizing Negroes and white Northerners. Distinguished members of the Confederacy were pardoned one by one, and one by one they returned home and assumed positions of power. Their strength was best evident in the growing ranks of the Democratic party. By 1870 Virginia and North Carolina fell into the Democratic column. Frightened, Negroes stayed away from the polls in droves, and the South's one-party system began to take form. Furthermore, the United States Supreme Court ruled that the Fifteenth Amendment (ratified in March, 1870) did not give Negroes the right to vote, that it only provided that they should not be discriminated against at the polls. This, of course, gave support to the white night riders then terrorizing the South.

Soon the old crusaders of the Republican party passed on. Stephens, Sumner and Butler were replaced by men like Hayes, Blaine and Conklin. These latter men were practical Republicans, more concerned about the industrial interests in the North than with the cause of the Negro.

The matter came to a head in the Presidential election of 1876. The Democrats campaigned on a promise to end Radical Reconstruction. The Republicans were divided on the issue, one wing of the party expressing a willingness to withdraw federal troops from the South, while the other faction supported continued federal supervision of the once rebellious states. The election of Rutherford B. Hayes, the Republican candidate, was disputed; the issue was thrown into Congress, and was finally resolved by a specially constituted electoral commission. Hayes succeeded in getting himself declared elected by obtaining the support of Southern Democrats in return for his promise to, among other things, withdraw the last of the federal troops from the South. Declared President, Hayes kept his word. That, for all practical purposes, was the end of Radical Reconstruction.

The Hayes compromise caused the Southern Democrats to flex their muscles, and they set about the business of destroying "Black Republicanism." Their principal gambit was confusion and intimidation at the ballot box. The state of South Carolina took the lead in destroying Negro voter effectiveness by enacting a labyrinthian voting booth procedure in 1882. A ballot for each office was placed in every voting booth; each vote had to be put in the right box or the ballot was thrown out. Moreover, no one was allowed to speak to the voter while he was in the booth. And since the majority of the Negro voters couldn't read, they couldn't cast votes that counted. This and similar practices spread over the South. By 1889 Henry W. Grady, an Atlanta newspaper publisher, could say, "The Negro as a political force has dropped out of serious consideration."

But the Negro voter almost returned to power. By destroying Black Republicanism Southern political forces also destroyed the political glue that held poor and aristocratic whites together as a political unit. All white Southerners had combined to defeat the Negro, but once the Negro was no longer a threat at the polls, the white population began to come apart along traditional lines. The depression of 1870 reopened old wounds between the poor whites and great landowning whites, commonly called the white Bourbons. The economic panic of 1873, during which thousands of poor whites lost their land, poured salt into the wound. The poor whites turned against the finance houses that foreclosed their mortgages, the railroads that charged high rates but received aid from both the state and federal governments, the corporations that pushed for higher tariffs while at the same time charging higher prices for farm machinery, and the governments, state and federal, that continued to raise taxes.

Another factor in the open break between the poor whites and the Bourbons was the changing guard of the Southern Democratic party. During the days when the party stood against Black Republicanism the leadership of the Democrats was largely in the hands of aristocratic plantation owners with whom the smaller white farmers had at least had some rapport. But now industrialists and merchants, whom the small farmers disliked intensely, rose to positions of power. In some states they became the leaders of the Democratic party.

This caused thousands of small white farmers to drift from the Democratic party and toward an alliance with small Negro landowners in the hope that together they could break the economic stranglehold the lords of industry had upon the rural South. Organizations such as the National Grange and the Southern Farmers' Alliance sprang up and urged "radical agrarian" reform as the only hope for the South. Negroes were barred from these organizations but they were encouraged to, and did, set up similar organizations of their own. Thus the Colored Farmers' Alliance was formed and prosecuted the same interests that motivated small white farmers. Fired by such white leaders as Tom Watson, Negro and white small landowners came closer and closer together. Watson's sermon was that poor whites and Negroes were being used by the white Bourbons, that they were being set apart deliberately, the better to be fleeced. Advocating restoration of the Negro vote, Watson went on to talk of a day when Negroes and poor whites would ally and drive the white Bourbons from power.

This advocacy found expression in the platform of the Populist party as it launched an all-out drive for the Negro vote in the election of 1892. Not only did the Populists go after the support of voting Negroes; they resorted to extreme means to get the franchise for Negroes in areas where the vote had been denied, then, for more than a decade. Alarmed, the Democrats pleaded with the Populists to abandon their drive for the "nigger vote." Rebuffed, the Democrats turned to the Negroes themselves and, during the 1892 election, wound up by loading the very people whom they once sought to disfranchise into wagons and driving them to the polls.

When Negroes refused to vote the Democratic ticket willingly, the Democrats resorted to violence. Fifteen Negro

Populists were murdered in Georgia alone during the 1892 election. There were widespread race riots in Virginia and North Carolina.

For a brief time—1892 to 1895—the agrarian revolt wielded some power. As a result Negroes returned to political prominence in several Southern states. The relationship between Negroes and poor whites was such that Professor C. Van Woodward, a noted American historian, says, "Never before or since have the two races in the South come so close together as they did during the Populist struggles."

But the Populist uprisings were, by and large, a revolt by the poor, the uninformed and the unequipped, and they could not long withstand an opposition that controlled the economy of the land as well as the government. The agrarian revolt collapsed in 1896, at the same time that the land-rich white Bourbons were bent upon disfranchising the Negro completely as insurance against another such coalition of the poor and the downtrodden.

Their agrarian dreams thwarted, poor white farmers accepted the reality of the hour and allied with the Bourbon white power structure. And it was during this era that white demagogues gained control over the South's political institutions. Their main gambit was to go "niggering" among the voters. That is to say, they took to the political stump and wooed the poor whites by launching vile charges against the Negro race. While the white Bourbons maintained a silent approval, these politicians embarked on a twenty-five-year-long denunciation of the Negro as an inferior creation, incapable of moral vitality or learning. "Niggering," of course, was a great psychological release for the poor whites, who had nothing but a dismal subhuman existence to look forward to, and their yells resounded from courthouse steps all over the South.

Within these courthouses, however, the real subjugation of the Negro—and the poor whites, for that matter—was taking place. The legal brains of the South were drafting laws that would disfranchise Negroes, allow equally ignorant white people to vote and, at the same time, not contravene the Fifteenth Amendment to the Constitution. In addition, bands of bloodthirsty "preservers of our way of life" roamed the land terrorizing thousands and killing hundreds of Negroes.

This was the birth of the Southern Alliance, the coming together of conservative Bourbons, opportunistic politicians and poverty-stricken farmers in an atmosphere of panic for the express purpose of translating a psychological aberration into a social institution.

And they did precisely that.

Taking the floor of the Virginia Convention in 1900, Carter Glass said: "We are here to discriminate to the very extremity of permissible action under the limitations to the federal constitution, with a view to the elimination of every Negro voter who can be gotten rid of, legally, without materially impairing the numerical strength of the white electorate."

The entire South followed the same pattern. The result was the maze of voting laws, literacy tests, poll taxes and the other ballot box curios that linger until now.

Meanwhile—Reconstruction had lasted the better part of twenty years—scores of educated Negroes had come out of freedmen's schools. Booker Washington had founded Tuskegee in 1881 and Dr. W. E. B. Du Bois had graduated from Harvard and was on the faculty of Atlanta University. But they too were caught in the web, for vengeful white Southerners were determined to subjugate all Negroes regardless of their accomplishments. J. K. Vardaman, Senator from Mississippi, expressed their view in lyrical language:

"I am just as opposed to Booker T. Washington as a voter with all of his Anglo-Saxon reinforcements, as I am to the coconut-headed, chocolate-colored, typical little coon, Andy Dotson, who blacks my shoes every morning. Neither is fit to perform the supreme function of citizenship."

√Since we were all Andy Dotsons then, the total humiliation of the Negro was under way. Tennessee led by passing the first Jim Crow law. All over the South the "white" and "colored" signs went up. Trains, busses, barbershops, schools and all other public places were segregated by law. Then, in 1896, the United States Supreme Court rendered the now-famous *Plessy* vs. *Ferguson* decision, which set forth the doctrine of "separate but equal." Segregation thus became an American institution, a way of life imbedded in the law of the land. But if "separate but equal" was the law, "separate and unequal" was the practice. And injustice is the Siamese twin of inequality.

4.

THE FAITHS THAT FAILED

THE AMERICAN NEGRO spent the first half of the twentieth century adjusting to and recovering from the all-pervading reality of legalized segregation. Fear of white people has been advanced as the basic motivation of Negroes during those years, and I suppose there is some validity in that analysis. But I doubt that fear was the only force shaping Negro attitudes and behavior; self-realization in an essentially hostile world, I suggest, is a more accurate description of what the Negro was about. Fear, to be sure, was one of the techniques of that self-realization. After all, when the entire legal structure is against you and your very life is in daily peril, fear is an understandable emotion. Denied modern weapons with which to defend yourself, and hauled before openly hostile courts when you fight back with sticks and stones, you will do well to pretend fear even when you are not afraid.

I was born just after World War I and spent my first seventeen years in south Georgia. Remembering our way of life, I am convinced that, for the most part, Negroes were not really afraid. Rather, we were clever; canny, actually, for that was the way to stay alive and get ahead. Living by our spiritual wits, then, we managed to stay alive and shape men for the big push to come. Perhaps the best proof of what we were doing lies in the fact that the Negroes who now carry the leadership burden were born and shaped between 1915 and the Second World War. It is further revealing that these men, with one or two notable exceptions, were born and shaped in the South. This makes sense, for, whereas the South's Negroes were by far the more deprived, they were also the more inspired. The Northern Negro was militant—at least his talk was— and it is indeed easy to talk loud and bad about the white man when the entire New York City police force stands between you and Mississippi; the Southern Negro was docile by comparison, something it is indeed wise to at least appear to be when the KKK tries your case long before it can get before the Supreme Court.

The American Negro was, then, split into two factions based on overt attitudes toward the white man: the militants and the dociles. The militants built the platform upon which the ultimate civil rights struggle would be carried out and the dociles produced men whose intimate relations with the race problem and the Negro masses shaped them as tacticians and decision makers. Let us here concern ourselves with the dociles, the Southern Negro; let us watch him as he shuffles his way to a position of strength and power. Then, in a subsequent chapter, we will examine the Northern Negro and put his contribution to the Negro revolt into perspective.

The orientation of the Southern Negro into a separate but equal way of life was based upon two assumptions, neither of which was questioned by Negro leaders at the turn of the century. The first assumption was that education would be a lever of racial progress; the second was the faith that the vaporous thing known as Negro Business would jell and become the economic foundation of our world within the white man's world. Both assumptions had flaws. The flaw in the assumption that education would be a lever of racial progress was not fatal, but it led to a serious illness that still afflicts the Negro people.

The burden of educating the Negro masses was assumed by Northern white missionaries even while the Union Armies were marching through the South. As swiftly as the slaves were liberated and brought behind Union lines, the missionaries arranged for their care, employment —usually on a farm—and religious education. This ingenious admixture of Jesus, farming and puritanical thrift was an oasis for the Negroes who had been forbidden to learn by their former masters. The knowledge-thirsty freedmen and their spinster missionary teachers formed one of the great tableaux of American history. Dr. Horace Mann Bond, dean of the Atlanta University School of Education and an eminent Negro historian, describes them in these compelling words:

> The missionary teachers from New England, fresh from the then-recent victories of Horace Mann and Henry Barnard in the battle for a free public school, encouraged the freedmen in their conviction. At no time or place in America has there been exemplified so pathetic a faith in education as the lever of racial progress. Grown men studied their alphabets in the fields, holding the "blue back speller" with one hand while they guided the plow with the other. Mothers tramped scores of miles to towns where they could place their children in school. Pine torches illumined the dirt floor cabins where men, women and children studied until far into the night. No mass movement has been more in the American tradition than the urge which drove Negroes toward education soon after the Civil War.

However, the education of the black masses could not be left to the chance efforts of the Union Army chaplains and Northern missionaries. The Freedmen's Bureau, a federal agency authorized by Congress after the Civil War for the express purpose of caring for the ex-slaves, unified these efforts toward education and made them their major work. Although the Bureau lived only five years and was faced with stiff Southern opposition every day of its life, Bureau agents set up more than four thousand schools for Negroes in the South. These schools employed upwards of ten thousand teachers and were responsible for the primary education of a quarter of a million Negroes. The Bureau accomplished this minor miracle by spending some six million dollars. The federal government contributed three and a half million to the project, philanthropic societies added another million and a half, while Negroes themselves contributed a million dollars in gifts and school fees.

The Bureau's intention was to teach Negro teachers who, in turn, could teach the people. This resulted in the founding of Howard, Fisk and Atlanta universities and gave rise to the term "higher education" among Negroes. Additional "higher education" for Negroes was provided by the American Missionary Society, which established a dozen schools and colleges in the years immediately after the Civil War, and by various religious denominations, Negro and white, which set up Negro colleges and universities of their own.

Without doubt, the most significant event in the history of Negro education was the rise and rule of Booker T. Washington.

Washington was the product of Hampton Institute, a Negro college founded by the American Missionary Society. Much of the philosophy of education followed at Hampton, however, came from General Samuel Chapman Armstrong, its first president. Armstrong had spent considerable time in Hawaii and had observed the training program at the Hilo Labor School. He patterned his curriculum after what he had seen there. His great urging was that the Negro student be given "moral as well as mental strength." He wanted Negro students to become "first rate mechanical laborers" but at the same time he felt the purpose of education was also to make them "first class men and women."

Booker T. Washington was about sixteen when he arrived at Hampton. He was a good student and responded well to General Armstrong's teaching that labor was "a spiritual force, that physical work not only increased earning capacity but promoted fidelity, accuracy, honesty, persistence and intelligence." Washington learned the fundamentals—reading, writing, arithmetic, grammar—and gathered a fair knowledge of good books. But intermixed

with this he absorbed and accepted Armstrong's teaching
that the greatest values, therefore rewards, lay in acquiring
land, homes, vocations and skills. Washington personalized
this philosophy and concluded that it would be his great
life's work to find ways in which his people could be most
useful to the world—that is to say, how Negroes could
acquire homes, property and wealth by performing some
service the world both needed and wanted.

When Washington accepted the invitation to build a
"normal" school at Tuskegee, Alabama, based on the
things he had learned at Hampton, it was as if fate had
cut his challenge to order. The white community at
Tuskegee was hostile to the idea of a Negro school in
their midst. This offered Washington the twofold challenge of (1) finding the resources necessary to build the
school and (2) appeasing the local white people who did
not want it. To Washington's mind the need was clear-
cut. He must show the hostile whites that the Negroes
would be trained to perform services that the white community needed. Washington's students learned the three
R's, but their great aim was to become well-trained construction workers, cooks, farmers and mechanics. In addition, Washington taught his students to respect the law,
stay in their place as Negroes and respect white people.

As Tuskegee began to turn out polite domestics and
eager farmers, white opposition to the school vanished.
Convinced that he was on the right road, that he had
carved out a unique service that the Negro could perform
for the white world, Washington went on to tell white
Southerners that their salvation and comfort were tied up
in the "proper" education of the Negro. Needless to say,
he gained immediate support.

Tuskegee Institute was something of a barony, run by
Washington but owned and supported by white philanthropy. Students and faculty members lived in an atmosphere dominated more by piety than by learning. Dr. E.
Franklin Frazier once told me that Washington went to
every length to make sure the white supporters of Tuskegee didn't get the impression that students there were

being taught to think. In his book Frazier recalls that, during the academic year 1916-17, he was once called in by the dean of Tuskegee and reprimanded for walking across the campus with books under his arms. Although Frazier was a full professor, the dean felt that white people seeing him walking around with books under his arms would get the impression that Tuskegee was training the Negro's intellect rather than his heart and hands.

The great moment at Tuskegee seems to have been the Sunday evening services in the now famous Tuskegee Chapel. Here Washington delivered his Sunday evening talks, many of which have survived in manuscript form and provide an amazing insight into what was going on in the name of education.

"Our greatest danger is that in the great leap from slavery to freedom," Washington said, "we may overlook the fact that the masses of us are to live by the production from our hands, and fail to keep in mind that we shall prosper in proportion as we learn to dignify and glorify common labor, and put brains and skills in the common occupations of life."

On another Sunday evening the assemblage was edified with this:

"We must not only teach the Negro to improve the methods of what are now classed as the lower forms of labor, but the Negro must be put in a position, by the use of intelligence and skill, to take his part in the higher forms of labor, up in the regions where the profits appear." For, after all: "Art and music to people who live in rented houses and with no bank account are not the most important things to which attention should be given. Such education creates wants without a corresponding ability to supply these wants."

Following this, Washington set forth his own formula for the good life:

"We might as well settle down to the uncompromising fact that our people will grow in proportion that we teach them the way to have the most of Jesus in a permanent form is to mix with their religion some land, cotton and corn, a house with two or three rooms, and a little bank account."

Washington's philosophy of education was pleasing to the white South, which, in the words of Mississippi's J. K. Vardaman, felt that white Northern missionaries who taught Negroes the classics were "ruining our Negroes. They are demanding equality."

✓It is now clear that the white South—to say nothing of some of his Negro contemporaries—misread Washington. He did not oppose teaching Negroes the arts and sciences; he merely felt these disciplines were impractical; he was convinced that Negroes would not be allowed to use these tools, so why learn them? Washington would have had the Negro learn how to make money performing the tasks allowed him and then use this money to build "as other races have done."

Since "industrial education" was generally accepted to be a way of life for Negroes rather than a type of education, the consensus emerged that Washington, as the proponent of industrial education and the acknowledged Negro leader, accepted segregation with all its grim trappings. Then, at the Atlantic Exposition of 1895, Washington made his famous "Let Down Your Bucket Where You Are" speech and removed all doubt.

"In all things purely social," Washington told Negroes and whites, "we can be as separate as the fingers, yet one as the hand in all things essential to mutual progress."

White people, North and South, welcomed Washington's speech. The South saw it as acceptance of segregation and a promise that racial conflicts would end. The North desperately wanted a peaceful Southland for purposes of industrial exploitation and, like Washington, mistook his program of industrial education for one that would produce a black industrial labor force.

Nothing could have been farther from the truth. First, Washington had no concept whatsoever of industrial labor in the proper sense, and the students who came out of Tuskegee were not trained for work in the nation's industries. Second—and this was by far the most important factor in the making of the modern Negro image—the students who finished Tuskegee and other "industrial" schools had no intentions whatsoever of working in plants. Rather, they returned to the rural South to teach school, something for which they were even less equipped than they were to work in industry.

Washington, as Negro leader and educational philosopher, was challenged by Dr. W. E. B. Du Bois, then a highly regarded sociologist at Atlanta University. Said Du Bois:

> I would not deny the paramount necessity of teaching the Negro to work, and to work steadily [but] I do say that this is industrialism drunk with its visions of success, to imagine that its own work can be accomplished without providing for the training of broadly cultured men and women to teach its own teachers, and to teach the teachers of the public schools.
> The Negro race, like all races, is going to be saved by its exceptional men. The problem of education, then, among Negroes must first of all deal with the talented tenth, it is the problem of developing the Best of this race that they may guide the Mass away from the contamination and death of the Worst, in their own and other races.

Du Bois had few adherents, white or Negro; only a few Negro intellectuals in the North and the last remnants of the white abolitionists supported his arguments. Not only did Northern philanthropy oppose Du Bois, but it became known that Atlanta University would not receive additional grants from some foundations so long as he remained on the faculty. Rather than endanger the life of the entire university, Du Bois resigned.

✓Du Bois, of course, was correct. Although Washington is to be commended for being able to secure any kind of education for Negroes in the Deep South, the fact remains that the Negro colleges that sprang up in his shadow produced a flood of miseducated Negroes who, almost by second instinct, acquiesced in segregation and all the indignities that went with it. These graduates became teachers of all the children of all the Negro people, elite and common.

In this connection the emergence of land-grant colleges in America must be remembered. Land-grant colleges were created by the Morrill Act of 1862 and provided that public land should be given to the several states for the erection of "at least one college that, without neglecting the arts and sciences, would . . . promote the liberal education of the industrial classes." When the South was forced to accept at least some of the burden of Negro education it established land-grant colleges which provided precisely the kind of education Booker Washington advocated. These colleges exist until this day, and every Negro student is required, in addition to his liberal arts training, to become proficient in some trade such as bricklaying, shoemaking, painting, automobile repair or—and these are "majors"—home economics and farming.

The rise of Negro land-grant colleges combined with such private institutions as Tuskegee to promote a philosophy of Negro education that rendered the Negro an inferior, second-class citizen. These Negroes, however, did not look upon themselves as inferior or as second-class citizens. Theirs was a world apart and separate; as "educated Negroes" their role was to provide the culture and intellectual leadership of a Negro community supported, at rock bottom, by Negro business.

In his *The Negro as Capitalist,* Abram L. Harris says:

> The Negro masses, urged by their leaders, were led to place increasing faith in business and property as a means of escaping poverty and achieving economic independence. Although ostensibly sponsored as the means of self-help or racial cooperation through which the masses were to be economically emancipated, Negro business enterprise was motivated primarily by the desire for private profit and looked toward the establishment of a Negro capitalist employer class.

At first blush this looks like nothing more than the rise of a group of enterprising Negroes who, in the American tradition, would let down their buckets where they were and dredge profits from the Negro masses. But it was more than that. The Negro businessmen realized that if they were to make profits from the Negro market, then Negro workers had to be employed. At the turn of the century Negro workers were in a mean and deadly fight with poor white laborers for menial jobs. The poor whites invariably won, and thus the Negro masses had little buying power for the Negro businessman to feed upon. Thereupon the Negro businessmen reasoned that the thing to do was to encourage Negro workers to turn some of their meager income into capital; this capital, in turn, would be used to capture control of some existing industries and to establish others. These Negro-controlled industries, would, of course, hire Negro workers and a self-supporting economy within the Negro tribe would be realized.

This was an interesting scheme, and, in 1900, Booker T. Washington founded the National Negro Business League to implement this philosophy. The move set off lively action and at one time there were fifty-odd Negro banks in the United States. Most of the Negro businesses were small retail shops and funeral parlors operated by their owners. Almost all of them failed, and none of them provided the self-perpetuating and expanding Negro economy the visionaries had predicted. However, the few Negro businesses that did survive—insurance companies, funeral parlors—did create a wealthy class of Negroes, and since the faith that Negro business would aid the Negro masses proved futile, the impression remains that Negro businessmen were interested primarily in profits from the impoverished.

It has been suggested that the Negro businesses failed primarily because the Negro people lack a merchant tradition. Several foundations and Negro colleges have launched studies on the failure of Negro business in the hope of reviving it as a lever of racial progress. The bare truth seems to have escaped most of these studies: Negro business failed because it was "Negro"; it assumed that a separate Negro economy could exist within the white economy, and it reckoned without the ingenuity of the white merchant, who not only could afford to sell at a lower price than the Negro merchant but who also welcomed Negro money as long as his Negro customer stayed in "his place."

I remember vividly the Friday a Negro woman—a member of my father's church—was slapped by a white chain-store manager because she picked over some fruit and then refused to buy it. There were rumors that Negroes would simply stop buying at the store, but there was never any suggestion that we take our trade to the Negro merchants, whose prices were a third higher than those in the chain store.

The collapse of the Negro business myth, as E. Franklin Frazier calls it, meant that the Negro worker had no alternative but to seek employment in white industries. Negro and white workers in the South have always been locked in a deadly fight over the crumbs that fall from the nation's table; never was the fight meaner, the crumb smaller, than during the second decade of this century. The labor depression that hit the South during 1914-15 sent wages down below seventy-five cents a day. The boll weevil all but destroyed the cotton market, and the floods of the summer of 1915 left thousands of Negroes homeless and penniless.

Northern industry, on the other hand, was flourishing. Foreign migration dropped from one million in 1914 to about three hundred thousand in 1915. This created a Northern labor shortage, which Negroes were more than willing to fill.

The North became the "Promised Land" for thousands of Negroes who responded to the lures of Negro newspapers and agents from Northern industries. The Chicago *Defender* headlined: "It Is Better To Die From Frost Bite Than At The Hands Of A Mob." The *Christian Recorder* suggested, "If a million Negroes leave the South for the North and West during the next year, it will be the greatest thing since the Emancipation Proclamation."

Negro migration reached its peak during the summer

of 1916. Jobless and weary of the South's civic and social injustices, a million Negroes fled the South between 1915 and 1918. (Dr. John Hope Franklin questions this generally accepted figure. He suggests that half a million is closer to the fact.) White families were without servants, Negro churches were vacant, farmers were unable to secure laborers. The Southern white press pleaded with Negroes to remain in the South, and the city of Jacksonville, Florida, went so far as to impose a one-thousand-dollar license fee on migration agents representing Northern industries. But it was the Negroes who remained who formed the Southern Negro as we know him today, and the basic structure of the Negro tribe.

Negro colleges and universities were sending forth an ever-widening stream of graduates. They poured back into the segregated Negro community as professionals. Meanwhile a small class of Negro businessmen emerged out of the reality of legal segregation. They opened their shops in the Negro community because they were not allowed to sell their wares elsewhere. The Negro churches and burial institutions were already celebrating their fiftieth anniversary. Thus it was, then, that a Negro world within the white world came into being. This Negro world was peopled by masses, most of whom could not read; it was led by poorly trained professionals who had translated their humiliation into the positive faith that theirs would be a separate but equal world; it was serviced by Negro businessmen who depended upon that community for their income, but who were forced to compete with white businessmen who had no qualms about selling a Negro woman a dress, provided, of course, she didn't wish to try it on before making the purchase.

This Negro world was an enclave of terror; white policemen kept the peace by wielding night sticks first and asking questions later, homes were entered without warrants, citizens were arrested without charges. There was no vote; Negro workers were restricted to the lowest of jobs, and, if things got rough, had to compete with poor white laborers for even those. Thwarted, the Negro masses turned to drink and bloodletting, and Saturday night became the bloodiest night in the week.

The Negro masses were trapped in this separate hell; and the Negro leaders, since their income and status depended upon the Negro masses, developed a vested interest in a separate society which they deluded themselves into believing would one day be equal.

White supremacy was enacted into law during the last two decades of the nineteenth century; it became a functioning reality in the first two decades of the twentieth century as the Negro masses, their leaders at their head, became a tribe. Being segregated and humiliated was our lot; we accepted it and within the confines of this misery set about creating a way of life.

5

THE EMERGING TRIBE

DESPITE THE ABSENCE of a classic culture, the American Negro is a people. There is now a tie that binds us all while yet allowing for the variegated lives we live. We call each other "brother," and we congregate together to eat "soul" food and listen to "soul" music. We are—from Muslim Leader Malcolm X to the United Nations' Ralph J. Bunche—"Lodge Members." Ask a Negro about soul music, soul food, his brothers, and what a lodge member is, and, chances are, he will laugh and walk away. But while laughing and walking he will bump into a fellow lodge member, and they will take off to eat some soul food while listening to soul music. And they will call each other "brother."

All American Negroes "pay dues." "Dues" is the fee one pays for being black in America. If you are a musician, "dues" is the price you pay when you see white musicians take tunes and concepts you created and make millions while you tramp the country on one-nighters; if you are a writer, "dues" is the price you pay for being relegated to "Negro" themes when your real interest could very well lie somewhere else; if you are a college professor, "dues" is what you pay for being confined, for the most part, to Negro colleges which don't afford you the academic challenge every scholar wants; if you are a college professor on an "integrated" campus, "dues" are what you pay when students make you a specialist on the Negro and approach you with sympathetic condescension; if you are just a common man—and that is what most of us are—"dues" are what you pay when rents are high, apartments are filthy, credit interest is exorbitant and white policemen patrol your community ready to crack heads at any moment. In a phrase, "dues" are the day-to-day outlay—psychological and economic—every black American must make simply because he is black. And a "lodge member," as anyone who stopped laughing at Amos and Andy long enough to think should realize, is a fellow Negro who, of course, also pays dues. Soul music and soul food are the mystical oneness with certain rhythms and the cooking we have enjoyed while forging ourselves into a people welded together by common suffering.

Not all Negroes will agree with this analysis, and I will be the first to admit that it is somewhat futuristic, but no Negro will doubt that we are becoming more and more tribal and that the patois I have set out above has a common ring. We were not always as much of a tribe as we now are, and the schisms that divide us have their roots in the days when we were completely asunder.

First, there were the traditionally free Negroes versus those who had once been slaves; then there were the former house slaves versus the former field slaves; while among those who had always been free there were the aristocrats versus the common men. Almost all of them suffered from a paucity of learning. There was a fusion of sorts into two groups, who, in turn, produced what Dr. E. Franklin Frazier calls "the only two valid cultural traditions in the social history of the Negro in the United States: one being the genteel tradition of the small group of mulattoes who assimilated the morals and manners of the slaveholding aristocracy; and the other, the culture of the black folk who gave the world the spirituals."

During the immediate post-Civil War period the mulatto class continued to stand apart from the Negro masses. They reveled in their "blood," cited their white ancestry

with great alacrity and pride, and spent their Sunday after-
noons in the enjoyment of English and, in the New Orleans area, French music and literature. These mulattoes
were steeped in the Southern tradition of "ladies" and
"gentlemen" and were among the main opponents of grant-
ing suffrage to the Negro masses.

When emancipation shattered the Southern way of life,
these mulattoes managed to hang on to their "culture"
and remained "ladies" and "gentlemen" even though they
were forced to give up employment as artisans and become domestics. They captured control of Negro leadership organizations, such as they were, and remained in
power until the work of Northern missionaries and philanthropy wrought a change in Negro life.

Washington, D.C., became the "capital" of the Negro
elite: the Schomburg Collection in New York City carries
a satirical account of "Negro society" in the District of
Columbia at the turn of the century. The critique was
written by John E. Bruce and contains this rib-tickling
paragraph:

There is another element in this strange heterogeneous
conglomeration, which for the want of a better name has
been styled society and it is this species of African hu-
manity which is forever and ever informing the uninitiated
what a narrow escape they had from being born white.
They have small hands, aristocratic insteps and wear blue
veins, they have auburn hair and finely chiseled features.
They are uneducated as a rule (i.e.) the largest number of
them, though it would hardly be discovered unless they
opened their mouths in the presence of their superiors in
intellect, which they are very careful not to do. In personal appearance, they fill the bill precisely so far as importance and pomposity goes—but no farther. They are
opposed to manual labor, their physical organization
couldn't stand it, they prefer light work such as "shuffling
cards or dice" or "removing the spirits of Frumenta from
the gaze of rude men" if somebody else becomes responsible for the damage. Around the festive board, they are
unequalled for their verbosity and especially for their apt-
ness in tracing their ancestry. One will carry you back to

the times of William the Silent and bring you up to 18 so and so, to show how illustrious is his lineage and pedigree. His great, great grandfather's mother-in-law was the Marchioness So and So and his father was ex Chief Justice Chastity of South Carolina or some other southern state with a polygamous record.

It is of no little significance that these mulatto Negroes of the "genteel tradition" were Episcopalians, Presbyterians and Congregationalists while the black masses were members of the "common" churches, such as the Baptist and Methodist congregations. The services in the former churches were of a much "higher" order, the meaning a good deal less exciting. Negroes in these "high" churches disassociated themselves from the black masses and they neither admitted their need to escape from reality nor accepted the mandate to change that reality. This is precisely what Reverend Thomas Lomax, my grandfather and a Baptist firebrand of the late nineteenth and early twentieth centuries, had in mind when he cracked, "If you see a Negro who is not a Baptist or a Methodist, some white man has been tampering with his religion."

The black masses who produced the spiritual and formed the core of the Negro tribe were centered in the South; their immediately discernible folkways revolved around the church and burial societies. It was in church that the Negro masses found both meaning for life and escape from reality. These are what the spirituals actually are, a plaintive reaffirmation of the dignity of the individual soul couched in a rousing denunciation of this world's ways:

"Soon I will be done with the troubles of the world."
"Swing low, sweet chariot, coming for to carry me home."
"O Lord, I want two wings to veil my face, two wings to fly away."
"Steal away, steal away to Jesus."
"Go down, Moses, way down in Egypt land, tell old Pharaoh to let my people go."

This was the litany of reaffirmation and escape. And although few of them realized it, had one probed these Negroes' minds, Pharaoh would have emerged looking suspiciously like a Southern white man. The burial societies, on the other hand, were organizations that provided some measure of economic security in the time of sickness and death. They also gave the mass Negroes another opportunity to congregate, socialize and worship.

The Negro church was born because Negro clergymen were denied the right to officiate and otherwise hold forth in "white"—actually integrated but white-controlled—churches. The Negro Baptist and Methodist churches are the direct result of overt discrimination. One has only to examine the African Methodist Episcopal Church, the African Methodist Episcopal Zion Church and the Colored Methodist Episcopal Church to grasp the reason for their existence. Now—and this is the historical point that was overlooked—if the Negro churches were formed by angry Negro Christians smarting under the abuses of the white man, it was inevitable that, in time, those churches would produce militant opponents of the white power structure.

Money, however, was the Negro church's initial undoing. The parishioners were, for the most part, menials and had little to spare for the collection plates. But even that was a harbinger of things to come. It followed, logically and economically, that once Negro parishioners were able to finance their own religious undertakings they would produce a free class of Negro ministers who would—as Dr. Martin Luther King proves—stand ready to die for their race.

Whenever a people are isolated—by choice or by force, to a limited or total extent—they develop a folkway. In classical cultural terms, there is no difference between the Negro Baptist Church and the Baptist Church proper. In folk terms, however, there is. Not only do we Negro Baptists have a way of preaching and singing, but there is a meaning to our imagery that is peculiar to us. After all, a theology is the result of man's groping with adverse powers —known and unknown, seen and unseen—and the function of a gospel is to speak to the frustrations of the people who espouse it. These were the deep rumblings that stirred in the Negro masses' breasts during those difficult days after slavery.

Superior even to the school was the position of the church in the world of the Southern Negro. By listening and fervently responding to the pure poetry of the Negro preacher, the Negro masses got a sense of history and moral philosophy. There is something incredibly informative about sitting Sunday after Sunday and year in, year out, listening to a minister trace out the history of the Jews from the day God spit out the seven seas to the time John the Revelator closed the Bible and said all truth had been revealed. Even those of us who couldn't read came to think of history as a moving, changing thing; we were never allowed to doubt that man as a created thing had purpose and that we, to be sure, were a part of that purpose. And the singing we did, in church and in school, was of the same meaning. "Jordan's waters were chilly and cold," and as we sang about it, we were readying ourselves for the great crossing. Indeed, we were climbing Jacob's ladder and practically every Negro home had a picture of Booker T. Washington lifting the veil of ignorance from his people. The fans we used in church were supplied by the local Negro funeral home; they, too, carried Washington's picture.

Many were the times white people would come to our church. We would give them the front seats and they enjoyed themselves as our ministers held forth about Moses using the rod to part the waters of the Red Seas. More than once the minister would go on to suggest that there were some "Black Moseses" in the making and I wondered even then if white people knew what we were really talking about. After all, Moses did set his people free and it happened only after the people and God visited plagues upon the Egyptian power structure.

We trudged off to school and learned our ABC's while reading about "Little Black Sambo" and "Ned," of First Reader fame, who, of course, was white. As a matter of fact, when I was in grammar school, we could always liven up an otherwise dull day by telling some student that he looked "like Ned in the First Reader." This was our way of calling each other a dirty name—that is to say, white—and it always started a fist fight. We were forced to use the textbooks issued by the white board of education and these volumes were chock-full of disparaging things about Negroes and their African background. Our teachers had no alternative but to teach us from these books. But they also taught us Negro history. Negro history, much of which I have rendered in the previous chapters, was almost a folklore with us. We didn't have Negro history books and the heritage of our people was passed on by word of mouth from generation to generation.

The public rendering of Negro history occurred on January first of each year. That was Emancipation Day and a cause for great speaking and celebration. The Emancipation Day services were mammoth things. They took the order of church services: A highly respected local Negro would read the Proclamation exactly as it had been rendered by President Lincoln. Then the choir—usually the school chorus—would sing. The emancipation paper, actually the history of the Negro race, was read by another local citizen, usually a woman and a schoolteacher. This is where we heard about Crispus Attucks, Paul Laurence Dunbar, Frederick Douglass, Phillis Wheatley and Booker T. Washington. The paper was our "Ark of the Covenant" and was passed on from one reader to another over the years. Each year the names of Negroes who had done well were added to the list. The climax of the celebration was the main speech, always delivered by some distinguished out-of-towner. Over the years practically every major Negro college president came to our town, Valdosta, as emancipation speaker. Following the main speech—and in lieu of the Doxology—we all stood reverently and sang the Negro National Anthem.[1] In recent years it has not been fashionable to refer to the song as the Negro National

[1] See next page.

Anthem; rather it is called after its opening line "Lift Ev'ry Voice and Sing."

Lift Ev'ry Voice and Sing
(The Negro National Anthem)

Lift ev'ry voice and sing
Till earth and heaven ring.
Ring with the harmonies of Liberty;
Let our rejoicing rise
High as the list'ning skies,
Let it resound loud as the rolling sea.
Sing a song full of the faith that the dark past has taught us,
Sing a song full of the hope that the present has brought us.
Facing the rising sun of our new day begun,
Let us march on till victory is won.

Stony the road we trod,
Bitter the chast'ning rod.
Felt in the days when hope unborn had died;
Yet with a steady beat,
Have not our weary feet
Come to the place for which our fathers sighed?
We have come over a way that with tears has been watered,
We have come, treading our path through the blood of the
    slaughtered,
Out from the gloomy past,
Till now we stand at last
Where the white gleam of our bright star is cast.

God of our weary years,
God of our silent tears,
Thou who has brought us thus far on the way;
Thou who has by Thy might
Led us into the light,
Keep us forever in the path, we pray.
Lest our feet stray from the places, our God, where we met Thee,
Lest our hearts, drunk with the wine of the world, forget Thee,
Shadowed beneath Thy hand,
May we forever stand,
True to our God,
True to our native land.

Words by JAMES WELDON JOHNSON
Music by ROSAMOND JOHNSON

The shift came when Negro spokesmen pointed out that we could not demand oneness with the American mainstream if we maintained an anthem of our own.

The Negro fraternal orders and burial societies formed another link in the emerging Negro folkway. We in Georgia were not so steeped in these societies as were our brothers in, say, Mississippi, but "Grand Lodge" turnouts were always big public meetings where we gathered to review the history of the race and urge the young on to higher things. The lodge "turnouts" were by far the most colorful and festive of our tribal ceremonies. Here one would see cooks, maids and butlers march alongside teachers, doctors and other professional men carrying banners carved with secret symbols. The Masons were particularly exciting to watch; they made much of their angular white aprons and there was much ado about "the stone that the builders rejected." Then there was more infectious magic about "going East" and "squaring a corner." But when the ritual was over, the lodges settled down to the business of the hour: establishing race pride and providing scholarships for worthy Negro children.

Then there was graduation night, for the elementary and secondary schools. The valedictorians gave addresses, the main theme of which was the progress of the race. Again, the roll of Negro heroes was called. The commencement speaker would then go on to exhort us to learn well, and fast, that we too might help lift the veil of ignorance from our people. But even then the search was on for the talented tenth. And, with the coming of fall, there was warm rejoicing in the community as two or three of the high school graduates left for college, usually to get an "industrial and mechanical" education.

It pains me, now, to remember those days, to recall just how close we Southern Negroes were to becoming a first-rate culture group. We had so many things going for us: a way of worship that, in time, would have produced a Negro God; a historical heritage that we passed on as if it were an Ark of the Covenant between the Almighty and us; although we shared the common language, we spoke a jargon of our own; and our social outlets satisfied the ambitions we then felt. But there was a fatal flaw in the foundation of our emerging way of life: We had come together as a tribe for negative, not positive, reasons; we were bound together by the animus of the white man, not by historical customs and traditions such as those that have fashioned the world's peoples into culture groups.

✓We lived on our enclave, but it was not a land of our own choosing; and the great cleavages that rent our tribe were the direct result of peoples of diverse backgrounds and interests being forced to live as one in the slums and other areas cast off by the white man. As a result, the Negro community was a troubled place.

There were killings and violence. However, much of it —most, I suggest—was against Negroes by other Negroes. Despite the efforts of the churches and the schools, there was little stability in the home life of the Negro masses. To be sure, much of the bloodletting among Negroes was a result of sheer frustration and despair brought on by their plight as black Americans. Some of it, however, was simply human. After all, white people raise hell too.

Indeed, violence was always in the air. Seldom a week passed that we didn't get word of some Negro who had been beaten or lynched by white mobs. (Some four thousand Negroes were lynched between 1889 and 1922, the year I was born.) And we lived in constant awareness that our lives were not ours to keep or to protect. Our only hope was to stay in our place.

Even that didn't always work. I remember a Negro boy who worked with me delivering groceries. He made a delivery to a white home, and by the time he got back to the store seven white men were there waiting for him. The white woman to whom he had delivered the groceries was home alone; she took the groceries through the back screen door and as she turned she felt a blow on her rear. The woman screamed and ran to the telephone; she called her husband and said the Negro boy had assaulted her. Only the insistence of the white store owner kept the boy from being whipped, if not lynched. While the matter was being talked out, the store telephone rang. It was the aggrieved woman. She said she had just felt the same blow in the same place, and upon checking for the source discovered that her five-year-old had been pelting her with his peashooter. But for the grace of God—we delivered orders by lot—I would have been the one to make that delivery.

On another occasion I was working as a shoeshine boy in an all-white barbershop. The owner was a garrulous man. His forte was telling how he attended and helped officiate at lynchings. Then he would squat down and do a duck walk showing the laughing white men how to get through a lynch crowd so they could "be up close to the nigger."

Not even Southern Negro professionals were exempted from the excruciating humiliations visited upon citizens of the Negro community. I know of one Negro school principal who was ordered to type his white supervisor's annual report and was warned not to "get any nigger funk on them papers." One of my close friends is the son of a Southern Negro undertaker whom city officials told, "It's better to let them damn niggers die than race your ambulance through town at fifty miles an hour." I once attended the church of a Negro minister who had been cornered by a group of young white hoodlums and made to dance in the street because he "wore white shirts even white people can't afford."

Whatever hope there was that Negroes would inherit a separate world was destroyed by the reign of terror and injustice visited upon that world by white people. And it was this reign of terror, coupled with denials of every tool of self-realization, more than the concept of a separate world itself, that moved enraged Negroes to demolish the foundation of their world shortly before it was completed. Had we been given time and equality of opportunity and, most of all, spared physical and spiritual abuse, there is a probability that the Negro would have emerged into American society in a role approximating that now enjoyed by the Jew. But the terror and injustice were more than we could bear; the use of our tax money to spawn and spread the spurious theory of Negro inferiority was more than we could stomach and still maintain our self-respect; the clear determination to make us the white man's servant rather than his brother rendered every Negro father a weakling before his son, a limp reed in the eyesight of his wife. These—more than segregation per se—were the moral flaws that made the Negro world an anathema; and because of these moral flaws we embraced integration, thereby changing the social history of this nation.

6.

BEYOND THE SOUTHLAND

I HAVE CENTERED MY DISCUSSION of the emerging Negro
tribe around the Southland because it is there that the
overt evidences, and thus the core of the Negro tribe, are
located. The Negro outside the South, however, is not only
a member of the tribe; he is apt to have Southern roots,
and regardless of where he lives, he suffers the humiliations common to Negroes all over the United States. Thus
it is that the Negro revolt extends far, far beyond the
Southland, and the current crisis in American race relations could well come to a head somewhere outside the
South.

The American Negro is now carrying out a major migration. This migration is primarily a shifting from rural to
urban areas, but a large body of the migration is from
the South to the non-South. The 1960 census shows that
New York has the largest Negro population of any state,
1,477,511. Over a million Negroes live in New York City
alone and they constitute 14 percent of the population of
that city. Thus the Negro population of New York City
exceeds the number of Negroes in every Southern state
but Texas, Georgia and North Carolina. Turning to other
areas of the non-South, the Negro population of California
as of 1960 was 883,861, an increase of 91.2 percent over
the 1950 figure, and Negroes are continuing to pour into

California at the rate of 1,700 per month; Illinois now has over a million Negroes, an increase of 60.6 percent over the 1950 Negro population figure; and in Washington, D.C., the Negro population is now 411,737 as opposed to 345,263 white residents. Here, in Washington, the bare facts of the Negro migration are clearly evident; the Negro population increased some 58.8 percent since 1950, while the white population increased only 18.8 percent.

Similar statistics from Detroit, Cleveland, Cincinnati and other cities of the non-South support those who contend that if the present trend continues, for Negroes and whites, most of the major cities of America will have decisive Negro majorities in the "Central City" by 1970.[1]

Housing and job discrimination are the major barriers faced by Negroes outside the South. The disturbing results of these barriers are evidenced by the fact that the income of the average Negro family is only 55 percent of that of the average white family;[2] when it comes to housing, although Negroes comprise 11 percent[3] of the population, we are restricted to 4 percent of the residential area. And the residential areas for Negroes are, by and large, Negro ghettos; this leads directly to *de facto* school segregation. As of the mid-1950's, 74 percent of the Negro population of Chicago was restricted, by practice more than by law, to six community areas. The situation in Los Angeles is about the same. There was considerable premature rejoicing in Los Angeles when the 1956 Federal Housing Administration report showed that the nonwhite occupancy of dwelling units had increased more than the nonwhite population in the past five years. On the surface it appeared that progress had been made, that nonwhite areas were being opened to Negroes. Then came the brutal facts behind the report: the increase in nonwhite occupancy had been brought about by Negroes acquiring formerly all-white property strips. The white families had moved out;

[1]"Central City" is a term used by social scientists to describe the heart of the city.
[2]See Appendix V.
[3]See Appendix I.

thus there had been no break in the segregation pattern. The same trend is evident in New York City, where there is every promise that by 1970 the larger part of Manhattan Island will be a nonwhite ghetto.

The effect of this residential segregation is alarming. The Chicago Urban League has argued and documented the following disturbing facts:[4]

First, although housing available to the Negro is poorer than that available to the white applicant, the rents charged Negroes are nearly as great as those paid by the whites. This, coupled with job discrimination, means that Negroes can only acquire housing by "doubling up," many families sharing an apartment unit. And here is the root of Negro family breakdown and crime.

Second, there is a direct correlation between housing discrimination and general community health. Chicago Negroes are 20 percent of the population, yet they account for 33 percent of the city's tuberculosis. City health officers have certified that this high TB rate is due to improper diet and poor sanitation. Referring to the 1956 polio epidemic that hit Chicago, the Chicago Public Health Service said: ". . . As the [polio] outbreak progressed, high rates developed only in those areas of the city characterized by a particularly dense population, a low socio-economic status and a high proportion of nonwhites." When the final sad total was in, Negroes, 20 percent of the population, accounted for 61 percent of the polio. And the hardest hit were the children under ten years of age.

Finally, housing discrimination results in increased welfare costs for the entire community. The Illinois Aid to Dependent Children (ADC) report for 1956 showed that unwed and deserted mothers comprised a sizable portion of the welfare budget. Housing for these mothers and their children was the major cost item in that ADC budget, and the published report shows that it cost Illinois taxpayers $83.77 a month to house the average Negro ADC case as

[4]Testimony of the Chicago Urban League to the Illinois House Executive Committee, 72nd General Assembly, in support of the Fair Housing Act of 1961.

compared with $64.84 for the average white ADC case. This discrepancy is caused solely by housing discrimination, and costs Illinois taxpayers four million dollars a year in Cook County (Chicago) alone. Virgil Martin, president of one of Chicago's largest department stores and chairman of the civic committee appointed to investigate mounting welfare costs in Cook County, made the blunt point when he said, "Public aid costs could be sliced in Chicago if racial discriminations were eliminated in housing and hiring." The Chicago Urban League concludes that housing discrimination costs Negroes a "color tax" of $26 million each year.

New York City Welfare Commissioner James Dumpson makes another point about why our relief rolls are swelling. "Much of our relief money," Mr. Dumpson says, "goes to help those families whose breadwinners are working but do not earn enough to support their families."

These facts and figures about relief and the Negro are true of any city outside the South. Sooner or later they will be turned into weapons against the Negro, and the controversial Newburgh, New York, plan is a case in point. The manifest object of the stringent thirteen-point relief plan authored by City Manager Joseph McD. Mitchell is to keep the Negro migrant worker out of Newburgh. His local support comes from those who believe that all of that 250-year-old city's problems can be attributed to the increase in its Negro population. It is so much easier to blame every problem from the rise in venereal disease to increased fire hazards on the Negro rather than to attack the real and complex causes of poverty and urban decay.

Another form of racism which every Negro faces is police brutality. A Negro does not have to be involved in a crime to hear a policeman's club ringing around his ears, and one of the large expenditures to be found in every big-city budget is the damage money paid to Negroes who have been beaten by policemen.

The Commission on Civil Rights has certified police brutality as one of the major injustices in America today and has adduced evidence that police in the non-South are the worst offenders:

Detroit, Michigan: A Negro police officer, Jesse Ray, was assigned to take part in a routine gambling investigation in 1955. Ray was in plain clothes and with one of the police car units dispatched for the investigation. Ray walked to the suspect's home and rang the doorbell. The light inside the house went out. Ray rang again; no response. Then Ray walked down the steps away from the house. At this moment, a white policeman—apparently not a part of Ray's unit—ran down the street after Ray and proceeded to whip Ray with a pistol. The entire confusion wound up at the Fifth Precinct before the sergeant, Ray's sergeant. Then, and only then, did the white officer believe Ray was a policeman. The sergeant asked Ray to keep the story quiet for the sake of the reputation of the police department.

Chicago, Illinois: The United States Supreme Court decided the case of *Monroe* vs. *Pape* on February 20, 1961. Monroe, the Negro plaintiff, charged Chicago police with unlawful entry, illegal search, illegal seizure and unprovoked violence. The Court decision did not completely dispose of the case but it did permit Monroe to sue the Chicago police department for violating the federal Civil Rights Act on the basis of a complaint that alleged that:

About five o'clock on the morning of October 28, 1958, thirteen Chicago policemen led by Chief of Detectives Pape broke through two doors and entered the apartment of one James Monroe. Monroe and his wife were roused from their bed and forced to stand in the center of the bedroom; the six Monroe children were roused and forced to line up in the living room of the apartment; Pape hit Monroe several times with a flashlight, calling him "nigger" and "black boy"; another officer physically assaulted Mrs. Monroe; several of the Monroe children were hit, kicked, and two of them thrown to the floor. Police then proceeded to search the apartment. Monroe was taken to the common jail, held for ten hours on an "open" charge, forced into police lineups, denied the right to go before a magistrate, and refused the right to call a lawyer. The final fact in the case is agreed upon by all, including the police records: Monroe was released without any charges whatsoever being placed against him. In November of 1962 the Monroes' civil suit against the Chicago police department was heard by an all-white jury. After hearing all of the evidence the jury awarded the Monroes fifty thousand dollars damages.

Cleveland, Ohio: A white policeman, identified only as "A" in the commission report, was on motorcycle duty. He alleges that a Negro motorist, twenty-three-year-old Jeffrey Perkins, tried twice to run him down after he had ordered Perkins to "pull over." "A" followed Perkins to the latter's home and shot Perkins dead as he sat at the steering wheel of the car. "A's" defense was that Perkins reached toward the glove compartment of the car and that he, "A," thought Perkins was about to shoot him. Alas, a search proved the glove compartment to be empty and a Negro woman testified that she was standing ten feet from the car when the incident occurred and that Perkins was shot with both hands on the steering wheel.

This roll call could go on ad infinitum. I don't know of a single Negro who doesn't get a flutter in his stomach when approached by a white policeman. Anything can happen; sometimes it does. There are at least four Negro lawyers in New York who make upwards of twenty thousand dollars a year each as specialists in police brutality cases. These men always work on a percentage basis, and one of them has told me that New York City taxpayers cough up over a million dollars a year to pay for unwarranted attacks policemen make upon citizens, most of them Negroes.

The problem is aggravated in areas like Harlem where police brutality is an accepted fact of life. Without such cases to report, Negro newspapers would have considerable blank space. On the other hand, "transition areas," such as the one in which I live, are far from exempt. The white people are moving out but many of them are still here;

the police are on the prowl for suspect Negroes, and some white family can be depended upon to sound the alarm that a Negro is lurking in the trees near their home. Any Negro who happens to be walking, or riding, for that matter, down that street is apt to be in for it. For this very reason, I always keep my press card in my hand when I am driving home late at night. I have been forced to pull my car to the curb by policemen four times in the past two years. Always my press card has ended the inquiry on the spot, but, in each instance, the police have told me they were looking for some Negro suspect.

Racism in the non-South is a very real thing, and I join with Southern whites in denouncing Northern white people who make a fetish of talking about Little Rock, and Mississippi, and Alabama, while practicing, or allowing to be practiced, the most debilitating kind of discrimination in their own back yard. The matters mentioned so far are the overt examples of non-Southern racism. Let us now turn to covert racism and examine "tokenism," economic exploitation and community domination.

Many white liberals argue that only lower-class Negroes face discrimination in the non-South. More than once I have been questioned after a lecture as to whether my wife and I are subjected to any forms of discrimination. "After all," the question goes, "you are a writer, your work has appeared in *Harper's,* you have been on the Jack Paar Show; surely you cannot say you have been discriminated against."

Then I must tell them the dreary truth: My wife and I have been late for a theater curtain because we couldn't get a taxi. In New York, of all places, white taxi drivers pass Negroes by on the assumption that the Negro wants to be taken to a Negro area where the driver might get robbed. My wife and I still rent because we find it difficult to get banks to finance our purchase of a house. That Negroes find it difficult to get mortgage money in New York, and must pay higher rates of interest when they do find financing, is an open and published fact of life. Nobody in this oasis of liberalism has seen fit to do anything about it.

Then there is the matter of job discrimination. I have done several TV documentaries, including *Walk in My Shoes,* but I have only been called in when the race issue was under study. There is not a single Negro employed as a writer or producer in TV documentary units. Of the major magazines, each of the "slicks"—*Life, Look, et al.* —has its one necessary Negro, the single writer or reporter who saves them from the charge of discrimination.

Then there is the matter of discrimination against the Negro who wishes to go into business; the formidable obstacles facing the Negro businessman are something even the advocates of integration have all but forgotten. Let me state the situation in terms of Harlem, which I know although I do not live there. I hasten to add, however, that I have researched the problem of the Negro businessman in Chicago, Los Angeles and Detroit. Their plight is identical.

To go into business one has to have capital; white businessmen execute this hurdle by obtaining loans from banks or by years of personal savings. The Negro cannot get the kind of job that permits him to save and banks simply will not lend him money to go into business. But some Negroes do manage to get enough money to get into business, and then comes the rank fact of discrimination in the non-South: To go into business one must rent or buy or build a building. A Negro can't do it just anywhere; the real estate interests will not let him. Los Angeles is the only place I know where a Negro has been able to rent store space outside of the Negro ghetto. And only one Negro has done that; and he did it because both he and his wife were so light that the owners thought they were white people.

Relegated to the Negro ghetto, then, the Negro businessman finds that white shopkeepers have a "gentleman's agreement" on store rentals. Again the realtors simply will not rent to Negroes. If a store is about to become vacant, the neighboring merchants get the word first, and when a

Negro finds out that the space is available, it has long since been leased to another white man.

The best example I know of is 125th Street in New York. One Hundred Twenty-fifth Street, as everybody knows, is the main stem in Harlem. For years white businessmen worked every trick in the book to keep Negroes from opening businesses along the "main drag." Of late the One Hundred and Twenty-fifth Street Businessmen's Association has gone out of its way to take in a few Negro members, but the Negroes involved are representatives of noncompetitive enterprises—Negro insurance companies, funeral homes and newspapers.

Take a walk along the Negro "Diamond Mile," 125th Street from the New Haven Railroad station to St. Nicholas Avenue. There are four Negro candy stores and three Negro restaurants, but not a single Negro-owned clothing store, furniture store, jewelry store or, for that matter, pawnshop.

This is no accident. The Negro ghetto is considered ripe for plucking; the prices are higher, the credit rates exorbitant; the buyers are less informed; their job status makes it difficult for them to get credit and, as a result, they leap for whatever buy-now-pay-later plans are offered them. Until a few years ago, these stores along 125th Street refused even to hire Negro clerks; it took a threatened boycott and a near race riot to get a few token Negroes in as salesmen.

Incidentally, the "Negro" radio stations that advertise these stores are brimming with Negro purveyors of gospel music and jazz; neither of the stations, however, is owned or operated by Negroes. The talent on these stations are not unionized, and their salaries are far below those paid for white radio personalities doing the same tasks. The management of these stations makes it clear that the Negro talent can leave if they don't like their working conditions. But where can they go? No white station will hire them! So they stay and suffer.

The economic life of the Negro community is controlled from without. The people who scream the loudest about

Negro crime and not wanting Negroes to move into their suburban communities come into the Negro community and reap unusual profits, which they stuff into a bag and drive home with at sunset. The businesses are white; the leading lending institutions are white (only recently have Negroes been hired in New York banks, and as a result of great pressure; there is not a single Negro bank outside the South except in Washington, D.C.); the realtors are white; and thus the Negro is frozen out.

The majority of the Negro slum buildings in which Negroes live and commit so many crimes and incivilities are owned not by Negroes but by white people. The dope traffic which has enslaved so many Negroes is controlled not by Negroes but by white people. The numbers game which bleeds so many thousands of Negroes is run not by the Negroes but by white people. The prostitution racket which flourishes in the Negro community is controlled by the same people who control race track betting and the dope racket. In this connection it is significant to note that when gangland war breaks out, not a single Negro is slain; alas, the lords of organized crime—betting, dope, prostitution and systematic theft—are white.

Stand with me in the Negro community. It has two sources of income: legitimate business and illegitimate business. At sundown, the white, legitimate businessman, the owner of the major stores and media of communication, leaves to go home to his family in suburbia. Enter then the white illegitimate businessman—the lord of dope, crime, prostitution and theft. From sunset to sunup he is the king of the black jungle. And when the morning newspapers carry shocking headlines of murder, depravity and violence, the removed white community reacts with one accord and shouts, "Niggers ain't worth a damn."

PART II

The Negro Revolt

7.

THE NEGRO IN THE FIFTIES

AS OF MAY 17, 1954, "separate but equal" was the law of the land; however, "separate but unequal" was, and still is, the practice and reality.

The American Negro of the fifties lived in a state of constant humiliation. His dignity as an individual was not admitted, in the North or the South, and his worth was so demeaned that even other nonwhite peoples of the world had little respect for him. School desegregation, disfranchisement, segregation of public facilities and overt police brutality aside, the true condition of the Negro is best reflected by his relative position as a wage earner and professional man in American society.

Professional Pollyannas, particularly among white liberals, point with pride to the fact that the American Negro has more income today than he has ever had before. That is not the issue; everybody has more income today than he ever had before, and consumer goods cost more today than they ever have before. The crucial issue is that the income of the American Negro family showed no progress in relation to the income of the white family during the decade of the fifties. As a matter of fact, the relative average income of the Negro family declined during the last two years of the fifties.[1] As of 1960, the median in-

[1]*Economic and Social Status of the Negro in the United States,* published by the Urban League, January, 1961.

come of the Negro family was only three-fifths that of the white family;[2] and there were almost three times as many whites as there were Negroes in business and professions.[3] The statistics are almost exactly reversed on the other end of the economic scale: there are three times as many Negroes as there are whites in such menial occupations as common labor and housework.[4]

Commenting on the current state of the Negro wage earner, the United States Civil Rights Commission concludes:

Although their occupational levels have risen considerably during the past 20 years, Negro workers continue to be concentrated in the less skilled jobs. And it is largely because of this concentration in the ranks of the unskilled and semiskilled, the groups most severely affected by both economic layoffs and technological changes, that Negroes are also disproportionately represented among the unemployed. . . . Negroes continue to swell the ranks of the unemployed as technological changes eliminate the unskilled or semiskilled tasks they once performed. Many will be permanently or chronically unemployed unless some provision is made for retraining them in the skills required by today's economy. The depressed economic status of Negroes is the product of many forces, including the following:

● Discrimination against Negroes in vocational as well as academic training.

● Discrimination against Negroes in apprenticeship training programs.

● Discrimination against Negroes by labor organizations —particularly in the construction and machinists' crafts.

● Discrimination against Negroes in referral services rendered by State employment offices.

● Discrimination against Negroes in the training and "employment" opportunities offered by the armed services, including the "civilian components."

[2]See Appendix V.
[3]Appendix IV.
[4]*Ibid.*

● Discrimination by employers, including Government contractors and even the Federal Government.[5]

This economic straitjacket has everything to do with the breakdown of family life and general morality in the Negro community; it is the basic explanation for the inordinate Negro crime rate; it is the fundamental cause of our high welfare rolls and abundant relief chiseling; this is why we live in slums, and this is precisely why we have to gang up —brothers, sisters, cousins, aunts, every family we can gather—to buy homes outside the Negro ghetto; and as a result of ganging up we bring social and economic deterioration to the once all-white communities.

Let us take a swift, but comprehensive, look at the relative social and economic status of the American Negro as of January 1, 1960:

● The Negro population had a net increase of 25 percent during the decade of the fifties; the white population's increase was only 18 percent.

● For the first time in history the end of the fifties found more than half of America's Negroes living outside the Deep South. The greatest numerical increase was in the Far West, where the Negro population doubled in the decade of the fifties.

● Seventy-two percent of the Negro population now lives in urban areas; only 70 percent of the white population is now urban. (This should be contrasted with the 1950 census, which showed that 63 percent of the Negro population lived in urban areas while 64 percent of the white population were urban dwellers.)

● As of 1960, one out of six nonwhite dwelling units was dilapidated, compared with one out of thirty-two white dwellings: 29 percent of the nonwhite dwellings were deteriorating, compared with 12 percent for white dwellings; nonwhites are less likely to own their homes and when they do the chances are one out of three that the

[5]United States Civil Rights Commission Report Number Three, *Employment, 1961.*

home is substandard; two-fifths of the nonwhite dwellings lacked some or all plumbing, compared with only one-tenth of the white-occupied units.

• These are national figures. The problem in the South is particularly serious: One out of four nonwhite dwellings (rentals) are dilapidated as compared with one out of ten for white dwelling units. Not only is nonwhite housing of an inferior quality; the nonwhite dweller must pay more for his housing.[6]

• To compound the difficulty, nonwhite families (4.4 members) are, on the whole, larger than white families (3.6 members).

• Whereas public housing has improved the quality of housing available to low-income Negroes, it has not noticeably increased the quantity of good housing available to Negroes. This seeming contradiction arises from the fact that public housing usually displaces slum units and the former slum dwellers cannot afford to occupy the new units. The lowest-income Negroes have slums and will travel, and that's precisely what they do: Chicago affords a classic case where Negro slum dwellers are moved out by public housing or urban renewal and transplant, sometimes en masse, into another section of town, carrying all of the "slum" elements with them. In a matter of months their new homes are slums also. Even so, Negroes, only 10 percent of the national population, occupy 47 percent of the public housing.

• These economic and housing factors are reflected in the Negro family characteristics: One out of three nonwhite women above fourteen years of age who have married was, as of 1960, separated or divorced from her husband; the corresponding ratio for white women is one out of five. The higher mortality rate among Negro males leads to a higher ratio of nonwhite widows. This creates another financial burden. The Negro crime rate—which takes the Negro man, principally, from the social scene—adds even more of a burden.

[6]Robert C. Weaver, *The Negro Ghetto*, Harcourt, Brace & Company, New York, 1948, p. 261.

● Broken homes lead to broken morality. One out of five nonwhite births is illegitimate, as compared with one out of every fifty white births. Moreover, nonwhite unwed mothers find the doors to many adoption agencies closed to them. Little wonder, then, that over two-fifths of the unwed mothers receiving public aid are nonwhite.

● The economic disadvantage suffered by the Negro family spills over into such areas as old-age assistance and aid to the blind. As of 1960, the number of Negroes receiving old-age assistance was three times that of white persons and one out of every three blind persons receiving federal assistance was nonwhite.[7]

These dreary facts rasp when heard against recent, and true, reports that the American Negro has developed quite an aristocracy based upon wealth and bloodlines. There are at least twenty-five Negro millionaires, some four hundred Negroes earn fifty thousand dollars a year or more, while about ten thousand of us earn somewhere between fifteen thousand and fifty thousand dollars a year. The Negro elite's penchant for conspicuous consumption has been well known to us for some time, but it did not come to the attention of the white public until the *Saturday Evening Post* of January 13, 1962, published an article on them. The important thing was not the increasing number of wealthy Negroes but what these Negroes are saying.

Mrs. Earl B. Dickerson of Chicago, a close friend of the Kennedys, the Roosevelts and the Rockefellers, lives in a luxurious apartment; when she comes to New York she and her husband, an insurance executive, live in a suite at the Waldorf Towers. Said Mrs. Dickerson: "How can Negroes like us who have our heads above the water be smug while there are masses of our people still struggling below the surface to attain first-class citizenship?"

Post writer Bill Davidson found the Negro elite hard at work for such organizations as the NAACP and the Urban

[7]*Economic and Social Status of the Negro in the United States*, the Urban League, January, 1961.

League; he found their homes larded with *Negro* paintings, expressing *Negro* themes, all mixed in with Louis XIV furniture and other status symbols.

Perhaps the most trenchant comment of all came from Claude Barnett, head of the Associated Negro Press and a member of the Chicago elite: "It's a shame that we have a separate Negro society in this country and a separate wire service for Negro newspapers. We are working toward the end that someday there will be no more need for my news service and no need for anything else—including society—which at present the white community does not allow us to share."

Ten years ago these rich Negroes and their predecessors would not have said these things. Something happened, a dream busted, in the fifties; times got better but things got worse.

For the better part of two decades the United States Supreme Court had been hinting that there was something rotten about segregation. While never striking down the "equal but separate" doctrine that flowed from the *Plessy* vs. *Ferguson* decision of the late 1800's, the Court explicitly said that Negroes were entitled to the same treatment as white people in public institutions. As early as 1935 the Court ruled that a Negro convicted by a jury from which Negroes had been systematically excluded was illegally convicted.[8] In 1938 the Supreme Court ordered the state of Missouri either to provide Negroes with equal law school facilities or admit them to the University of Missouri Law School.[9] A decade later, the Court sharpened and defined this ruling: A Texas Negro was ordered admitted to the University of Texas because the Negro Law School, upon examination, did not afford equal facilities.[10] And in a separate opinion the Court held that even when admitted to a "white" university a Negro student was not given equal treatment if he was required to sit at a separate

[8]*Hollins* vs. *Oklahoma*, 295 U.S. 394.
[9]*Gaines* vs. *University of Missouri*, 305 U.S. 337.
[10]*Sweatt* vs. *Painter*, 339 U.S. 629.

table in the library and a specific seat in the classroom.[11]

The Browns, a Topeka, Kansas, Negro family, got fed up. Their daughter was a student at an inferior all-Negro school; she had been denied admission to the "white" school. Aided by the National Association for the Advancement of Colored People, they sued, not for equal but separate facilities but for the right of their daughter to attend the "white" school. For two years, while the case dragged through court after court, we waited. This, in a very real sense, was it. Now we would find out if, as we suspected, the United States Supreme Court would rule against segregation. The longer the Court deliberated, the more we became convinced that we would win. We felt—later developments proved we were right—that the Court was deliberately stalling, giving the Southern and border states time to swallow the hint and prepare for the inevitable. Then, on Monday, May 17, 1954, came the verdict: Segregated schools were legally wrong; school districts must prepare to integrate Negroes into previously all-white schools; to give everybody concerned time to prepare for integration, the Court would stay its implementation order for one year.

The Supreme Court school desegregation decision was an electric thing, coming—as it most certainly did—just as the Negro was at the breaking point. Negro soldiers had come home from a war against Hitler's race madness only to face incredible insults and police brutality at the hands of the nation they had risked their lives to defend. Later other Negroes were filtered back from Korea.

It would be impossible for a white person to understand what happened within black breasts on that Monday. An ardent segregationist has called it "Black Monday." He was so right, but for reasons other than the ones he advances: That was the day we won; the day we took the white man's laws and won our case before an all-white Supreme Court with a Negro lawyer, Thurgood Marshall, as our chief counsel. And we were proud.

[11]*McLaurin* vs. *Oklahoma*, 339 U.S. 637.

But we were also naïve.

"The people of the South will never accept this monstrous decision," Mississippi Senator James Eastland cried. "I predict this decision will bring on a century of litigation."

We heard Eastland when he said it; we knew there was some truth in what he said; but we did not—refused to, actually—believe that Eastland spoke for the South. Rather, our sentiments were voiced by Negro Congressman Adam Clayton Powell: "This is a great day for the Negro. This is democracy's finest hour. This is Communism's greatest defeat."

Those of us who really believed the desegregation order would be carried out were twice bemused, each time by a false faith. We knew there would be wild speeches, rallies and Klan gatherings; we expected to hear again all the epithets we had been called all our lives. We were prepared for all this and felt we could withstand it. We—particularly those of us who were Southern born—had faith in a class of white people known to Negroes as *good white people*. These were the respectable white people who were pillars of the Southern community and who appeared to be the power structure of the community. It never occurred to us that professional white people would let poor white trash storm the town and take over. Not that the good white people wanted integration—indeed, we knew they did not —but we expected them to be law-abiding and to insist that their communities remain that way. Let me state it in terms of typical Negro naïveté: It was incredible to a Negro woman who had been a servant in a white home for twenty years that her employers would cringe and hide while white trash threw bricks at her grandson on his way to school.

The second false faith that bemused us was the belief that local school boards would recognize the Court order and submit their own integration schedules. This, of course, did not happen. With few exceptions, Negroes have had to institute court action before local boards submitted integration schedules. And when submitted the plans called for "token" integration and did little to unburden the current generation of Negro students, almost all of whom will go forth to life from segregated schools.

Senator Eastland's timetable is on exact schedule. As of June, 1961, seven years after the school desegregation decision, 7 percent of the South's public school Negroes were attending integrated schools. These figures, as the table shows,[12] are even more discouraging when one realizes that this 7 percent includes the District of Columbia, where 84 percent of the Negro students are integrated, and other border states where race relations have been fairly good.

Even less luster clings to this 7 percent figure when it is remembered that to achieve this paltry breakthrough Negro organizations have spent millions of dollars in lawsuits. More, scores of Negro families have been disrupted in the process; many were forced to leave their homes, others have been subjected to economic reprisals and physical abuse.

✓So far, the Deep South has thwarted our efforts toward school desegregation. But in the process they have done something even worse: they have destroyed the Negro's faith in the basic integrity of the white power structure. The report of the Louisiana State Advisory Committee to the Commission on Civil Rights shows why Negroes have lost faith in white people. Commenting on why attempts to desegregate New Orleans schools resulted in riots, the report says:

Insofar as the issue of public school desegregation is concerned, by far the largest segment of leaders in New Orleans may be classified as "neutrals." Included in this category are influential leaders in business, labor relations, politics, the professions, and civic and social affairs.

During the long and bitter controversy over the legal, moral and social aspects of desegregation, the vast majority of the "top" leadership in New Orleans made no statements in regard to this all important issue. *The truth is that, time*

[12]See Appendix II.

*and time again, they refused to speak out, despite the fact
that certain other responsible citizens urged them to do so.*
[Italics mine.]

The Negro masses were more than just resentful and
angry; they were also informed. For decades, Negro newspapers have devoted their columns to glaring accounts of
racial injustices. These reports were stepped up beginning
with the Emmett Till case and became a floodtide with
the outbreak of violence at Little Rock. On the surface
the school integration cases involved the right of children
of taxpayers to attend public schools. But the real issue
was deeper than that; it involved the entire status of the
black man, as an individual, in American society. The
lynching of Emmett Till—the murderers were exonerated
and then confessed in *Look* magazine—and the harassed
Negro students ducking in and out of previously all-white
schools were but current symptoms of a malady that had
afflicted the nation.

Instead of token integration making the mass Negro
more content with his lot, more willing to suffer for the
sake of the future then, it has made him more impatient.
There is nothing more humiliating to a Negro man who
cleans cuspidors and bows before white patrons in an all-
white barbershop than to see a nine-year-old Negro child,
head high, face well scrubbed, walk through a howling
mob and flying bricks to go to school. He hates himself—
God, how he hates himself!—and he will never forgive the
white man who forced him into impotence.

And the Negro's view of himself is not brightened by the
African renaissance. True, the mass Negro is proud of the
new African states and feels a tangential kinship to them,
but the Africans have forced the American Negro to take
a second and much harder look at himself. Segregation and
colonialism are not the same shackle, yet the Negro masses
inevitably say, "If the Africans can do it, why can't we?"
Nor is the matter relieved when American State Department officials go to great lengths to pave the way for

African diplomats to visit restaurants and hotels that deny service to Negroes. There is something macabre about an African who has been denied restaurant service along some highway being rewarded with tea and talk at the White House. If every Negro who met with discrimination was given the same treatment, Washington wouldn't be able to hold the crowd. We are glad to see the African's feathers smoothed; the hideousness of all this is what it says about this nation's view of the Negro: We are the least of the black and despised.

"At the rate things are going," James Baldwin wrote, "all of Africa will be free before we can get a lousy cup of coffee."

"The most wonderful thing that can happen today," the Reverend Gardner Taylor told me, "is to be black in America so long as you are not an American. Black Americans meet these refusals every day, but the President does not invite them to the White House."

This is the voice of deep hurt and bitter disappointment. Baldwin and Taylor speak for us all. This hurt and disappointment are vital factors underlying the Negro revolt. While in the South I talked with the Negro masses—the cooks, the butlers, the maids and the shoeshine men. They still serve white people but they no longer trust, respect nor love them. And with the breakdown of faith in the integrity of the white power structure there is a concomitant loss of respect for law as an effective means of social change. This, I submit, is the main reason why the Negro revolt has come now and as it has.

With the Negro's deepening disillusionment also came widespread doubts about goals which had hitherto been unquestioned. Assuming school integration had proceeded as expected, how much would this have affected the current lives of the Negro masses? Not very much, Negroes discovered once they stopped to think about it. Most of them would still be Jim, Mary, Sue, Aunt Grace and Uncle Charles. The school desegregation decision said nothing about the right of a Negro laborer to become plant foreman if he had the ability to do so. Negro homes were searched without warrants; the victims' heads were bloodied and their jobs were threatened if they dared protest. Negroes darted in and out of department stores where they dared not sit down; they were denied free access to the polls; and if they received a just day in court it was usually when all parties concerned were Negroes.

I remembering standing in the back yard of a Tennessee washerwoman. Her face was drawn, her hands literally bleached from years of "taking in" white people's washing. "Lord, honey," she said, "I sure wish some of these drops of integration would ooze down on me."

The point is that a generation and a half of today's Negroes are doomed to live out their lives under exactly the same conditions they have always suffered, and would be so doomed even if the 1954 school desegregation decision had been implemented.

With the Negroes' deepening doubt and disillusionment and the concomitant decline in their faith in legalism as a weapon of social change came a decline of faith in the Negro leadership organizations that sponsored and seemed married to it. This decline in stock was brought about by three factors:

First, Negro leadership organizations, dominated, as they most certainly are, by middle-class Negroes and white liberals, lost touch with the mood of the Negro masses. The result was a concentrated attack on segregation that reflected "class" rather than "mass" concerns.

Second, even after it became apparent that legalism and "class" concerns could not accomplish the swift change demanded by both the temper of our times and the mood of the Negro people, these organizations persisted in their basic philosophical approach to the problem of segregation; more, they interpreted any desire to debate the question as an attack upon the organizations and the individuals who head them.

Finally, these organizations failed to make room for the

younger, educated Negroes who were coming to power in the Negro communities. The irony of this is that many, if not most, of the younger educated Negroes are educated and inspired because of the work of the very organizations which now refuse to make room for them.

These factors, coupled with a certain estrangement between the local and national offices of Negro leadership organizations, led local Negroes in various parts of the country to express themselves. And these expressions made it crystal-clear that the traditional Negro leadership class, epitomized by the National Association for the Advancement of Colored People, could no longer be considered the prime mover of the Negro's social protest.

Thus the current Negro revolt is more than a revolt against the white world. It is also a revolt of the Negro masses against their own leadership and goals. The full nature of this aspect of the revolt will become clearer in later chapters. It is sufficient to say here that there is a basic disagreement between the Negro masses and some of their leaders, centering on these questions: What are the aims of the battle against segregation, and what should be the main points of attack? What methods should be employed? What should be the role of national and local leadership in the fight? Should there be *one* Negro leadership organization? If not, should the several Negro leadership organizations define their respective roles and each take care not to overlap the other?

These are the questions now being raised by a people who for four hundred years have waged a battle for the right to be ordinary, to be, as individuals, like everybody else: some good, some bad; some wise, some foolish; here and there a genius, now and then a fool. The people are asking these questions of their leaders, who have, at one time or another, tried economic determinism, education and legalism as weapons against the crude, basic reality of segregation. Individually and collectively, these methods have failed and the Negro people are beginning to wonder if, indeed, their leaders have yet come upon the weapon that will accomplish their full deliverance. The Negro consensus, I suspect, is captured in John Ruskin's exhortation that in order to do that which has not been done, we must try that which has not been tried.

8.

THE BIRTH OF THE REVOLT

"LORD, CHILD," a Mississippi woman once said to me, "we colored people ain't nothing but a bundle of resentments and sufferings going somewhere to explode."

The explosion—and no one would have then taken it for that—came on December 1, 1955, the day Mrs. Rosa Parks boarded the Cleveland Avenue bus in Montgomery, Alabama. And the Negro revolt is properly dated from the moment Mrs. Parks said "No" to the bus driver's demand that she get up and let a white man have her seat.

There have been scores of attempts to discover why Mrs. Parks refused to move. The local white power structure insisted that the NAACP had put her up to it, but this charge was quickly disproved. The extremists spread the word that Mrs. Parks was a Communist agent, that the whole thing had been hatched in the Kremlin; that rumor collapsed under the weight of its own preposterousness. The truth is that Mrs. Parks was a part of the deepening mood of despair and disillusionment that gripped the American Negro after World War II. She had been an official in the Montgomery NAACP; Mrs. Parks was an alert woman, a dedicated Negro and fully aware of the continuing injustices Negroes all over the nation were enduring. The only way to account for Mrs. Parks is to say she was a part of the times; that, at long last, her cup ran over.

Word of Mrs. Parks' arrest swept the Negro community. By nightfall an *ad hoc* committee of Negro women was calling for action; they telephoned their clergymen and other civic leaders and demanded that a boycott of the busses be called. On Friday evening, little more than twenty-four hours after Mrs. Parks' arrest, the largest gathering of local Negro leaders ever assembled met to map a plan of action. The meeting almost broke up before it started because the chairman, Reverend L. Roy Bennett, was so angry about the arrest that he didn't wish to tolerate discussion from the floor. "It is time to act," he shouted. "Let's act!"

Calmer heads prevailed, however, and, after several members had asked questions about the wisdom of the action, it was decided to call a bus boycott for the following Monday morning, three days away. This meant that word had to be gotten to the seventeen thousand Negroes —75 percent of the bus-riding population—that they were to walk to work on Monday morning. The clergymen promised to take to their pulpits Sunday and spread the word; but there was still the monumental task of mimeographing and distributing printed material among Montgomery's fifty thousand Negro citizens. A young Baptist minister, Dr. Martin Luther King, accepted that task.

As the busses moved through the Negro section on Monday morning, they were empty. The boycott was on. So was the Negro revolt. That night, hundreds of Negroes jammed a church for a mass meeting to formalize the boycott and the organization that was to direct it. Martin Luther King, a man who, three weeks earlier, had rejected the presidency of the local NAACP because he felt he was too new in town, was elected president.

Formed into the Montgomery Improvement Association, the group did not ask for the end of segregated seating. Rather they asked that:

1. Negro bus riders be given courteous treatment.
2. All bus riders be seated on a first-come, first-served

basis; that Negroes would sit from the back toward the front, the white passengers from the front toward the rear.

3. Negro drivers be hired on routes that served predominantly Negro sections.

The program was much too mild for the local NAACP and that organization refused to enter the boycott, principally because the demands did not ask for the outright end of segregated seating.

The white reaction was bitter. First, the bus company officials proved absolutely intransigent. Second, charged with racist emotions, white gangs began terrorizing Negroes and committing acts of violence; Martin Luther King and other leaders of the protest were jailed on various charges. Despite these acts the protest continued; and because of these acts King and the other Negro spokesmen decided to redirect their forces and attack segregated seating per se. This, of course, led to increased violence, but it also brought the NAACP into the Montgomery story. On May 11, 1956, Robert Carter, legal counsel for the NAACP, argued the case before the Federal District Court. On June 4, six months after Mrs. Parks' arrest, the Court ruled against segregated seating on municipal busses. Four months later, the United States Supreme Court upheld that decision and bus segregation came to an end in Montgomery.

"Praise the Lord," one Negro woman shouted, "God has spoke from Washington, D.C."

Their God had indeed spoken, and He had talked about more than segregated busses. The Montgomery struggle had involved fifty thousand Negroes; it sprang up overnight out of deep resentment over a situation that had aggrieved the local community for almost two decades. As they walked to work or organized car pools, Montgomery Negroes struck back for cursings, slappings and jailings that had been their daily fare for more years than they had the courage to remember. They at first did not ask for integration; they only wanted decent treatment. When even this was denied, they struck for more, and got it.

Meanwhile, the Montgomery story inspired Negroes in other Southern cities who had been bearing the same cross for years. King, along with clergymen from other Southern cities, formed the Southern Christian Leadership Conference and made segregated bus conditions their prime target. The Tallahassee, Florida, and Birmingham, Alabama, stories that grew out of this are now history along with Montgomery.

Montgomery was the launching pad for Martin Luther King; he soared into orbit before he himself realized what had happened. Once he had a quiet moment to reflect and assess his life, it was too late. He had gained international fame, the applause of the world was ringing in his ears, eighteen million Negroes were calling him "Savior" and world ethicists were comparing him to Gandhi and Thoreau.

This was heady stuff for a twenty-seven-year-old whose main ambition had been to become a great preacher. Now, some six years later, Martin Luther King is a somewhat troubled man. He left Montgomery, his work undone; the busses are integrated, but the schools are not; neither are the parks, playgrounds or any other public facilities. And one of the questions now plaguing social scientists is why such a deep-rooted movement as the Montgomery boycott resulted in nothing more than the integration of the busses.

Martin King left Montgomery and returned to his home, Atlanta, where he became associate pastor, along with his father, of Ebenezer Baptist Church and settled down as executive head of the Southern Christian Leadership Conference. It was about as difficult for Martin King to go home again as it was for Thomas Wolfe. The established Negro leadership in Atlanta was wary about his return, and there are those who say that King returned under a truce agreement which calls for him to concentrate, by and large, on national matters and leave local affairs to the entrenched Negro power structure.

Whatever the uneasiness of his return Martin King has been in Atlanta for two years now, and the organization which he heads from there has become a major force in the Negro revolt. Dr. King is, by far, the most popular Negro in America today and it is all but impossible to assess him, his leadership and his organization, without incurring the wrath of thousands, Negro and white, who call his named blessed. Although I am among those who venerate Martin King, I happen to believe he is quite human. He was created by the Negro revolt and it could well be that he will be destroyed by it. The French Revolution ended in victory, with the beheading of those who started it; the Negro revolt could go the same path, for there is something about a revolution that makes it impatient with the strong and the powerful.

The honeymoon between Dr. King and others close to the Negro revolt is over; for the first time since Montgomery criticism of Dr. King is now appearing in print, and comes from, of all people, the Negro students. His crime seems to be that he has not gone to jail enough to merit the badge of continuing leadership. Students are not only idealistic, they are impatient. Then again they could be right; not that Dr. King's jail record is not impressive, but rather that there may be something lacking in the leadership Dr. King and his organization have given. The students are not the only ones who speak critically of Martin King, although none of Dr. King's adult critics will allow themselves to be quoted. In *Harper's Magazine* of February, 1961, writer James Baldwin talked of "The Dangerous Road Ahead for Martin Luther King." When pressed to state just what Martin King's future was, Baldwin halted, pirouetted, and then took refuge in a quote from William James to the effect that "all futures are rough."

The problem facing Martin Luther King is created by his admirers, who would make of him more than he is and therefore obscure what he is in so much controversy that his real merit is almost impossible to determine. The first thing any accurate appraisal of Martin King must do, then, is to establish clearly just what he *is;* and this can best be done by listing the things he *is not.*

Martin Luther King is not an administrator.

Dr. King is the son of one of the most imposing men I have ever met in my life. The Reverend Martin Luther King, Sr. and the Reverend James L. Lomax (my uncle, but the person who took over my rearing when I was ten years of age and bore all the responsibilities for my education) are fellow Baptist ministers in Georgia and have been colleagues in the Baptist State Convention for thirty years. As a youth I attended every session of the convention, as well as those of the auxiliaries, and got to know Dr. King, Sr. rather well. He is a powerful preacher, a brilliant church politician, and is of the dying order of Negro clergymen who have the uncanny ability to make people do things by the sheer power of their presence and oratorical ability. Martin Luther King, Sr. was, and is, what we used to call a "hard" preacher. That is to say, on Sunday morning he preaches as if Heaven and Hell were coming together and only he, sustained by the God-given power of oratory, could keep them apart.

Being a "hard" preacher also meant something else: The Negro Baptist Church is a nonorganization. Not only is each congregation a sovereign body, dictated to by no one, but it would appear that the members who come together and form a Baptist church are held together only by their mutual disdain for detailed organization and discipline. Each congregation elects its own minister after hearing several applicants preach. The only requirement is that it be announced three Sundays "hand running" from the pulpit that on a given date there will be a special church meeting for the purpose of "calling" a pastor. (Even this rule can be evaded. I know of one Negro Baptist church in Washington, D.C., where the members were so anxious to get a certain minister that they voted themselves out of the Baptist connection—thus eliminating the need to wait three weeks—voted the man in as pastor and then, with great shouts and amens, voted themselves back into the Baptist brotherhood.) The "calling" of a minister was always an exciting affair and it is not unknown for the local police to come in and preside over this election in the interest of community peace and security. Almost without exception, particularly in the Deep South, a minister is called to a pulpit over the opposition of some of the members who had other choices. This means trouble, a constant running battle between the "pastor's faction" and the dissidents. More than once in my youth I saw instances where the dissidents got the upper hand and ran the pastor out of town; then they put *their* man in the pulpit, and this meant that the other "faction" became the dissidents and the whole ruckus was on all over again.

A "hard" preacher, then, was a man who could, somehow, keep unity and understanding in his church. To do this the minister had to know the Baptist Discipline, Roberts' Rules of Order and the Holy Bible almost from memory. He had to cajole some members, pray with others: much of his time was spent outwitting love-starved widows in his congregation, particularly those with money or who had influence with some of the brothers on the "deacon" board. Having mastered all this, the Negro Baptist minister still had troubles. His only recourse was the pulpit on Sunday morning; there his mission was clear: he must preach love into the congregation by scaring the hell out of them.

This is the mold in which Martin Luther King, Jr. was shaped. I know what it can do to a young man for I was shaped in the same mold. But men who come out of this mold are not disciplined to become executives. Rather they are emotional men; they think in spiritual rather than practical terms of reference; and as an inevitable result they periodically confuse God's will with their own personal desires and ambitions. They can run a big Baptist church because their churches are, largely, personality clubs; the people come, and give, and respond, because they like the minister. But faced with the task of administering the affairs of a complex and diffuse organization, particularly a secular one, the men molded in the fashion of Martin Luther King, Jr. tend to flounder. Men such as Martin are natural-born revolutionaries; they have what it takes to get people out into the street yelling and dying for a cause. But when the revolution is over, the republic would be better off if someone else took over the executive leadership.

This is part of what has happened to Martin Luther King, Jr. And it is symbolic that he did not have an office at his Southern Christian Leadership Conference's headquarters in Atlanta. (The headquarters have been moved since I was there and I do not know if Dr. King has an office in the new quarters.) Dr. King was seldom seen at SCLC; his private secretary was ensconced at Ebenezer Baptist Church and King's private mail was answered from there. And as I studied the SCLC office on Auburn Avenue I got the impression that the movement was being run in King's name but by somebody else.

Perhaps this incident will illustrate my point: Dr. King held a press conference during the SCLC's annual convention in Nashville in the fall of 1961. During the conference King was flanked by his principal aides, Wyatt T. Walker and James Lawson, a quasi-mystic educated in India and a follower of Gandhi. A reporter asked, "What is the program of your organization for next year?"

Martin King paused, and then replied, "This question should be directed to Reverend James Lawson, here on my right. He is our program director." The reporter turned to Lawson, expecting a reply. Lawson paused, rolled his eyes to the ceiling, and then replied: "We plan to send a nonviolent army through the South next year."

The reporter gulped and then continued: "About how many will be in your army?"

"Oh . . ." said Lawson, "I would say about a quarter of a million Negroes."

Dr. King looked a bit dazed but kept silent.

It was clear to everybody present that this was the first Dr. King had heard of the nonviolent army; it was equally clear that there would be no army. The entire episode was so disturbing that most of the reporters present did not use the exchange in their stories. This could not have happened to a skilled administrator.

Martin Luther King is not an intellectual.

When the news broke that the hero of Montgomery was

a twenty-seven-year-old Baptist minister with a Ph.D. from Boston University, many Negroes saw Martin King as Harry Emerson Fosdick, Albert Einstein and Gandhi all rolled into one. True, King has some of all these men in him; he is more Fosdick than Einstein and more Gandhi than either. Martin King is an excellent preacher, an even better orator; when it comes to nonviolence and suffering for what he deems to be deeply spiritual causes, he is without parallel in American history. But as an intellectual, Martin himself would be the first to testify to the narrowness of his training. This is not Martin's fault, nor is this a criticism of him; rather this is a commentary on the seminary in America and the kind of men the seminary produces. The education of the American clergyman is incredibly narrow, and the limitation is compounded by the fact that seminaries teach men to believe, not to think. Then there is society's view of the clergyman: Our ministers are the only members of the tribe upon whom we impose chastity belts, in the broad sense of that term. They are expected to be of the spirit, not of the flesh, and thus their intellectual and social horizons are limited.

Asked to explain why Mrs. Rosa Parks refused to move when the bus driver issued his demand, Martin King wrote: "She had been tracked down by the *Zeitgeist*—the spirit of the times."

Pressed to explain the Montgomery bus boycott, King replied in terms which show why he should never be called an intellectual:

"Every rational explanation breaks down at some point. There is something about the protest that is suprarational; it cannot be explained without a divine dimension. Some may call it a principle of concretion, with Alfred N. Whitehead; or a process of integration, with Henry N. Wieman; or Being-itself, with Paul Tillich; or a personal God."

This, of course, is what they taught Martin Luther King, Jr. at Crozer Theological Seminary and Boston University. And this course of study is designed to turn out theologians, not scholars; Martin Luther King, Jr. is one of their outstanding products. Only a sycophant would even compare him with such Negro scholars as John Hope Franklin, E. Franklin Frazier, Dr. Jean Noble and high-school-educated James Baldwin.

What, then, is Martin Luther King?

Watch:

The church had been packed since five o'clock; three thousand people stood on the outside waiting to hear the call for action over hastily installed loudspeakers. This was the Montgomery Negro's finest night, the night they came to hear the call for an all-out boycott of the busses. A slight, almost diminutive man (five foot seven) parked his car five blocks away from the church and began to make his way through the crowd. He was not an imposing man; there was nothing uncommon about his light brown face or his thick lips, of which the white press had made so much. He was a new man in town, the preacher over at Dexter Avenue Baptist Church, and many of the crowd would not have recognized him if his picture hadn't been in the local papers.

The meeting began a half-hour late, something of an improvement for such meetings run by Negroes. The audience stood and sang "Onward, Christian Soldiers." Their voices, according to the man who was to give them the call to action, were "a mighty ring like the glad echo of heaven itself."

Then, after other speakers had had their say, it was time for the leader, Martin Luther King, to issue the call. True to the tradition of Negro Baptist ministers, he walked to the rostrum without notes and faced the people. The *Zeitgeist* was forgotten; so were Whitehead, Wieman and Paul Tillich. Maybe, on second thought, they were not forgotten; they were just translated. And this is how they came out:

"There comes a time when people get tired."

"Yes, Lord."

"We are here this evening to say to those who have mistreated us for so long that we are tired—"

"Help him, Jesus!"

"—we are tired of being segregated and humiliated."

"Amen."

". . . *tired!* . . . did you hear me when I said *'tired'?"*

"Yes, Lord!"

". . . tired of being kicked about by the brutal feet of oppression. Now we have no alternative but to protest. For many years we have shown amazing patience. We have sometimes given our white brothers the feeling that we liked the way we are being treated. But we come here tonight to be saved from the patience that makes us patient with anything less than freedom and justice."

By then, as you can well imagine, the angry Negroes were ready to walk, march and, if necessary, fight. Only the nonviolent preaching of Martin Luther King kept them from doing the latter. As for walking and marching, what they did is now history.

✓First of all, Martin Luther King is the foremost interpreter of the Negro's tiredness in terms which the mass Negro can understand and respond to. This is the magic about King's many speaking engagements; in some instinctive way he helps Negroes understand how they themselves feel and why they feel as they do; and he is the first Negro minister I have ever heard who can reduce the Negro problem to a spiritual matter and yet inspire the people to seek a solution on this side of the Jordan, not in the life beyond death.

Second, as a disciple of nonviolence, Martin Luther King is able to involve thousands of American white people in the Negro's struggle. I have watched white people react to King close up and, without exception, they are caught up by his addiction to nonviolent protest. The American Negro is the only group in the world today that takes a nonviolent approach to its problems. India marched into Goa; the Africans rioted against their European colonial masters; the Communists have resorted to bloodshed in Korea, Laos and other areas of Southeast Asia; the West responded, gunfire for gunfire, bloodshed for bloodshed. And when it comes to national defense, anyone who suggested that America remain nonviolent in the face of a Communist attack would be accused of treason. Yet faced with subjugation strikingly similar to that the Communists impose on peoples under their domination, the American Negro elects to stage nonviolent protests.

I remember attending a rally in Chicago where King spoke. I sat next to a white reporter from a daily newspaper and watched him frown with disbelief as King said, "The nonviolent man not only refuses to shoot his opponent but he also refuses to hate him."

"Is he *serious*?" the reporter whispered to me.

And that is precisely the point: Dr. King is quite serious about nonviolence; he actually believes that the man who turns the other cheek will win the battle, or if he happens to lose the battle his children will win the war. Regardless of what one may think about nonviolence, it cannot be denied that such a stance makes Dr. King of extreme value, particularly as far as reflective white people are concerned.

As far as Negroes are concerned, Martin Luther King's role is that of a symbolic leader. Martin is to the Negro revolt as Paul was to the early church; not only does he go from town to town inspiring Negroes to take action, but he returns to suffer with them in the time of trouble. This was his role in Montgomery during the freedom rides and in Albany, Georgia, during the ill-fated move against segregated bus terminal facilities there.

This is Martin Luther King, Jr., the man and civil rights advocate. Now let us turn to an examination of Dr. King as the head of the Southern Christian Leadership Conference.

The Southern Christian Leadership Conference was founded on the theory that clergymen in various Southern cities were ready to assume civil rights leadership in their communities. In essence, this is what had happened in Montgomery; the clergy gained the leadership and took the project to a magnificent conclusion. Dr. King's efforts to organize his influence and project it across the South have met with some success, but his South-wide impact as an organization man is nothing comparable to the stature he achieved in the local Montgomery situation.

There are two main reasons for this: First of all, Southern Negroes are highly denominational—bigoted, actually—when it comes to religion. The Montgomery movement involved Negroes of all major denominations and, although the men closest to King were Baptists, there were Methodists, of all shades, on his board. One Methodist minister, the Reverend E. N. French, was the first corresponding secretary of the Montgomery movement, known then as the Montgomery Improvement Association. The Southern Christian Leadership Conference does not enjoy this degree of denominational integration. The key men in the Conference are all Baptists and there is a good deal of mumbling among Methodists about this very fact.

A second reason why the Southern Christian Leadership Conference has not made the expected impact upon the South is that local leaders in various towns saw themselves as potential Martin Luther Kings, and they did not want his organization moving into their parishes to capture the power and the glory that come with a successful desegregation move. What these men *did* want, and still demand, was Martin Luther King, the symbolic leader; they want King to come to town and help them inspire their people to action, but they do not want the Southern Christian Leadership Conference to move in and take over local movements.

As a result, the Southern Christian Leadership Conference is a loose organization with some sixty-five affiliate organizations in various Southern cities. Except for the Atlanta headquarters, SCLC is an amorphous organization. This is not to say that the SCLC is ineffective, but in comparison with an organization like, say, the NAACP, with identifiable chapters in every major town and city, the SCLC leaves much to be desired.

Under the dynamic leadership of the Reverend Wyatt T. Walker, the executive director of the movement, the SCLC has turned in an amazing job considering the problems it faces and its lack of branches. During the fiscal year September 1, 1960–August 31, 1961, the SCLC raised over $193 thousand; its expenditures exceeded $179 thousand. Where, in terms of civil rights advancement, did this money go and for what?

According to Wyatt Walker, the SCLC was active in four general areas during the time period involved:

Voter Registration. The SCLC conducted voter registration drives in Birmingham, Alabama, in conjunction with other civil groups, and in Montgomery, Alabama, in conjunction with the Montgomery Improvement Association, the organization that brought Martin King to power. There were also voter registration drives in Atlanta, Georgia, and McComb, Mississippi. Both drives were conducted in conjunction with other groups. In each of the above instances, according to Walker, SCLC provided funds and in three instances it provided staff workers.

Nonviolent Action. The SCLC acted as the Southern coordinating center for the freedom riders; according to Walker, the SCLC housed, fed and purchased bus tickets for freedom riders passing through Atlanta en route to trouble spots in Mississippi and Alabama. The SCLC provided staff workers and money for the students who kept the freedom rides going after the initial ride had been ended by a bus burning. The SCLC, through the Reverend Fred Shuttlesworth, fed, housed and gave sustenance to freedom riders in Birmingham, Alabama. The same was done, through Reverend Ralph Abernathy, for freedom riders in Montgomery.

Student Liaison. One of the major programs of the SCLC, says Reverend Walker, is supporting the Student Non Violent Coordinating Committee that sprang up in the wake of the sit-ins. The SCLC gave money and staff workers to aid the students in various voter registration drives and during their freedom rides.

Citizenship Training. This is a relatively new area of operation for the SCLC and the present program was made possible through a forty-thousand-dollar grant from the Field Foundation. Although the SCLC supervises the program, the citizenship training school is located at Dorchester Institute, in McIntosh County some fifty miles south of Savannah, Georgia.

This program is aimed at what Reverend Walker calls "the second-line leadership." It calls for Dr. King's peers in various Southern cities to send their seconds-in-command to the citizenship training school, where they will be taught how to teach basic citizenship skills to the masses back home. The second-line leadership is given courses in how to teach reading and writing, civics, voter registration techniques, the measurement and evaluation of candidates and state politics. This last item is a detailed course on the government and politics of individual states. Persons from Virginia, for example, get a course in that state's political machinery, while people from other states get courses built around the political makeup of their individual states.

This program was inaugurated early in the fall of 1961. By the end of the year, 101 persons had taken the citizenship training course. The idea was that each of these persons would return to his home town and set up basic citizenship training schools for the Negro masses. By February, 1962 fifty-one schools had been set up as a result of the SCLC program. The schools are located in Mississippi, Georgia, Alabama, Virginia and South Carolina.

There can be little doubt that the SCLC has just begun to hit its stride. The key move was made by Dr. King in 1961 when he brought the Reverend Walker—then pastor of the Gillfield Baptist Church and leader of the Petersburg, Virginia, Improvement Association—to Atlanta, where he became executive director of the SCLC. Walker seems to have more patience with executive detail than King; at least he has the wisdom to surround himself with persons who can do an administrative job. Most important, Walker so far seems perfectly willing to remain in the background at SCLC while the public glory goes to Dr. King. This is no easy feat; Walker was master of all he surveyed in Petersburg, his home-grown protest movement was one of the best in the nation. By resigning his church and coming to the staff of the SCLC, Walker not only interrupted a promising pulpit career but relegated himself to the civil rights shadows.

At the time Walker joined the SCLC staff the annual budget was approximately $65 thousand; Walker met his budget by June and went on to get it oversubscribed by $130 thousand. His projected budget for 1962 was $200 thousand.

But Wyatt Walker also brings problems to the SCLC. The major problem is his tendency, according to local civil rights leaders, to come into a town where a mass program is under way and take over. This is precisely what local men feared King would do. "Now we have both King and Walker to contend with," one small town Southern leader said to me.

An example of the conflicts the SCLC engenders is the much debated Albany movement, which ended in the first real failure Negroes have had since Montgomery.

In capsule, this is what happened:

Early in the fall of 1961, the youth chapter of the Albany, Georgia, NAACP decided to test bus terminal facilities in that town. They had a ready-made situation; Albany is a college town, hundreds of Negro students were available for the test. Also, Albany is the site of an army base and discrimination against Negro servicemen in downtown Albany has been a source of friction for more than fifteen years. In typical NAACP style, the youths made a quiet test of the bus terminal facilities. They were refused service. The issue was joined and began its slow journey through the courts.

At this juncture, the Albany situation caught the eye of the Student Non Violent Coordinating Committee in Atlanta. As will become clear in a subsequent chapter, the Albany situation posed the great question under debate by American Negroes: Shall we wend our way through the courts in order to get civil rights or shall we set off mass demonstrations and by dint of strength, numbers and moral right crush segregation on the spot and now? The NAACP youths were willing to let the case snake through the courts; the leaders of the Student Non Violent Co-ordinating Committee were not. The student leaders, with money gotten from the SCLC, launched freedom rides into Albany. In the meantime, other student leaders came into Albany and began to mobilize the Negro masses to support the freedom riders. This put them in a head-on clash with the local NAACP.

"I wouldn't say we didn't want the students here," an NAACP spokesman told me. "I would say, however, that they found us not too receptive to them."

Put bluntly, the clash between the NAACP and the students in Albany was such that it was necessary to form the Albany Movement, an organization that would involve all civil rights groups, and give it the leadership of the protest movement. This was the only way the various civil rights groups could be persuaded to work together.

At first, the Albany protest didn't look as if it would be much of an eye-catcher, but as students from all over the South began to pour into town, and into jail, and as students from the local college—several hundred of them—joined the movement, the entire world began to look upon Albany, Georgia, as another U.S. trouble spot. Then it emerged that the Albany Negro community was not only well organized but was behind the students. Negroes of all classes began to march and protest; here was Montgomery, Alabama, all over again.

Feeling justified—after all, their money had financed the students—Wyatt Walker and Dr. King flew into Albany to give aid and assistance. Martin Luther King's personal presence was a magical inspiration, but his organizational presence, in the person of Wyatt Walker, put local noses out of joint. Martin Luther King spoke, marched, prayed and went to jail along with Dr. W. G. Anderson, an Albany physician and leader of the Albany Movement. Wyatt Walker began to issue organizational orders and commands. Local Negroes got mad.

"Dr. Walker can't come to Albany and take over," one of the leaders cried.

"We can bake our own cake," another shouted. "All

we need from the Atlanta boys is some more flour and sugar."

But, as Negroes across the South are now learning, when you get flour and sugar from Wyatt you also get Wyatt. The local Negroes were not the only ones angry when Walker came to town and began issuing orders; the students, whom Walker had helped finance, were also disgruntled.

"After all," one of them told me, "we did the spadework for this thing. Why didn't Walker stay the hell in Atlanta, send us more money, let us have Martin to speak and walk with the marchers! If he had done that we could have won. No, he had to come running into town like an Alexander who has stopped crying because he's just found a new world to conquer."

The local white powers were not only obdurate; they were also smart. They knew about the troubling of the Negro leadership. They elected to remain firm and bide their time.

Martin Luther King and Dr. Anderson, along with several hundred others, went to jail. The world cried out in dismay; headlines in Moscow told the story of white meanness in Albany; the arrest of Martin Luther King pushed their own problems off the front pages and caused West Berliners to forget the wall that separates them from their friends and relatives. Those of us who have watched such moves closely through the years began to smile; the Albany white power structure had made a fatal mistake by arresting Martin Luther King. And when the news flashed that Martin, along with Dr. Anderson, had been moved to a jail outside of Albany, one located in a nearby county noted for Negro-baiting, Albany moved to the brink of a race riot.

The King arrest and transfer caused the battling Negro factions to forget their differences and move in concert. Things got quiet; local leaders met with city officials and came away empty-handed. Each night there was a mass meeting at a Negro church. Steam was building up; something had to give or something would burst.

Then Martin Luther King changed his mind. He had promised that he would stay in jail until a change came; he invited others to come and spend Christmas in jail with him. Had he stuck to this, as Gandhi would have done, Albany would have been desegregated. But Martin came out on bond.

"A Major Defeat For Martin Luther King," the New York *Herald Tribune* said, and this was the big news item around the world. Negroes everywhere looked at each other in shocked dismay; King's long-standing critics chanted, "I told you so."

There was nothing but gloom in the Negro community as Martin Luther King packed and left Albany. The Albany Movement verged on collapse; Negro leaders, from students to old-line moderates, admitted a terrible defeat.

One day, perhaps, Martin will tell the true story of Albany; he is the only man who can tell it. A few people —about a dozen—know the truth, but Martin Luther King is the only man who can tell it. Knowing Martin as I do, I doubt he will ever part his lips. When I unearthed the truth and asked him to confirm it, his only reply was, "If you print it I will not be nonviolent with you!" And then he smiled.

There, then, are the two Martin Luther Kings, the symbolic leader and the organizational man. Martin the symbolic leader had victory in his grasp at Albany; then, still the symbolic leader, he made the sacrifice of his life and suffered humiliation, silently, for the sake of a better day—a day that will come soon now—for Albany Negroes. But because he did this, as well as because of the resentment stirred up by Walker, Martin the organizational man is in deep trouble. The next town he visits to inspire those who are ready to suffer for their rights he will find people saying, "Remember Albany." And there will be the old, ugly self-criticism Southern Negroes used to level at each other when Martin and I were young boys in Georgia. I can see and hear it now:

"Lord, child," some big mouth will say when Martin

comes to his town, "we got to watch our nigger leaders. They'll lead you into trouble with the white folks and then run off and leave you like he did them people in Albany. Now I got a sister who lives on a farm near Albany and she wrote me last week and she said . . ."

And so the tale will go. Whatever the outcome—and I wouldn't dare predict it—the emergence of Dr. King with all he stands for and means has provoked a serious debate over Negro leadership and methods. Montgomery was the first major battle in the Negro revolt; the crucial encounter lies not far ahead. But before we can deal with the days ahead we must pause and recount the rise and programs of other civil rights organizations that are major forces in the encounter.

9.

THE NAACP

THE NAACP ANNUAL CONVENTION of 1959 should have been a festive affair. The organization was fifty years old, it had racked up a remarkable series of legal victories in the name of the Negro people, and could justly lay claim to being the most important of the Negro leadership organizations. Yet the fifteen hundred delegates who gathered in New York's Coliseum were troubled; there were deep rumblings of unrest and discontent.

The issue many of the delegates wanted resolved was whether the NAACP would, as a matter of official policy, employ direct action to storm further the bastions of segregation. Direct mass action had paid off handsomely for Negroes at Montgomery, as well as in other areas where Martin Luther King's Southern Christian Leadership Conference had given guidance. The precise legalism of the NAACP, on the other hand, while gaining spectacular courtroom results, had made relatively little practical headway. This was the issue the delegates wished to debate. But even as they sought to bring the issue to the convention floor, the delegates knew that, at best, they could only suggest that the NAACP adopt a broader attack upon segregation. While the constitution of the NAACP allows the delegates to offer resolutions, they cannot fix policy. The rank-and-file NAACP members' views have no effect whatsoever upon the policy of the organization, unless the executive board, upon hearing these views, decides to take a given action. Convinced that the organization needed a broader base for its desegregation program, and hoping to use the floor debate on this issue as an opportunity to persuade the executive board to relinquish its absolute power and institute a more democratic procedure, a coterie of delegates moved on the floor of the convention with fire and determination.

But the debate bogged down from the outset. Rather than raise their point on the clear-cut issues of mass action and more democratic procedure within the NAACP, the crusading delegates couched their case in the cause of one Robert Williams of Monroe, North Carolina:

Earlier that year, Williams, the president of his local branch, had held a press conference during which he said that Southern Negroes would use arms, if necessary, to protect their persons and property.[1] Every American, of course, has the right to protect himself, but the sound of Williams' voice was too much for the Southern white power structure. A cry arose that the NAACP was exhorting Negroes to violence; the national office of the NAACP took note of the incident and Williams was dismissed from his post. The national office defended this exercise of their constitutional right to dismiss a branch officer by saying that whereas they reaffirmed the right of a person to protect himself, they felt it was not in the interests of the organization for a local branch chapter to state this as a general policy.

The rebel delegates took to the floor in the name of the Williams cause, and, through muddy thinking, allowed the leadership of the convention to make the Williams case *the* issue. The delegates somehow equated the Williams advocacy with mass action, and assumed that by corraling a rousing floor vote against the dismissal of Williams they

[1]The NAACP national office also claims that Williams advocated "getting" one white man for every Negro assaulted in the South. Williams denies this but the original press release on the Williams case supports the contention of the NAACP national office.

would inspire the executive board to pay more attention to the rank and file.

The national office not only controlled the platform; they subjected the Williams forces to a heavy bombardment from the NAACP's big guns. Jackie Robinson and other "names" spoke in defense of the dismissal, but the issue proved a bit much for the former Brooklyn Dodger and his cohorts. In a desperation move, the NAACP leadership called in Mrs. Daisy Bates, then riding high as the heroine of Little Rock. The delegates were stunned. Mrs. Bates herself had just survived a covert attack by the national leadership of the NAACP. Yet she made an impassioned speech in favor of the dismissal of Williams, and the ensuing emotional tide doomed the Williams forces.[2]

With that, the issue fell dead. The NAACP was still on record as a friend of Martin Luther King and others who engaged in direct mass action, but the question of the NAACP itself becoming involved in this tactic was left unsettled.

Why, then, did the NAACP certify a false issue for debate? One must conclude that it was either because the NAACP is unwilling to become involved in direct mass action—an impression that many of the semicentennial delegates came away with—or because it cannot decide what, if any, role it should play in the mass action movement, and is unwilling to commit itself. My feeling is that the latter is the case. Had this issue been debated on its merits during the convention, there is little doubt that the forces desiring direct mass action would have won. Indeed, the NAACP leadership would have been embarrassed to oppose direct mass action openly. On the other hand, despite many opportunities to do so, the NAACP has consistently failed to take a positive and meaningful lead in

---

[2] Late in the fall of 1961, race trouble erupted in Monroe, North Carolina. In the melee a white couple was kidnaped and taken to Williams' home. Faced with prosecution Williams fled the country and is now in Cuba.

initiating or giving concrete support to various mass action movements and demonstrations.

It is my opinion that the issue of direct mass participation, raised by the being and actions of Martin Luther King, presents a grave dilemma to the national leadership of the NAACP, a dilemma that they have been unable to face directly and resolve. Despite the real cordiality that exists between King and Roy Wilkins, King's phenomenal rise has been a profound embarrassment to the NAACP. It is a credit to both these men that cordiality still exists, and that their joint press releases indicate an outward solidarity of purpose. However, this show of unity only begs the rather obvious question of why there are, then, two separate organizations functioning in the same field, ofttimes—as in the case of voter registration—overlapping each other.

It is extremely difficult to get at the NAACP's precise position on mass action. On one hand, the national leadership of the organization says it supports mass action and exhibits directives and press releases to prove it; on the other hand, local NAACP people complain that they are not getting national leadership and help in the area of mass action.

The truth seems to be this:

The NAACP national leadership does believe in mass action but it does not believe that national leaders should go into local communities and set off such demonstrations. If local NAACP-ers want to hold a mass demonstration, fine; the national office will support them with funds and, if necessary, legal aid. This dumps the responsibility for mass action into the laps of local NAACP leaders, who are now deeply troubled because CORE and the SCLC have come into their towns and set off demonstrations that not only changed things but received world-wide attention and acclaim.

Looking at it from the local NAACP point of view, however, two points should be made: First, they feel there is some value in the kind of symbolic leadership Martin Luther King exerts; although local leaders wish to run their own towns, they do feel the need for national figures to come in and suffer along with them. Second, although the NAACP national leadership supports mass action, it has failed to call its various local branch leaders together and outline a plan of attack to be followed in concert.

√"We are a highly organized outfit," NAACP Executive Secretary Roy Wilkins told me. "I don't sit here in New York and tell other people what to do. We let them know our general policy and we help them when they attempt to carry it out."

√ My own view is that the NAACP, both locally and nationally, suffers from its own history. It was created by upper-class Negroes and still reflects this view although the rank-and-file membership has shifted from the elite to the common Negroes. True, the NAACP has fought many battles for the common man, but one gets the feeling that its main involvement is with the "talented tenth," the exceptional Negro who proves the Negro's right to equality. Compared with other civil rights leaders, the NAACP leadership tends to be conservative, at both the top and the bottom. This remains despite the fact that the very makeup of the NAACP has changed. Whereas the NAACP once drew its membership from white liberals and upper-class Negroes, today 80 percent of its members are Negroes—not only professors, lawyers and teachers, but postmen, maids and bus drivers. But, as I said earlier, the NAACP is victimized by its own history; it has had long years of splendid success and has become almost impervious to the changing conditions and attitudes of recent years.

The history of the NAACP begins during the time Southern Negroes were being forced to forge themselves into a reluctant tribe. The story is set in the North, which, for all of its faults, has always been a fairly free place. Men of conviction could take to the public platforms there and protest without fear of being lynched or driven out of town. This basic freedom caused another sort of migration around the turn of the century: Whereas Negro workers came North in search of work, hundreds of Negro intellectuals came in search of a free platform where they could work for the betterment of their race.

Having become the bane of legalized segregation and therefore Northern philanthropy and thus of Atlanta University, W. E. B. Du Bois left Atlanta and joined several other young Negro intellectuals who were determined to correct the Negro's situation. Du Bois and his cohorts were opposed not only to white segregationists but to the teachings and preachments of Booker T. Washington as well. The group held its first meeting in Niagara Falls, Canada, in June of 1905, and incorporated themselves as the Niagara Movement. Their platform was adopted during their 1906 meeting at Harpers Ferry in what Du Bois himself has called "a tumult of emotion."

This passage from the platform perhaps best conveys the atmosphere in which they met:

> . . . Never before in the modern age has a great and civilized folk threatened to adopt so cowardly a creed in the treatment of its fellow citizens, born and bred on its soil. Stripped of verbose subterfuge and in its naked nastiness, the new American creed says: fear to let black men even try to rise lest they become equals of the white. And this is the land that professes to follow Jesus Christ. The blasphemy of such a course is only matched by its cowardice.

The movement met annually for two years and picked up some support from Negro and white militants. Most Americans, Negro and white, considered Du Bois and his followers too radical, however, and their efforts had little impact. Then, in 1908, came the bloody race riot in Springfield, Illinois. (Springfield had also had a race bloodletting in 1904.) Several white Northerners of stature were shocked by these events and resolved to do something about them. These distinguished white Northerners, some of whose names live until now—Jane Addams, William Dean Howells, John Dewey, Arthur B. Spingarn—announced plans to set up an organization to be called the National Association for the Advancement of Colored

People. They invited the young militant Negroes of the Niagara Movement to join them. Most of the Niagara men, including Du Bois, accepted the invitation. Some of them, however—notably Monroe Trotter, who flatly said he didn't trust white people—refused to join. The NAACP became a formal organization in 1910 with Du Bois the only Negro officeholder. These were the organization's announced goals:

- Abolition of enforced segregation.
- Equal educational advantage for colored and white.
- Enfranchisement for the Negro.
- Enforcement of the Fourteenth and Fifteenth Amendments of the United States Constitution.

The NAACP's program was "denounced by every white man who gave to Negro institutions," according to Mary White Ovington, a white New York social worker who was among the founders of the movement. Negroes, particularly those who were associated with institutions receiving aid from Northern philanthropy, also spoke against the objectives of the Association.

Undaunted, the leaders of the NAACP stuck to their guns and achieved remarkable success. Leaning heavily upon the legal process as a weapon of social change, the NAACP achieved three major court victories in the first fifteen years of its life. In 1915 the Supreme Court ruled against the "grandfather" clauses that had kept Negroes from voting in several states; in 1917 the Court struck down a municipal ordinance requiring Negroes to live in certain sections of town; and in 1923 the Court overturned a murder conviction against a Negro because, among other things, Negroes had been excluded from the jury which had convicted him.

These cases were of far-reaching significance and gained the NAACP much popularity and support among Negroes and liberal whites. The mass migration of Negroes swelled the ranks of the NAACP, and by 1921 there were more than four hundred branches of the organization scattered throughout the nation, collecting information for the national office, and carrying out the general principles as much as their local situations would allow. The NAACP has been criticized for its failure to exert pressure on the labor unions of that era to accept Negroes, but has defended itself by saying it chose to concentrate on the great evils of disfranchisement, lynching and legalized segregation.

The Urban League, formed two years after the NAACP, made the Negro worker its main concern, but it too shied away from the touchy question of the role of the Negro in labor unions. The League concerned itself with helping the Negro migrant adjust to urban life—that is to say, the League helped him find a job. Standing between the worker and the employer and then bringing them together, the League accomplished a Herculean task, and was instrumental in relieving the doubts of both the Negro newcomers and the white industrialists who hired them. Like the NAACP, the League received the bulk of its economic support from white donors. It should be said that the national office of the Urban League did speak in favor of desegregated unionism, but the local League branches, left to their own devices, evaded the matter whenever local employers so dictated.

Barred, by law and practice, from white labor unions, Negro laborers began, in 1920, to organize their own locals. The moves were ineffective, however, until A. Philip Randolph organized the Pullman Porters and Maids in 1925 with the aid of several white unionists. After much behind-the-scenes haggling, Randolph was able to get the support of the national offices of both the Urban League and the NAACP. The railroad interests were obdurate, however, and Randolph's local was not granted full recognition and bargaining power until 1937. Even so, Randolph was able to get a million and half dollars in salary increases for his eight thousand workers. This near-miracle made the Negro labor movement the third of the major Negro leadership organizations working for the general betterment of the race.

The NAACP, the Urban League and the Brotherhood of Sleeping Car Porters, as Randolph's organization was named, were the Big Three. Walter White, Lester Granger and A. Philip Randolph—these were the Negro leaders. These men and these organizations—with a lusty assist from the depression of the thirties, World War II and the continuing Communist menace—led the Negro closer to freedom and equality than he had ever been before.

✓The NAACP rose in power during the decade of the forties by winning a series of court victories which broke down restrictive covenants and ordered Southern states to equalize the salaries of Negro and white schoolteachers and the facilities of Negro and white public schools. Its position was further strengthened when the Urban League fell into disfavor, as far as Negroes were concerned, because of its reluctance to give aid to Negro labor unionists. Then, in 1949, two of the Negro members of the League's board of directors resigned, claiming that white real estate operators controlled the League and advocated segregated housing.

The NAACP, on the other hand, saw the sign in the sky and was more definite in its support of the Negro labor unionists. As a result, the NAACP also eclipsed A. Philip Randolph and his Pullman porters' union—the third of the "Big Three" Negro leadership organizations—and at mid-century it stood atop the heap.

The NAACP's main ally was the upsurge of freedom that swept the world in the wake of Nazism and in the face of Communism. Far-reaching social change was in the air. It could happen here. Who would bring it? How? The NAACP had the center of the stage; its position was based on solid performance; Negroes, smarting under the charge that they forever fought among themselves, closed ranks around "Twenty West Fortieth Street," the New York headquarters of the NAACP.

Negro writers, clergymen, schoolteachers, lawyers, social workers—all who commanded a public platform—agreed in public with the NAACP. Many of us felt that the NAACP was too committed to legalism and not committed enough to direct action by local people. There was an endless parade in and out of the NAACP's national office of Negroes who felt that the desegregation fight should take on a broader base. But until the spring of 1958, four years after the school desegregation decision, not a single desegregation-minded Negro engaged in serious open debate with the NAACP. Even then, unfortunately, the debate came in terms of personalities rather than policy.

Since 1939 the entity known to the public as the NAACP has actually been two organizations: the NAACP headed by the late Walter White and now by Roy Wilkins, and the NAACP Legal Defense and Education Fund, headed by Thurgood Marshall, now by Jack Greenberg. The initial reason for the separation was to provide tax relief for contributors to the Legal Defense and Education Fund, which functions solely as a legal redress organization. The NAACP, on the other hand, maintains a lobby in Washington and so its contributors are not entitled to tax exemptions. For a long time, however, the two organizations maintained quarters in the same building and shared an interlocking directorate. In 1952 the Legal Defense and Education Fund moved to separate quarters and in 1955 the interlocking directorate was ended. The tax matter aside, the cleavage came about as a result of deep internal troubling, the details of which are still in the domain of "no comment."

Despite the march of well-scrubbed, carefully selected Negro students into previously all-white schools, it was crystal-clear that the fundamental question of the Negro's dignity as an individual had not been resolved. The glory was the NAACP's and nobody begrudged it. Yet there was a widespread doubt that a nationally directed battle of attrition that took so long and cost so much to bring so little to so few would ever get to the heart of the issue.

There were many local heroes during the decade of the fifties; they all had a brief hour, were clasped to the breasts of national leadership organizations, but when their public-relations and fund-raising value slipped they fell into disuse.

Mrs. Daisy Bates, the president of the Arkansas State NAACP and the undisputed moving spirit behind the integration of Little Rock's Central High School, affords an example of life behind the monolith's curtain.

The Spingarn Medal of 1958, voted annually by the NAACP to the person or persons who have contributed most to racial advancement during the previous year, was awarded to the Little Rock Nine. When the students received notice of the award and realized that it did not include Mrs. Bates—whose home had been bombed, and whose business was destroyed—they rejected the citation. The powers-that-be at Twenty West Fortieth Street reversed themselves and Mrs. Bates was included in the award, which she and the students accepted with smiles, amid thunderous ovations. The Negro press reported the Bates case in great detail and interpreted the incident as overt evidence of the covert pressure the NAACP had been exerting on local Negro leaders for some time.

Today the NAACP is beset by dissension within and criticism from without. Even so, it is the largest, best-organized and most efficiently run of the Negro leadership organizations. As of 1962, the NAACP numbered 471,060 members scattered through 1,494 branches in 48 states. Its general fund income for 1961 exceeded one million dollars, more than half of which came from branches in the form of membership fees and contributions.

To ask, "What is the NAACP's program?" is, to some, like asking, "What does God do for a living?" But when one wades through the prestige, heritage and lore, these general program items emerge:

● The NAACP maintains an excellent lobby in Washington.

● The NAACP maintains a thorough research department that relentlessly unearths facts and figures to support their efforts against discrimination in private and federal employment.

● The NAACP is without parallel when it comes to lodging protests in high places, with the people who are able to do something about the problem.

● The NAACP, through its local branches, assumes all the burden of integrating schools in the Deep South. This effort involves getting parents to send their children to previously all-white schools. One must not confuse this work, however, with the legal prosecution of these cases. This work, on the whole, is done by the NAACP Legal Defense and Education Fund.

● The NAACP stands ready and willing to help any Negro, or Negro organization, that yells for help in a racial matter.

Why, then, is there criticism of the NAACP? Why, then, have other organizations come into being and eclipsed the NAACP as far as dramatic mass action is concerned?

When Roy Wilkins mounted the rostrum of Spelman College's famous Sisters Chapel on March 16, 1961, he was up to his graying temples in history, and he knew it.

Spelman was born with the aid of white philanthropy (largely Rockefeller money, and Sisters Chapel is named after the Rockefeller sisters) in the days when the American Negro was young. Now the Negro has grown up and students from Spelman were among those engaged in sit-ins and freedom rides. But most of all, from an historical point of view, Wilkins was in Atlanta, the same town where Booker T. Washington cheered the hearts of whites and doomed the hopes of Negroes with his "separate as the fingers, yet one as the hand" speech.

"I am honored by the invitation to speak to the students at this historic college at what may be an historic moment in the evolvement of an old, old issue," Wilkins began.

Then Roy went on to compliment the students for the nonviolent protests against segregation.

"Everything, of course, is tied to the school desegregation fight; not only here, but throughout those Southern areas still resisting the inevitable. Virginius Dabney, the scholarly editor of the Richmond, Virginia, *Times Dispatch,* wrote in 1953 that school segregation was the keystone in the arch and that if it should be knocked out the whole segregated structure would collapse.

"The principal task before any community," Wilkins

added, "is the abolition of the segregated school. The inadequate and unequal education our children are receiving under this system is literally placing them in leg irons to run the race of life."

There, I suggest, in Roy Wilkins' Atlanta speech, is the key to all the troubling about the NAACP, its philosophy and action program.

To be certain, school segregation is an abominable thing, particularly when one realizes that Southern schools are not only segregated but still unequal. I do not know of a single concerned Negro who denies for a moment that school desegregation must be accomplished as quickly as possible. Nor does anyone doubt Wilkins' assertion that inferior schools place Negro children in leg irons for life.

The central failure of school desegregation as the cornerstone of a civil rights policy is that it simply does not involve enough people. All of its merits admitted, the desegregation of a local school is a tight little drama carried out by a few Negro actors while a white mob throws bricks and epithets. Yet each of the embattled towns have thousands of Negro citizens who must become involved if total desegregation is to become a reality. The case of James Meredith and his heroic bout with prejudice and violence at the University of Mississippi is a classic illustration of just this point. Our hearts leaped with joy when it became clear that Meredith was going to brave it out; yet, now that he is there, under daily protection of federal officers, the victory seems small. It took so much to get so little done, and the so little is of benefit to so few people. Meredith's courage is more than commendable; it is akin to saintliness. But—and this is precisely the point —such efforts as these are simply too restricted, too narrow in scope, to serve as a broad base of general desegregation.

Another failing of school desegregation as a central policy is that it provides no immediate relief for those who have already finished school or for those who have no intentions of attending school. Nor, indeed, does it provide any relief for those Negro children who elect—as

most of them so far have done—not to attend integrated
schools. Integrated schools have become an article of faith
for Negro leaders and white liberals but it overlooks the
fact that most people, Negro and white, are not sufficiently
school-minded to sustain integrated schools as the central
thrust against discrimination.

A third weakness of the theory that school desegregation
is the key matter is the question of time. It has taken seven
years to get 7 percent of the Negro children of the South
into integrated schools. I know of no one who envisions
that the job will be completed in less than a decade. Is the
entire desegregation process to wait until school integration is accomplished?

Then there is this: The very nature of the school desegregation battle sidelines the best Negro brains in the
various local communities. The bulk of the trained
Negroes are schoolteachers; they work for the embattled
cities and states involved, and their brains and efforts
must thus be done without. Moreover, little has been done
along the lines of securing the future of the Negro teachers
in the embattled areas. Some of the border states have
quietly integrated a few dozen Negro teachers, but there
is little likelihood that this will be done on a mass scale
in the Deep South even when every Southern white school
is integrated. I have talked with scores of Negro teachers
in the South and, almost to a man, they question whether
the matter of integrated schools has been clearly thought
out. Not that they are opposed to it; rather, they don't
feel the captains of the legal victory were ready to deal
with the ultimate practical results of the future of Negro
teachers.

NAACP people are hesitant to talk about it, but they
are having a most difficult time getting local parents to
start integration suits. Why? There seem to be two reasons: Parents, on the whole, don't seem to be interested in
doing so; some of them fear reprisals, but the major
explanations for this lethargy seem to be that school integration simply isn't something that large numbers of
Negroes get excited about. The second reason for the

dearth of plaintiffs in school desegregation cases is that local NAACP officials simply don't know how to get their cases properly under way.

I suspect the real problem with school desegregation is psychological. The process always involves taking Negro children to previously all-white schools. This is because the unequal tradition has rendered the white schools superior, but the integration process always gives the Negro the feeling of changing schools in order to be with white people. This is a difficult psychological hurdle for Southern Negroes to overcome. The truth is, on the whole, they don't want to be with white people as such. They do want the best schools, however, and I predict that if a Southern city ever built a new school and announced that all children were welcome to come, making sure that the school never got the stigma of having once been "the white school," Negroes would come in droves.

The residue of my argument against the theory that school desegregation is the key to total desegregation is this: School desegregation does not involve the Negro masses; it proceeds with the best local Negro brains on the sidelines and suggests that relief for those Negroes not attending school is to be delayed, or less emphasized as of now.

Looking at this from a purely organizational point of view—and I am a member of the executive board of my local NAACP—I am convinced that the NAACP has failed to launch a program whose visible goals capture the imagination of the Negro masses. Any organization that fails to elicit the moral and financial support of its rank and file will wither, no matter how worthwhile its aims. The NAACP has begun to do just that: its 1961 membership was several thousand less than in 1960 and, for the first time in years, the national office is running a deficit and must draw on its reserves.

The criticism of the NAACP over the past three years has taken its toll. Things are changing down at Twenty West Fortieth Street. For one thing Roy Wilkins has become less intransigent, more willing to talk with his critics than he once was. Also, a member of the NAACP youth division has been placed on the board of directors for the first time. The NAACP national office no longer ignores the fact that the sit-ins and freedom rides have relieved more common indignities for more common people in two years than legalism has accomplished in a quarter of a century. And, of late, the NAACP national office has flirted with quasi-mass action. On December 4, 1961, Gloster Current, national director of branches, sent a directive to all NAACP branches in metropolitan cities urging them to demand more jobs for Negroes in large retail outlet stores such as Sears and Montgomery Ward. The branches were urged to press their demands and, if necessary, demonstrate or picket. The last exhortation was that the branches should publicize their activity and keep the national office informed.

Praiseworthy though this may be, it is still a far cry from the kind of mobilization and on-the-spot leadership Dr. King managed to accomplish.

The internal unrest within the NAACP stems from two sources which are closely allied: Rank-and-file members, including several branch presidents, complain that they are unable to control organizational policy and that the over-all political structure of the NAACP is undemocratic. Their argument is that they would institute a program of vigorous mass action if they had the political power to control national officers and national policy. The national office, as we have already noted, contends that it does support mass action, but that it leaves it to the several branches to carry out such programs.

"The gripes about the organization being undemocratic come from people who want to wreck the NAACP," Roy Wilkins told me.

After an examination of the complex political and policy machinery of the NAACP, I am convinced that Roy is right when he says that those who are griping would wreck the NAACP; that is to say, if the reforms urged by the dissidents were put into practice they would indeed wreck the organization as it now is. However, I hasten to add that this begs the question whether the NAACP as it now functions does not need to be wrecked.

The National Association for the Advancement of Colored People is the most political organization I know of outside the two major political parties. Trying to determine the source of power and policy in the NAACP is a tedious endeavor and is made even more difficult when one realizes that the letter of the NAACP constitution is but a hoop skirt under which hides a number of chillingly political maneuvers. Let us start at the bottom, using my branch, the Jamaica, New York, NAACP, as an exact example of how the power flow within the NAACP works.

When interested persons desire to form a branch of the NAACP they are required to indicate this desire to the NAACP national office along with a petition for a charter carrying at least fifty signatures. Upon examination of the names and the request, the national office issues a charter which allows the interested parties to organize themselves as a branch of the NAACP.

To become a member of an NAACP branch one must pay his dues in advance. There are five adult membership categories, all of which give the member full rights and responsibilities:

● Two-dollar memberships. This membership fee is divided equally between the treasury of the local branch and that of the national office.

● Three-dollar-and-fifty-cent memberships. This is a two-dollar membership plus a subscription to the NAACP magazine, *The Crisis*. The balance is divided equally between local and national offices.

● Five-dollar memberships. This membership includes a subscription to *The Crisis*. The national office gets two dollars of the remainder, and a dollar and a half stays with the local branch.

● Ten-dollar memberships. This includes a subscription to *The Crisis,* the national office gets four and a half dollars of the remainder, and the local office four dollars.

● The life membership. This is a five-hundred-dollar

membership, three hundred of which goes to the national office.

We of the Jamaica, New York, branch elect our officers by a simple majority vote and for a term of one year. We elect the members of our board of directors in the same manner. I am a member of the board and, upon recommendation of my branch president and confirmation by the board, I am a member of the Political Action Committee of the branch.

The Jamaica branch is a member of the New York State Conference of branches, which comprises all of the NAACP branches in this state. The New York State Conference, in turn, is a member of Region Two, one of the seven regions of NAACP organizations.

The political meaning of all this becomes clear during the national NAACP annual convention.

The national NAACP is run by a forty-eight-member board of directors; these members are elected for three years, which means that, under the staggered system, sixteen vacancies occur on the board each year. This is the procedure for electing board members:

Each year the convention names a seven-man nominating committee to prepare a slate of candidates for the board of directors. Four members of this nominating committee are named by the delegates but only one can come from a given region. Since there are seven regions the stage is thus set for political horse trading; this brings on political campaigning within regional delegations and between regions. The other three members of the nominating committee are named by the board of directors itself.

These seven people meet shortly after the annual convention and agree upon a slate of candidates for the board (no member of the nominating committee can himself be a candidate). This slate is mailed to the various branches for voting confirmation. At the same time the various branches are invited to name independent candidates for the board. Any person may be named provided his nomination is supported by a petition signed by thirty members of a branch. These independent candidates are voted upon along with the committee nominees by the various branches at their annual meetings.

The sixteen candidates receiving the highest number of votes from each local branch receive that branch's unit vote. The size of a branch's unit votes varies according to its membership. The smallest branches have two unit votes, the largest have ten. These unit votes are forwarded to the national office and the sixteen persons having the highest number of unit votes are elected to the board.

That, in theory, is how the board members are selected. In practice, however, several things tend to occur. First, it is all but a political impossibility for any independent nominee to be elected to the board. Only one person has executed this feat in the fifty-three-year history of the NAACP. The political machine is simply against this occurrence. What actually happens, according to dissidents, is this:

The board appoints the executive secretary of the organization; he, at present Roy Wilkins, recommends his staff people to the board, which, in turn, confirms their appointment. One of these staff persons (there are several, one for each region) is the NAACP field secretary. His job is to keep in close touch with the local branches in his region. The charge is that the field secretary acts as the political liaison for the national office and that, through a number of horse trades, he influences the selection of the regional members of the nominating committee, who, in turn, determine just who will appear on the slate of candidates for the board. This, according to the dissidents, amounts to control by the national office.

This complex political machinery has everything to do with the policy of the NAACP. The delegates to the national convention are elected by their local branches. On the convention floor they can pass any resolution for which they can muster majority support. But the resolutions passed by the delegates are not binding upon the national office; the board of directors reviews these recommendations and decides whether they will become a matter of organizational policy. Since the final policy of the organization rests with the board, the entire decision depends on who the members of the board are and their attitude toward certain matters. Thus the matter of policy is tied to the political election of board members; thus also, according to the dissidents, the political and policy machinery of the NAACP is, as a practical matter, controlled by the national office.

Roy Wilkins, of course, denies this. It will take more than denial, I suspect, to stem the rising tide of unrest within the NAACP. In all fairness, I must state that I am with the dissidents on this issue, although I do not necessarily agree with all of the minor charges some of them make against the national office.

The disturbing thing is the unwillingness of the NAACP national office and the board of directors to realize the burning need to do two things: First, the elected delegates should be allowed to make basic organizational policy on the floor of the convention. Second, the elected delegates should have the right at least to nominate, if not elect, the men who will head the organization. Both the executive secretary and the national president of the organization are appointed by the board, much to the embarrassment of local members, who are trying to overthrow just such white political power structures in their home towns. This is an embarrassment, but the political obstacles faced by rank-and-file NAACP members are the precise blank wall faced by Negroes when they assault the "white primary" in the Deep South. Even when they can vote they cannot get into the councils where the men to be voted upon are selected. My own view is that if the political doors were opened at, say, the NAACP annual convention in Atlanta this year, we, the delegates, would return Roy Wilkins and his cohorts to power. We are not after Roy Wilkins; we are after freedom to vote and control our own organization.

But, I suspect, there would be one major change if the dissidents gained the right to elect national officers and fix policy: The national office would do more than issue directives urging mass action; they would plot and plan them, and then get out and lead them.

It is not incidental that the internal crisis of the NAACP has come at a time when other organizations—particularly Dr. King's SCLC and CORE—are in the ascendancy. The NAACP's troubling is born of the fact that the events of the past three years have shaken our faith in legalism as a tool of deliverance; we now want our major civil rights organization to look beyond the courts to the people themselves as the final and quick arbiters of public policy. First came Montgomery with its bus boycott, then came the sit-ins; these were enough to make us wonder if mass action didn't bring on a settlement beyond the power of naked legalism. Then came the freedom rides, and we knew legalism alone was not enough.

To understand the full meaning of the Negro's changing attitude we must now examine the roots and rise of the sit-ins and the freedom rides.

10.

THE SIT-INS

ON FEBRUARY 1, 1960, four freshmen from the all-Negro Agricultural and Technical College at Greensboro, North Carolina, walked into the local Woolworth dime store and sat down at the all-white lunch counter. When told to move, they refused; when the manager closed down the counter, the students opened their textbooks and began to study their lessons; when the local radio station interrupted its program to flash the news, scores of other students from A. & T. poured into town and joined the demonstration.

The second major battle of the Negro revolt was under way.

Like the first battle—the Montgomery bus boycott— the sit-ins were a revolt against both segregation and the entrenched Negro leadership; again, as in Montgomery, the sit-ins erupted in territory that the white South had long considered "safe," in areas that the militant Negro North had considered "docile." In the case of Montgomery it was the churchmen, backed up—indeed, driven forward —by enraged laymen, who spearheaded the move. As to the sit-ins, it was poorly educated Negro youths, squirming in the classrooms of admittedly inferior schools and allegedly more interested in making "Greeks" than becoming men, who startled the world—and, I suspect, themselves—by the militancy of their inspired actions.

✓As white opposition mounted, the students realized they needed adult aid. A committee of them called upon Dr. George Simpkins, respected as the most militant Negro in Greensboro and president of the local branch of the NAACP. Dr. Simpkins listened to their problem and then made a phone call that was to give the revolt an ever-deepening character. Despite his role as president of the local chapter of the NAACP, Dr. Simpkins placed a call to the New York office of the Congress of Racial Equality. CORE, at that time, was a little-known organization, some twenty years old, that had achieved spotty but impressive success in desegregating housing projects and restaurants in New York and Chicago. CORE's technique involved nonviolent, direct mass action, and through persistent use of this tactic, they had shaped it into an art at the very time the NAACP was locked in a bitter debate over whether, as a matter of national policy, that organization would embark on direct mass action.

I asked Dr. Simpkins why he called CORE instead of the NAACP national office.

"I had just finished reading a pamphlet CORE prepared on nonviolent protests," Dr. Simpkins told me, "and I called CORE because I was certain they were ready and able to give aid to the students."

To put it bluntly, Dr. Simpkins knew the NAACP national office was not equipped to handle the matter with the immediate precision the situation called for; and he was certainly aware of the nagging question of methodology left unsettled at the semicentennial convention. Dr. Simpkins knew well that all hell would pop in the wake of the sit-ins; his phone call was the act of a troubled man seeking help immediately from the people best qualified and most disposed to give it.

✓Greensboro happened by itself; nobody planned it, nobody pulled any strings. Negro students simply got tired and sat down. Once they made their move, however, three national civil rights organizations came into town to help them. This was the beginning of a pattern that would spread over the Deep South. Local Negroes would set off a demonstration and then find themselves flooded with money and advisers from national leadership organizations.

Three key national figures came to Greensboro; only one of them was a big name, but each came in the name of an organization. And since these three organizations—along with a fourth born out of the sit-ins—are the central figures in the current crisis of Negro leadership, it will be profitable to pause now and see precisely what each organization did at Greensboro.

Within hours after Dr. Simpkins placed his phone call, CORE sent several field workers, headed by Len Holt, into Greensboro to conduct institutes for students interested in nonviolent mass protest. Although NAACP youth groups had been the first to use the sit-in method, CORE had by far the most experience in training people in the philosophy and techniques of nonviolent protest.

I watched Len Holt and his assistants from CORE as they schooled Negro students for nonviolent protest:

The students were seated at a long table resembling a lunch counter. Holt, or one of his assistants, would play the part of the white man. The white man walked along the counter blowing smoke in the students' faces; he called them names: "nigger," "coon," "black bastard." When they failed to provoke any reaction, the white man would push and shove, and, finally in desperation, hit. The Negro student who fought back or got angry flunked the course. The only way to pass—and thus be allowed to participate in a real-life lunch counter sit-in—was to bear it all without a whimper, without anger.

The second man to come to town was Dr. Martin Luther King, who left Montgomery and came into the area to speak and give on-the-spot advice in the light of his experience. King was the patron saint of the students; they could read about Gandhi and Thoreau, but they could touch the hem of King's garment. More, Martin Luther King was a Negro.

Several days after the demonstrations began, the NAACP national office sent Herbert Wright, its youth secretary, into the South, where he set up additional training institutes for students desiring to participate in the demonstrations. The dispatching of Herbert Wright was significant. As youth secretary, Wright's job had been to interest youth in the program of the NAACP and offer them guidance as they made the transition from youth to adulthood. Several years before the Greensboro sit-ins, Wright and his colleagues conducted similar demonstrations in Albuquerque and brought about the first civil rights ordinance to be adopted by any city in the nation.

By sending Wright into the South, then, the NAACP deployed its surest link to restless Negro youth. Although his personal views on mass action are not the stated policy of the NAACP national office, Wright's work recouped much of the public respect the NAACP lost during the first days of the sit-ins.

I asked Herbert Wright for his viewpoint on direct mass action. This was his reply:

"I think that any and all kinds of demonstrations and direct actions by youth and adults and everybody else to end discrimination are badly needed, and certainly ought to be supported by all American citizens."

✓The sit-ins spread to every state in the Deep South and several border states such as Ohio, Illinois and Nevada. They involved more people than any other civil rights movement in history; some seventy thousand Negroes and white people were actively involved in favor of the demonstrators, who staged over eight hundred sit-ins in more than one hundred cities. Upwards of four thousand persons, most of them Negro students, were arrested before the sit-ins came to a halt. As a direct result of the sit-ins restaurants in at least eight cities have been desegregated.

It is a striking commentary on the relative ineffectiveness of legalism that the legal argument raised by the sit-ins reached the Supreme Court in October of 1961. The decision in favor of the sit-ins came a month later, but the practical issue involved in these demonstrations had already been settled.

The sit-ins raged throughout the spring of 1960 and convinced even more people that direct mass action was the shorter, more effective route to their goal of desegregation. But, from an internal viewpoint, more significant than the stale coffee and soggy hamburgers was the brand of Negro that was emerging. They were no longer afraid; their boldness, at times, was nothing short of alarming. And although few people know it, a new religion, peculiar to the Negro, was being born.

This faith, given incipent articulation by Martin Luther King, was the culmination of a hundred years of folk suffering. Like all faiths, it is peculiar to the people who fashioned it; it was a hodgepodge, as every faith is, of every ethical principle absorbed by my people from other cultures. And so the best of Confucius, Moses, Jesus, Gandhi and Thoreau was extracted, then mixed with the peculiar experience of the Negro in America. The result was a faith that justified the bus boycott and inspired Negro college students to make a moral crusade out of their right to sit down in a restaurant owned by a white man and eat a hamburger.

As Pastor Kelly Miller Smith walked to the lectern to begin his Sunday sermon, on that first Sunday of March, 1960, in Nashville, Tennessee, he knew his parishioners wanted and needed more than just another spiritual message. The congregation—most of them middle-class Americans, many of them university students and faculty members—sat before him waiting, tense; for Nashville, like some thirty-odd other Southern college towns, was taut with racial tension in the wake of widespread student demonstrations against lunch counter discrimination in department stores.

Among the worshipers in Pastor Smith's First Baptist Church were some of the eighty-five students from Fisk and from Tennessee Agricultural and Industrial University who had been arrested and charged with conspiracy to obstruct trade and commerce because they staged protests in several of Nashville's segregated eating places. Just two days before, Nashville police had invaded Mr. Smith's church—which also served as headquarters for the demonstrators—and arrested one of their number, James Lawson, Jr., a Negro senior theological student at predominantly white Vanderbilt University, on the same charge.

"Father forgive them," Mr. Smith began, "for they know not what they do." And for the next half-hour, the crucifixion of Christ carried this meaning as he spoke:

"The students sat at the lunch counters alone to eat, and when refused service, to wait and pray. And as they sat there on that Southern Mount of Olives, the Roman soldiers, garbed in the uniforms of Nashville policemen and wielding night sticks, came and led the praying children away. As they walked down the streets, through a red light, and toward Golgotha, the segregationist mob shouted jeers, pushed and shoved them, and spat in their faces, but the suffering students never said a mumbling word. Once the martyr mounts the Cross, wears the crown of thorns, and feels the pierce of the sword in his side there is no turning back.

"And there is no turning back for those who follow in the martyr's steps," the minister continued. "All we can do is to hold fast to what we believe, suffer what we must suffer if we would forgive them, for they know not what they do."

This new gospel of the American Negro is rooted in the theology of desegregation; its missionaries are several thousand Negro students who—like Paul, Silas and Peter of the early Christian era—are braving great dangers and employing new techniques to spread the faith. It is not an easy faith, for it names the conservative Negro leadership class as sinners along with the segregationists. Yet this new gospel is being preached by clergymen and laymen alike wherever Negroes gather.

The sit-ins were a major and, I think, decisive victory; they were a rousing triumph over segregation and a clear-cut vindication for the proponents of direct and mass action. And for these very reasons, the sit-ins marked the end of the great era of the traditional Negro leadership class, a half-century of fiercely guarded glory.

The sit-ins produced two unexpected results, one a movement, the other a method that would greatly augment the efforts of the sit-ins:

Despite the fact that they received financial aid and guidance from the three major civil rights organizations, the students decided to form a protest organization of their own. It was their feeling that they could accomplish more if students on each campus set up their own non-violent protest movement under the coordinating guidance of a South-wide committee. Thus was formed the Student Non Violent Coordinating Committee with offices in Atlanta. This, I feel, was something of a blow to all three civil rights organizations; after all, they had invested time and money in the student-directed sit-ins and the assumption was that the students would continue their protests under the guidance of the NAACP, CORE and Dr. King's SCLC.

Instead, SNICK (as the Student Non Violent Coordinating Committee is called) came into being and began to compete with the established organizations for public support and funds. The president of SNICK is Charles McDew, but the man who has already begun to capture national attention as the driving power in the organization is James Forman, a thirty-three-year-old Chicagoan and former public school teacher, the organization's new executive director.

SNICK operated on a budget of fourteen thousand dollars in 1961 and is out to raise thirty thousand for its 1962 program. The organization's headquarters is a windowless cubicle along Auburn Avenue in Atlanta, and its program is carried out by sixteen staff people, fourteen of whom receive subsistence pay of forty dollars a week. The other two, including Forman, receive sixty dollars a week because they are married and have families.

When I asked Forman to recap SNICK's program for 1961, he made these points:

• SNICK was active in voter registration programs in

McComb, Mississippi; Albany, Georgia; and Atlanta. SNICK's activity in McComb led to beatings and jailings, and its presence in Albany triggered the Albany Movement, which I have already discussed.

• SNICK joined with other organizations and staged freedom rides into Mississippi and Alabama.

• SNICK organized several sit-ins during 1961, the most effective of which occurred in Cambridge, Maryland.

Most of SNICK's operating funds come from the Northern Student Movement, an organization of students on non-Southern campuses which dedicates itself to helping the Negro students of the South. The SCLC is SNICK's next highest donor, Forman said. He added that the NAACP has arranged bail money for SNICK demonstrators, but it has not made a contribution to the operating fund of the student organization.

Despite its meager budget and staff, SNICK has a powerful impact. Not only do the students get a warm hearing from the Negro masses, but they are now called in for consultation by the white power structure, which has learned that the established Negro leaders cannot negotiate in the name of the Negro people. More than once—Nashville, Tennessee, was an example—the whites have arranged a truce with the established Negro leaders only to find that the students will not respect it.

Forman is new on the job at SNICK but he demands some attention. I have talked with white moderates in the Deep South who are greatly impressed by him.

James Forman is a light-brown-skinned, pipe-smoking man. He was born in Chicago but spent many of his young summers visiting his grandparents in Marshall County, Mississippi, which borders on Fayette County, Tennessee. Forman graduated from Englewood High School in Chicago and took his college degree in public administration from Roosevelt University. After a stint in the army, where he was a personnel classification specialist, Forman entered the Institute of African Affairs at Boston University.

Then the thing that happens to so many Negro students nowadays happened to James Forman. He picked up the newspaper one day and the headlines told of Negro share-croppers in Fayette County, Tennessee, being put off their land stake because they attempted to register and vote.

"This was like my home county," Forman said to me. "I had to go and do something about it."

And so James Forman left Boston University and headed for the Deep South. He didn't see the logic in learning about African affairs if he couldn't help his own people in America; whatever the problem of the Congo, it was no worse than the one in Marshall County, Mississippi, and Fayette County, Tennessee. Forman's work in Fayette County was Herculean but unsung (he helped raise money and clothes for the tent city victims), but he caught the eye of members of the student movement.

Edward King, Jr. was then executive director of SNICK. He was giving full time to this post but was preparing to return to law school at Wilberforce University. When the post became vacant it was offered to Forman and he took it.

At first blush Forman's age—thirty-three—is against him; one thinks of a student as head of a student movement. But on deeper reflection it becomes clear that Forman is the turning point in SNICK's life; the movement is much more than an aggregation of students, it is an organization of young Negro Americans who are determined to end segregation at all sacrifice. Forman brings both maturity and experience to his job, and I, for one, would not be surprised if SNICK became *the* organization to be reckoned with in the Deep South.

This, of course, puts SNICK on a par with and in competition with other civil rights organizations. This is one of the key factors in the crisis of Negro leadership which must be dealt with shortly. Suffice it to say here that SNICK was one of the major, and unexpected, results of the sit-in movement and its continued growth reflects most the dissatisfaction of many Negroes with the established Negro leadership.

The second thing that grew out of the sit-ins was the use of the economic boycott by Negroes to implement the demonstrations staged by the students. This has happened in several cities, but Nashville, Tennessee, is the best example of it.

Negroes spend seven million dollars a year in downtown Nashville. Shortly before Easter of 1960, 98 percent of Nashville's Negroes simply quit buying. The reason was simple: Nashville merchants had not responded to the student sit-ins' demands for integrated lunch counters. Upwards of a hundred students had been arrested during the demonstrations; many others had been beaten by white hoodlums. Nashville Negroes were just plain mad.

Established adult citizens like Reverend Kelly Miller Smith and Dr. Vivian Henderson, professor of economics at Fisk University, led the move and Nashville Negroes decided not to buy any Easter finery. The result was economic chaos:[1]

• The local transit company, most of whose bus riders are Negroes, found its business dwindling seriously.

• Twenty percent of Nashville's business comes from people who live in a seventy-five-mile radius of the city. They, Negro and white, stayed home or bought somewhere else, because of the tension created by the demonstrations and boycott.

• Department store managers reported that Nashville Negroes represented up to 20 percent of their business. Practically all of this was lost for Easter.

• Then Nature got into the act: April and May of 1960 were the coldest April and May Nashville had had in years. Even without the Negro boycott the unseasonable weather would have been disastrous for retail clothing stores.

• In addition, hundreds of white moderates felt sympathy for the Negroes and, without making a public issue of it, decided to wear old clothes for Easter too.

By early May, the white city fathers, to say nothing of the white businessmen, wanted to sit down with Negro leaders and talk. There were two conditions laid down by

[1] All the material in this section is based on a report made by Wallace Westfeldt for the Nashville Community Relations Conference.

the merchants: they wanted the negotiators for the Negroes to represent both the Negro community and the sit-in movement, and they wanted no white persons on the Negro negotiating team.

In a statement to Wallace Westfeldt of the *Nashville Tennessean,* one of the white merchants explained why these demands were made:

"We discovered, much to our surprise, that the Negro members of the Mayor's biracial committee, although both of them were university presidents, were not representative of the Negro community. We also discovered that whenever any white persons joined the Negro negotiators they started preaching to us about the morality of the question. We didn't need anybody to orate to us about that."

The Negroes readily accepted the conditions and talks began. On May 10, 1960, a selected group of Negroes entered the lunch departments of six downtown Nashville stores and ate along with white customers. The sit-ins had won, but not until the adult Negro community had rallied behind them and forced white merchants to their knees with an economic boycott.

The Savannah, Georgia, NAACP used the same technique in 1961 and accomplished the integration of lunch counters there. Without the support of the NAACP-organized boycott in Savannah, the sit-in efforts in that town would have ended in failure.

Thus, from the sit-in movement emerged a new technique: the economic boycott used by adult Negroes with purchasing power to augment the efforts of the militant students. It is providential that this alliance with the adult community did emerge during the sit-ins, for once Negroes embarked on freedom rides they needed all the help they could get from every quarter.

11.

THE FREEDOM RIDES

THE NAACP REPORT for 1960 is an attractive seventy-two-page document. Replete with pictures and charts, the report chronicles the organization's achievements for the year. On page 72, the report gets around to the dreary chore of listing its executive staff. Roy Wilkins, the executive secretary, of course, heads the list; then way down, four names from the bottom, one learns that James Farmer is program director for the NAACP.

As program director of the NAACP James Farmer was directly responsible to Roy Wilkins. His duties were (1) to draft suggested plans for direct mass action and (2) to develop the NAACP's educational program. He was the author of the NAACP's nationally voiced suggestion that Negroes withhold their patronage from certain chain stores that had been obdurate on the matter of lunch counter integration. This was the nearest thing to a call for mass action the NAACP national office had uttered in recent years, and was interpreted by some as a sign of hope. Then came the matter-of-fact press release that James Farmer was resigning to become national director of the Congress on Racial Equality.

With that announcement the question of the NAACP and mass action took on new and dramatic significance. For if the NAACP official charged with the responsibility of planning mass action resigned, took a post with another civil rights organization and unleashed a program of bold, direct, mass action, the inescapable inference would be that he had been chafing at the bit all along and that his suggested programs of mass action were lying in state— killed by cautious politics, embalmed by inaction, neatly tucked into coffins of conservatism and rowed off, one by one, on a spit-polished mahogany table top in an NAACP committee meeting room.

On February 1, 1961, forty-year-old James Farmer became national director of the Congress of Racial Equality. On March 13, CORE announced that it would conduct freedom rides through the South to test racial discrimination in interstate travel terminals. On April 28, CORE wrote President Kennedy and advised him that the rides would soon be under way and asked for federal protection. On May 4, after three days of training and indoctrination, the freedom rides began their journey from Washington, D.C.

It had taken James Farmer exactly three months to get the freedom rides on the road.

The freedom rides were born in James Farmer's anxious mind and spirit. Even as he was packing his bags and moving from the NAACP office along New York's West Fortieth Street to CORE's Spartan quarters down on Park Row, Farmer was planning what he would do and how he would do it.

Farmer, a former Methodist clergyman, has always been an "action man." He was among the concerned group of Negroes and whites who formed CORE in 1942 because they felt legalism was not sufficient to win the battle against segregation. He served as CORE's first national chairman, but divided his time among CORE and several other organizations in the field of civil liberties and world peace. Five years later, James Farmer was among those who took a freedom ride under the sponsorship of the Fellowship of Reconciliation. The main objective of this 1947 freedom ride was to test discrimination on trains engaged in interstate travel, and to discover to what extent the states of the upper South had complied with a decision rendered by the Supreme Court in 1946 when it declared that different racial regulations by various states imposed an undue hardship on interstate travel facilities.

As he assumed his duties as national director of CORE, Farmer remembered another Court decision that had not been implemented. In 1958 Bruce Boyington was refused service in a bus station in Richmond, Virginia. When Boyington refused to leave the lunchroom, he was arrested and charged with trespassing. The Court disregarded the constitutional arguments advanced by Boyington and NAACP lawyers and ruled that, under the Interstate Commerce Act, segregation in terminal stations was illegal whether the terminal was owned by the bus company or not. The ruling turned on that section of the statute which forbids busses to "subject any particular person to any unjust discrimination or any unjust or unreasonable prejudice."

The Boyington decision had been a paper decision. Practically every bus terminal in the South maintained segregated facilities. Everybody knew it, but Jim Farmer decided to do something about it.

After talking the plan over with his own staff, particularly with Marvin Rich, the executive secretary of CORE, Farmer sought the counsel and aid of Roy Wilkins, his former boss at the NAACP. Wilkins listened sympathetically and promised Farmer aid from local NAACP branches along the way. Wilkins wrote various branch heads along the route Farmer planned to take and asked them to give aid and comfort. Most branches responded favorably, but some did not. The Jackson, Mississippi, branch, for example, wrote Farmer that whereas they wished him God's blessings they could be of little aid on the day the freedom riders were scheduled to arrive in Jackson. Not that the Jackson NAACP leaders feared white reprisals; their inability to help the proposed freedom riders stemmed rather from the fact that the local NAACP would be having its annual Freedom Fund drive at the time and could not afford to divide its energies.

On May 4, the biracial group of freedom riders left Washington, D.C., en route to New Orleans. There were thirteen participants, six whites and seven Negroes, including James Farmer. The riders ranged in age from eighteen to sixty-one, and their number fluctuated during the course of the ride. The Southern Regional Council has compiled a chronology of the ride; it reads like an American nightmare:

May 4 Ride begins from Washington; arrives in Richmond.

May 7 Arrival in Danville (Va.); dispute over restaurant service settled quietly at Trailways terminal.

May 8 Arrival in Charlotte (N.C.); arrest of one Rider for trespass while demanding shoeshine at Union bus terminal.

May 9 Arrival in Rock Hill (S.C.) and attack in Greyhound terminal; white waiting room at Trailways terminal is closed when bus pulls in.

May 10 Defendant in Charlotte trespass case acquitted. Two Riders arrested in Winnsboro (S.C.) and released after several hours; charges dropped.

May 12 Arrival in Augusta (Ga.); all facilities used.

May 13 Traveling through Athens (Ga.), where all facilities are used, and arrival in Atlanta; restaurant closed at Greyhound station. The Court of Appeals of the Fifth Circuit directs a lower court to "obliterate" the distinction between interstate and intrastate passengers at the train terminal in Birmingham. This is one of the many stations in the South with one waiting room for white and Negro interstate passengers, and a second for Negro intrastate passengers.

While in Atlanta, James Farmer received word of his father's death in Washington, D.C. Farmer temporarily left the ride and flew to Washington for his father's funeral.

May 14   Some Riders are served at Trailways terminal
         in Atlanta. Entire group leaves for Birmingham,
         riding in Trailways and Greyhound busses.
         Department of Justice advises Birmingham
         police it has received warnings of planned vio-
         lence when busses reach their city. Greyhound
         bus met by mob in Anniston; passengers pre-
         vented from getting off. Tires slit and go flat
         six miles out of Anniston. Men following in
         automobiles attempt to board but are prevented
         by a state law enforcement officer who has been
         riding bus. An incendiary device thrown
         through a window sets fire to the bus, which is
         completely destroyed. All passengers are re-
         moved, and 12 admitted to hospital, mostly for
         smoke inhalation; they later resume their ride
         to Birmingham. The Trailways bus also en-
         counters the mob in Anniston, and faced by
         it the driver orders Negroes to the rear. One
         Negro and two white Riders beaten. Bus con-
         tinues on to Birmingham, where Riders are at-
         tacked when they get off; one of them requires
         over 50 head stitches. At neither Anniston nor
         Birmingham is anyone arrested. Despite warn-
         ings of probable trouble, no police are on hand
         at Birmingham, and none arrive until ten min-
         utes after fighting begins.

May 15   Greyhound bus drivers refuse to drive group on
         to Montgomery. Riders take plane for New
         Orleans, arriving there late at night. Governor
         Patterson issues his first statement, advising
         Riders to "get out of Alabama as quickly as
         possible."
         Attorney General Kennedy asks the state to
         provide police protection; the Governor first
         agrees and then changes his position.

May 16   Riders stay in seclusion in New Orleans. In
         Birmingham, three men are arrested for taking
         part in the attack of the 14th.

May 17   Riders meet at church in New Orleans and then disband. This ends the original CORE-planned ride.

The freedom ride had caught national attention, however, and several groups began to send riders of their own into the Alabama trouble spots. Although the original CORE-planned ride disbanded on May 17, several members of CORE's ride remained in Montgomery; James Farmer rejoined the ride there and they, along with other groups, carried the ride to its dramatic climax in Jackson, Mississippi. From May 17 on there were four organizations involved in the ride: CORE, the Nashville Student Movement, the Student Non Violent Coordinating Committee and Martin Luther King's Southern Christian Leadership Conference. Several concerned individuals—rabbis from Chicago, white college professors from Eastern universities and a Negro-white lawyer team from New York —also joined the ride at this point.

May 17   A bus arrives in Birmingham from Nashville, carrying new contingent of Freedom Riders. This is a group of college students affiliated with Southern Christian Leadership Conference. Two white students are in the group. Police meet bus on outskirts of city, arrest 2 Riders who refuse to change seats. Two policemen ride bus into Birmingham, where a crowd is waiting at the terminal. Drivers refuse to carry group on to Montgomery, and 10 Riders (8 Negro and 2 white) plus 5 sympathizers taken into protective custody.

May 18   Riders stay in jail; one of the white students released in custody of her father. The 5 Birmingham Negroes released. Attorney General Kennedy tries unsuccessfully to reach Governor Patterson by telephone.

May 19   Two of the jailed students (1 white, 1 Negro) receive suspended fines and are released. The remaining 7 are carried by Police Commissioner Connor in the early morning 120 miles to the Tennessee line and are put out of the car. They are back in Birmingham in the afternoon, where, joined by 10 or so others, including 3 whites, they unsuccessfully seek bus service to Montgomery. Spend the night in waiting room. An Alabama court enjoins CORE and its followers from further "freedom rides." Patrolmen read order on incoming busses. Both President Kennedy and the Attorney General try unsuccessfully to reach the Governor by telephone; the President talks with the Lieutenant Governor.

John Seigenthaler, administrative assistant to the Attorney General, confers in Montgomery with the Governor.

May 20   The Governor says: "We are going to do all we can to enforce the laws of the state on the highways and everywhere else, but we are not going to escort these agitators. We stand firm on that position."

At 8:30 A.M., after 18 hours of waiting, the Riders are taken on a Greyhound bus for Montgomery. The F.B.I. advises local police in Montgomery of probability of violence; are assured that local authority sufficient. On arrival, a "race riot involving hundreds broke out." At least 6 Riders are beaten, 3 severely. The mob attacks Negroes who have no connection with the Riders, and whites who appear sympathetic. News photographers are attacked. John Seigenthaler is knocked unconscious and left on a sidewalk for more than 20 minutes. Police arrive about 10 minutes after fighting begins, and do not for some time succeed in dispersing the mob, which continues its attacks. The police arrest at least 8 "integrationists." After again trying to reach the Governor, the Attorney General orders federal marshals to Montgomery, and also obtains in Federal District Court an injunction against the Ku-Klux Klan, the National States Rights party, and other individuals interfering with "peaceful interstate travel by bus." President Kennedy appeals to state and local officials of Alabama for order.

May 21   Federal marshals continue to pour in.

The Reverend Martin Luther King, Jr., president of the Southern Christian Leadership Conference, cuts short a speaking tour and flies to Montgomery from Chicago, to address a Negro mass meeting at a church. A mob, composed largely of white youths, forms outside. It is dispersed after bitter rioting by the federal marshals and state patrolmen, with some aid from the local police. The Negroes are penned in the church until early the next morning. Governor Patterson proclaims martial law in Montgomery, and National Guardsmen appear. Deputy Attorney General Byron White comes to Montgomery to take charge of federal activities; the Governor angrily denounces federal intervention during a conference with Mr. White. The American Nazi party announces plans to send a "hate bus" from Washington to New Orleans.

Alabama Associated Press Association condemns "the breakdown of civilized rule" in Alabama. It singles out Alabama Public Safety Director Floyd Mann as "the one notable example" of an officer carrying out his duties. Negro leaders at the mass meeting also praise Mr. Mann.

Governor Barnett of Mississippi wires an offer of support to Governor Patterson.

May 22   Eight hundred National Guardsmen on duty. More federal marshals ordered in. The Attorney General says that they will stay until the situation is brought under control by the state. He says further that Public Safety Director Mann is acting with vigor and skill, but that the Governor is not cooperating. The Montgomery Ministerial Association calls for all "necessary steps" to prevent further mob action and violence.

The "hate bus" leaves Washington.

Federal agents arrest 4 men on charge of firing the bus at Anniston.

Additional students begin arriving in Montgomery, from Nashville, New Orleans and New York.

Deputy Attorney General White says that arrests of Freedom Riders for violating the state injunction against them will not cause federal intervention.

Eighteen hundred pupils evacuated from two white junior high schools after phoned bombing threats.

May 23   "Hate bus" passes through Montgomery, escorted through the town by federal officers. Reaches New Orleans, where passengers have difficult time finding lodging.

Montgomery is quiet; National Guardsmen patrol city. One person arrested in connection with riots.

In reply to a protest from Alabama Congressmen, the Attorney General calls for action on the part of the Governor and local police, "not merely words of intention."

The Governor at a press conference blames the Sunday night riot on the federal marshals.

Justice Department officials are in continuing telephone discussions with Mississippi officials.

A press conference is held by M. L. King, Jr., CORE Director James Farmer, Montgomery minister Ralph Abernathy, and students Diane Nash and John Lewis. They announce that the

Ride will continue at no matter what cost. A few more students arrive in Montgomery.

The Rotary Club of Montgomery demands withdrawal of federal marshals. The Board of Directors of the Chamber of Commerce calls on local law enforcement agencies to "maintain and preserve" law and order. The Junior Chamber of Commerce condemns agitators and regrets failure of local police. The Louisiana legislature commends Governor Patterson.

Governor Barnett has Mississippi National Guard on stand-by alert.

May 24   Heavily protected and escorted by National Guardsmen, some of the Riders leave Montgomery on a Trailways bus about 7:00 A.M. Before leaving they eat at the bus terminal, thus achieving an objective. Later in the morning a second bus carries the rest. The escorts convoy the busses to the Mississippi line, where patrol cars of that state take over. On arrival in Jackson, 27 Riders, including James Farmer, are arrested when they seek service at the white lunch counters and use of the white rest rooms of the terminal, on charges of breach of peace and refusal to obey an officer. There are no disturbances otherwise. In Montgomery, additional Riders show up, the small group including professors and students from the North. The Department of Justice asks in Federal District Court for an injunction to prohibit the heads of the Birmingham and Montgomery police departments from interfering with interstate travel. The complaint asserts that all have been derelict in performing their duties.

The Attorney General also issues a statement appealing for a "cooling-off period." Southern Christian Leadership Conference executive Martin King promptly says "no."

The Greyhound Corporation orders disciplinary

action against its employees in Montgomery who refused food service to Negroes.

In New Orleans, the "hate bus" passengers are jailed for "unreasonably" alarming the public.

In La Grange (Ga.), 5 men attempting to organize an obstruction to the bus carrying the latest group of Riders to Montgomery are arrested.

May 25   The Reverend S. D. Seay, Sr., Negro leader, is shot in the wrist in Montgomery by a bullet from a passing car.

The latest group of Riders is arrested while eating at the Trailways terminal in Montgomery, along with Wyatt T. Walker, executive director of the Southern Christian Leadership Conference, and two Negro ministers: the Reverends Abernathy and Shuttlesworth. Charge: breach of peace.

The Reverend Abernathy and 6 Riders file suit in Federal District Court asking invalidation of Alabama's bus terminal segregation laws. The Department of Justice promptly agrees to the judge's request that it enter the case as a friend of the court; the Department also asks for a speedy hearing.

The New Orleans city council urges police to escort Riders, if they come, through city nonstop.

May 26   Meeting in Atlanta with a few others, M. L. King, Jr. announces that there will be a "temporary lull but no cooling off" in the Rides.

Police heads in Birmingham and Montgomery are under subpoena to produce records of their activities. The Northern professors and students post bail and are released from Montgomery jail.

In Jackson the 27 are convicted, fined $200 each, and given 60-day suspended jail sentence. Stringent measures are enforced during the trial, including use of police dogs to drive persons away from the front of the courthouse.

Alabama and Georgia authorities arrest a man in Rome (Ga.) for attack on Birmingham TV reporter during riots there.

The executive secretary of the NAACP dissents from the plea for a "cooling off."

May 27   Six white teen-agers, arrested in Montgomery for wounding of the Reverend S. D. Seay, Sr., released in parents' custody.

The vice-chairman of Americans for Democratic Action urges Freedom Riders to disregard the Attorney General's plea for a "cooling off."

A Freedom Riders Coordinating Committee is formed in Atlanta, composed of representatives of SCLC, CORE, the Nashville Student Movement, and the Student Non Violent Coordinating Committee; M. L. King, Jr. explains the nonrepresentation of the NAACP on the grounds that it is primarily a "legalistic body."

Both the Negroes in jail in Montgomery and the Nazis in jail in New Orleans are fasting.

Five of the 27 in Jackson are released on bond; 4 accept bail so that they can stand trial in New Orleans on earlier charges growing out of the picketing of downtown stores.

May 28   Seventeen Riders, coming from Montgomery and Memphis, are arrested in Jackson when they attempt to desegregate the waiting room. The contingent coming from Montgomery were escorted to the bus terminal by Guardsmen, where they found facilities closed.

May 29   Trial begins in federal court in Montgomery on the government's complaint against Montgomery and Birmingham police heads; C. V. Henley, a former Montgomery reserve policeman, has been brought into the suit. At issue also is the continuation of the restraining order against the Klan leaders.

Martial law is ended in Montgomery.

In Jackson, 19 of the first group of Riders are put to work at a prison farm; 3 others are released on appeal bond. The 17 who arrived May 28 are convicted on breach of peace charges, and sentenced to 60 days or $200; they choose jail.

In La Grange (Ga.), 3 of those arrested on May 24 are convicted and 2 bound over to a higher court.

Attorney General Kennedy requests the Interstate Commerce Commission to ban by regulations segregation in interstate bus terminals.

Sept. 22 The Interstate Commerce Commission issues an order banning segregation in interstate terminal facilities.

Nov. 1   The ICC order banning segregation in terminal facilities becomes effective.

✓On final count the freedom rides (actually, there were at least a dozen of them) involved over a thousand persons representing four major organizations. The rides themselves cost an estimated twenty thousand dollars and the legal expenses that grew out of them exceeded three hundred thousand dollars. ✓The rides did the job, however, and, as of this writing, interstate terminal segregation is all but a thing of the past. Some cities in the deep, deep South are still holding out, but the issue is about settled.

The rides completed the emergence of CORE as, without question, the boldest and most imaginative organization in the civil rights field. Since its organization in 1942 CORE had achieved a number of quiet, though very real, gains but was not thought of as among the top Negro leadership organizations. Even the sit-ins were not CORE's work; the students launched the movement and then CORE came in to help them along the way. The freedom rides were something else, however; the original ride was planned and financed by CORE, and its national director, James Farmer, was among those who were beaten and jailed. True, other organizations moved onto the freedom ride trail and SCLC's executive director, Wyatt Walker, and his wife joined the rides and were both jailed. But, without question, the glory and the victory of the freedom rides belongs to CORE and to James Farmer.

The proof of this is to be found in what has happened to CORE since the rides. CORE's membership now stands at about forty thousand, an increase of several thousand over 1961. The significant thing, however, is that CORE's membership is now approximately one-half Negro; although the organization does not keep tabs on the racial backgrounds of its members, CORE officials estimate that prior to the rides less than a fourth of its members were Negroes.

CORE's budget for the fiscal year ending June 1, 1961 was $233 thousand; this budget was oversubscribed by $10 thousand. The current budget is for $750 thousand, and upwards of $500 thousand of that has already been raised as of February 1, 1962. However, it must be noted that CORE has spent approximately $600 thousand since June 1, 1961.

Budget-wise this puts CORE on a par with the Southern Christian Leadership Conference. In terms of membership CORE is second only to the NAACP. (This does not include the Urban League, which cannot be considered as an action civil rights organization.)

The rides have catapulted James Farmer into the front rank of Negro leadership; it is inevitable, then, that CORE now has its critics. *Time* magazine of January 12, 1962, comments that CORE's leadership is fragmented and quotes an unnamed NAACP official as saying that CORE's membership is "a bunch of loonybirds and crackpots."

The latter criticism stems from the fact that a number of the people in CORE, particularly among the office leadership, have, at one time or another, been affiliated with various pacifist and antiwar organizations. However, CORE's membership roster also contains such names as Eleanor Roosevelt, who is also a member of the board of the NAACP, Tallulah Bankhead and Helen Hayes. On the whole, however, the members of CORE are not drawn from the conservative element that supports the NAACP. They tend more to be action people, the kind of Americans who believe in picket lines and marches.

As to the leadership of CORE being fragmented, I have worked closely with James Farmer and Marvin Rich and have some idea what the critics are trying to say. What they call "fragmented leadership" is actually fluid leadership, a leadership that is constantly involved in spot planning and immediate execution of these plans. There is nothing grand about CORE; its quarters are run-down, its staff poorly paid, and its program is as impetuous as a cat. The genius of CORE, however, is its insistence that direct mass action is the only way for Negroes to realize the practical results of the towering legal decisions the NAACP has won. CORE's argument for mass action embraces a good deal more than gathering people together for a demonstration; it goes to the root of having the job done by the people rather than for them; it underscores the fact that better response is gotten from the masses when the issue involved is a service open to great numbers of people rather than to a few. Financial troubles plagued CORE throughout the summer and fall of 1962. But now that many of the sit-in and freedom-rider cases are being settled by the Supreme Court—all were vindicated—much of the bond money posted by CORE will be returned and this will make it possible for CORE to resume and enlarge its direct action attacks.

Because it is bold, CORE can be relied upon to keep the South in turmoil as long as segregation exists. CORE's current plans now call for another kind of ride into the South. Encouraged by the nature of decisions recently rendered by the Supreme Court, CORE plans to test segregation in Southern hotels and motels.[1] This, of course, will set off considerable anguish and troubling. But such is the nature of CORE; it is convinced that real civil rights

[1] CORE has already staged demonstrations against segregated housing in New York.

gains are achieved only by people who are willing to force the issue to a test. CORE moves in peace but, to a man, its demonstrators are ready to endure the hardships of war. And this, in essence, is the underlying spirit of the Negro revolt.

12.

THE CRISIS IN NEGRO LEADERSHIP

WHILE DESCRIBING THE EMERGENCE of the Negro revolt I have attempted to set forth the organizational structure and program of the several Negro leadership organizations. They obviously overlap and, in many senses, compete. This not only confuses those who attempt to follow or study race relations in America, but it has led to a leadership crisis that must be resolved if civil rights organizations are not to become part of the very problem they are attempting to solve.

Shortly after Martin Luther King returned to Atlanta from his heroic defeat at Albany, Georgia, he commented that there is a great need for a "summit meeting of Negro leaders to decide just where we go from here."

Dr. King sounded a note one hears frequently nowadays[1] and there can be no doubt that the swift pace and explosive nature of the Negro revolt will force such a

[1] The call for a Negro "summit" meeting reached a crescendo during the summer of 1961. I asked Roy Wilkins to state his views on the need for such a meeting. He said: "Your question implies that there is a difference [between Negro leadership organizations], and, of course, when you have a summit—this is the only reason the two Ks are at the summit—you admit a difference. There are no differences of objectives between the NAACP and other organizations in the field."

meeting in the not too distant future, for this is the only way the current Negro leadership crisis can be resolved. To put this crisis into perspective it is necessary to review briefly the tangled paths these organizations have followed to the present impasse.

Once the Montgomery Improvement Association decided to strike for bus desegregation rather than for a protected section of seats on the bus, the Association moved into an area heretofore occupied by the NAACP. Dr. King rose to prominence because of Montgomery and his Southern Christian Leadership Conference was an attempt to project the spirit and meaning of Montgomery over the entire South. Thus the SCLC and the NAACP were mining for the same gold from the outset. Then came the sit-ins, launched and run by the students with a lusty assist from CORE; the students chose to form their own continuing organizations and thus they, too, moved into the area occupied by the NAACP and the SCLC. This was followed by the freedom rides, which brought CORE to the foreground. Thus, four major organizations are now working in the area of civil rights.

Further confusion developed when it was announced that the NAACP had taken over the legal expenses, some $300 thousand, for the freedom rides. The assumption was that this was the NAACP's role in the demonstration. This is but one of the scores of errors brought about by the continuing confusion over the NAACP and the NAACP Legal Defense and Education Fund. It was the latter group, headed by Jack Greenberg, not the former, headed by Roy Wilkins, that assumed the legal debt for the freedom rides. This is further complicated by the fact that the NAACP does maintain a legal staff of its own. A case may arise in, say, Little Rock; the NAACP national office is called in, but refers the case to the NAACP Legal Defense and Education Fund to handle. The press releases say, "The NAACP today filed a brief with the Court asking that . . ." and only the most knowledgeable observers know just who did what. Even they know only after exhaustive investigation, which sometimes brings charges that the investigator is trying to stir up trouble and division.

When all of this confusion is sifted a fairly clear leadership picture emerges:

CORE provides imaginative and bold leadership. It backs up this leadership with adults who are willing to risk danger to carry out demonstrations; these demonstrations are financed by CORE to the limit of its ability. (I was in the CORE office during a hectic week of the rides and there was doubt that any of the staff workers there, including Jim Farmer and his wife, would get paid. As I recall it, the staff workers agreed that only those who absolutely needed immediate food and rent money would draw pay until more funds could be raised.)

The student movements provide dedicated students who are willing to risk dangers for the sake of a cause. They have little or no money and rely upon the NAACP and the Southern Christian Leadership Conference for funds. They get some money from CORE, but, for obvious reasons, the amount is small. The bulk of their money comes from Northern white students.

Dr. King's Southern Christian Leadership Conference has one major asset: Martin Luther King himself. Through speaking engagements and private contacts, Dr. King raises the bulk of the organization's budget. As to program, the organization has sixty-five branches in eight Southern states, but they are not too active. The SCLC of late has devoted most of its energies to backing the student groups in various projects and toward organizing a South-wide voter registration drive.

The NAACP Legal Defense and Education Fund is, by charter and by law, relegated to legal activity. Were it to move one step beyond this it would lose its tax-free status. The Fund consistently comes to the aid of any persons testing segregation—and this includes local NAACP branches—and, as I have already pointed out, has assumed the staggering legal bill run up by the freedom riders. The Fund has also assumed the legal expenses involved in the sit-ins. The Fund does not initiate demonstrations, but it does give counsel to anyone who takes the trouble to ask about the legal questions involved in a proposed plan of action.

I have already discussed the NAACP's general program structure. The specific issue, as far as the current crisis of Negro leadership is concerned, turns on two questions: Does the NAACP endorse mass action? If so, why doesn't the NAACP national leadership make a bold point of the fact and offer on-the-spot leadership?

As one probes these questions he finds that members of the NAACP national leadership team differ in their versions of just what the organization is doing and should do in the area of mass action.

Executive Secretary Roy Wilkins denies that the NAACP is primarily a "legalistic" organization as charged by Dr. King and Reverend Walker. Mr. Wilkins goes on to lay claim to being a "mass" organization and cites his huge membership role to prove it; he then argues that the NAACP is involved in mass action and sustains his thrust by pointing to the number of local NAACP-ers who were involved in the sit-ins. In his "Summary Report" before the fifty-second annual NAACP membership meeting in January of 1961, Mr. Wilkins took pride in the fact that "NAACP college youth members were among the four who made history in 1960's first sit-in in Greensboro, North Carolina." Mr. Wilkins then went on to note that "300 NAACP youth demonstrators" were attacked and mistreated by police in Orangeburg, South Carolina.

Does this mean that the NAACP national office approves and sponsors mass action? I have been unable to unearth a single directive in which the NAACP national office has called for such action as the sit-ins and freedom rides. And the feeling that the NAACP national office does not condone such actions remains. This feeling is given confirmation when Jackie Robinson, a member of the NAACP national board, says bluntly, as he did to me, "Either the NAACP must adopt mass action as a matter of policy or accept the consequences. There are no two ways about it; the students, and many of the adults, want mass action. Either we employ it or suffer."

Now, to compound that confusion, is this: I asked NAACP Public Relations Officer Henry Moon for a direct statement on their mass action policy. This is his reply: "We approve of mass action. We adopted a resolution at our last convention in Philadelphia sanctioning mass action."

Then I asked if the national office had issued directives calling for mass action.

"Yes," Mr. Moon said. "We called for our members to conduct mass action by supporting the sit-ins; we called for them to form picket lines around department stores which refused to serve Negroes at their lunch counters."

Reminded that this kind of action was somewhat different from urging members to organize sit-ins and freedom rides, Mr. Moon quoted Roy Wilkins: "We do not sit here at Twenty West Fortieth Street and tell people what to do. We let them know our general policy and our availability to defend them when they act. The rest is up to the local people."

But NAACP board member Jackie Robinson has a different view: "We are not meeting the needs of the masses. We don't know the people; the people don't know us. I have been asked by many people to form another civil rights organization that would be closer to the masses. I'm all for a new organization if we can do it without interfering with what the NAACP is doing. Maybe a new organization is the answer. We must do something; we can't go on as we are now."

And there is at least one NAACP national official who feels that the NAACP cannot embrace sit-ins and freedom rides without violating the fundamental philosophy of the organization. This is what Dr. John Morsell, executive assistant to Roy Wilkins, had to say about the techniques of Martin King and CORE: "We [the NAACP] can hardly advocate or condone a policy of mass civil disobedience, except under such extreme conditions that would warrant the complete abandonment of the entire philosophy of operations which has sustained us for fifty years."

Does all this amount to a crisis in Negro leadership or is it nothing more than utter confusion?

As far as the Negro revolt is concerned this is mostly confusion; but from the point of view of the various civil rights organizations, particularly the NAACP, the current situation is nothing less than a crisis. The revolt will go on regardless of what these organizations do; the Negro masses are angry and restless, tired of prolonged legal battles that end in paper decrees. CORE, the students and Dr. King sense this and their magnificent accomplishments are due directly to the fact that they realized the people are ready to act, and that the people want to help do the job themselves rather than have the job done for them. The organizations that understand this unrest and rise to lead it will survive; those that do not will perish.

It is significant, then, that every civil rights organization but the NAACP reported an increase in 1961 membership over 1960. The NAACP national office admits to a fifteen-thousand drop in membership and there are indications, based on talks with branch presidents, that the final figure may be higher. And, as I have already stated, the organization is running a deficit. National office spokesmen say this decline in membership is due to the economic recession. While this cannot be disputed it is doubtful that this is the full explanation. I have talked with NAACP workers in several large cities and they all say the same thing: When they launch their membership drives they find the Negro masses asking questions like "Why don't you stage freedom rides?" "Why don't you engage in mass action?"

Because of the internal politics of the organization, most of the NAACP local leaders will not be quoted. Some of them, however, are willing to speak for the record. Raymond Brown, president of the Jersey City branch of the NAACP, is blunt and candid about the national leadership. During a television interview I asked Brown if he felt the national leadership was asleep at the switch. His tart reply was: "Hell, they don't even know where the switch is."

Roy Wilkins tends to blame himself for much of the crisis now facing the NAACP.

"Let's face it," he told me, "I am not a dramatic personality. I can do all right on a platform but I am not the spellbinder some of the other fellows are. This," he continued reflectively, his head tilted toward the floor, "is some of our problem. Maybe a man with a more dramatic flair should be sitting in this chair; I don't know."

Then, flanked by his public relations officer, Henry Moon, Roy moved on to another of his recurring themes: "You have to give it to CORE and Martin King; they know how to dramatize their wares; people know what they have to sell. Somehow we have failed to do this; people don't know about our apples and peaches and potatoes. And because they don't know, they conclude we don't have anything for sale."

This was the dilemma Roy Wilkins faced when he spoke to the students at Spelman College; he congratulated them for what they had done, but he was not with them, at their sides, when they did it. There is more to this than just the matter of going to jail; at rock bottom there is the question of the rapport between Negro leaders and the Negro masses. Current Negro leadership, such as it is, is devoted to doing the job for the people, rather than to having the people do the job themselves; current Negro leadership wants the job to be done in the nice, clean quiet of the courtroom, but the opposition will have none of it. Thus it is that the Negro masses must be mobilized to go beyond legalism to action. This is the NAACP's great failure and Mr. Wilkins' Atlanta speech was a major symptom of that all-pervading malady.

One might say that Roy Wilkins went to jail twenty years too soon. In the mid-forties, Roy was among those who were arrested while picketing Constitution Hall in Washington, D.C., because the Daughters of the American Revolution, managers of the hall, refused to allow Negro artists to perform there. The students who are now demanding militant action weren't born then, and they will be surprised to read here that Roy Wilkins was ever in jail for a civil rights cause.

I have sat with these students in their private meetings and I know the demands they make upon themselves and their leaders. But the students are not alone in this; adult Negroes everywhere are also demanding that their leaders come from behind their desks and walk and suffer with them. As far as the Negro masses are concerned, Roy Wilkins will never be able to explain why he didn't take a freedom ride or participate in a sit-in; many local NAACP officials did engage in these demonstrations, but this does not explain away the absence of national NAACP officials during these important demonstrations.

But, as Roy well knows, he and the national office are not all of the problem. Although there are many NAACP rank-and-filers who want mass action the NAACP local branches, particularly in the larger cities, are larded with professionals who have vested interests and ambitions at stake. Many NAACP branches are, for instance, headed by lawyers; their roles as NAACP presidents give them a base from which they can exert considerable power in political circles. But when such a mixture of personal ambitions and race leadership occurs the result is something less than militant.

There is a classic case of this in the two NAACP branch presidents who were scheduled to participate in a freedom ride; the plans were all laid, the other riders reported at the arranged time and place. Then came word that the two NAACP presidents would not participate. Only after the ride was over, its objective more than accomplished, did word leak out why the two NAACP presidents failed to appear. Both men are lawyers and consider themselves in line for judgeships. They simply weren't willing to jeopardize the possible judgeships by getting arrested.

I am not being critical of these men; indeed, we Negro reporters are in something of the same fix. Many of us have wanted to become freedom riders or sit-ins but our editors and lawyers warned us that if we were arrested

we would experience trouble getting security clearance if
an assignment that involved it arose and that we would
have difficulty getting visas into certain countries where
we might well be assigned. For this very reason many
of us who realize our professional lives would be imperiled
by becoming personally involved in certain protests have
refused to accept positions of leadership in civil rights
organizations.

The question raised here, then, is whether a man who
cannot afford to risk jail on charges of trespass should be
at the head of any civil rights movement. It is increasingly
clear that Negroes must be called upon to present their
bodies to bring about the fulfillment of the law; the chances
are that the leaders of such movements will be jailed, for
that is the price of being a modern Negro leader.

The slogan of the Negro revolt might be rendered as:
*"Direct Action to Augment Legalism; Legalism To Aug-
ment The Conference Table."* Central in this is the Negro
masses' loss of faith in the white power structure. They
don't believe the white power structure intends to obey
the desegregation law; thus they demand mass, direct action to force implementation of the law. They don't believe
the white power structure intends to keep bargains made
at the race relations conference table; thus they demand
legalism to reduce these verbal agreements to court decrees. This attitude by the Negro masses has forced the
issue by demanding militant, immediate action. A clear
example of this and how it places a strain upon leadership
organizations can be found in the burgeoning lawsuits
claiming school segregation in the North.

The issue of segregated schools in the North came to a
head in New Rochelle, New York, in 1960 and set a pattern that was to be followed in several non-Southern states.

Negro parents in New Rochelle became disgruntled because their children were forced to attend the Lincoln
School, which, for all practical purposes, was segregated.
The explanation seemed to be twofold: The school board
had gerrymandered school districts so that Negro pupils
were all caught up in one school district; and, second,

housing segregation led to *de facto* school segregation. The matter came before the New Rochelle branch of the NAACP; the issue set off internal wrangling and the branch did not act on the matter. In the meantime the Negro parents hired Negro attorney Paul Zuber of New York. Zuber took immediate action; he filed a law suit demanding that the New Rochelle school board provide open enrollment; this would allow Negro parents to send their children to schools other than Lincoln. To the amazement of many Negro skeptics, Zuber, with help from Thurgood Marshall, won the suit and the New Rochelle case is now a pacesetter for other such suits in the North.

Once the New Rochelle case was won Zuber found himself flooded with invitations from Negro parents in other Northern communities to come and represent them in similar cases. Early in the fall of 1961 Zuber accepted the case of a group of parents in Chicago, Illinois. It developed that the parents had wanted action from the Chicago NAACP but failed to get it. Some parents said they had been asking the Chicago NAACP for help over a period of two years. Zuber filed his case against the Chicago board of education and created a mild sensation. The case is still pending, but the entire matter has caused a deep schism in the Chicago Negro power structure and the Chicago NAACP has suffered.

"It is no accident," one Chicago NAACP member told me, "that our membership is off seven thousand this year. People ask us why we didn't file the suit against the board of education and we have nothing to tell them; we can't explain it."

An even more interesting development has occurred in Newark, New Jersey. The Newark NAACP retained Mr. Zuber to come and represent them in their suit against what they deemed to be segregated schools. Needless to say, this was not pleasing to NAACP lawyers, but the explanation seems to be that the people feel Zuber will act, quickly and without compromise.[2]

[2] In March, 1962, the Newark school board gave in and established "open enrollment." Zuber then withdrew his suit.

A similar thing was developing in Englewood, New Jersey. The NAACP members wanted Zuber to come in and represent them in a school desegregation case; the NAACP national office did not speak against this, but asked that NAACP lawyers be consulted first. The entire matter erupted into a stormy membership meeting during which both local NAACP-ers and national officers lost their tempers. Meanwhile the parents moved independently, outside the NAACP, and retained Paul Zuber. The local NAACP then voted to support the parents and Zuber; they also asked the NAACP national office for financial assistance in the case. The national office denied this assistance but did offer the services of their lawyers as consultants to Paul Zuber if Zuber so desired.

Thus it is that the crisis is developing; the Negro masses are demanding action, immediately, and leadership organizations are being circumvented when they hesitate or stand in the way.

The NAACP national office is acutely aware of the situation. For this very reason the board created a new post, staff assistant for education, to deal with the growing demands for legal action against Northern school boards. The post was given to June Shagaloff in September, 1961 and she has spent the better part of four months preparing school programs in several Northern states. So far Miss Shagaloff has been engaged in a constant race to get local NAACPs to act before parents call Paul Zuber into the case. She lost the Englewood case to Zuber not so much because the NAACP didn't act but because the people simply wanted Zuber to represent them. As of this writing, it is a toss-up whether Miss Shagaloff or Zuber will represent Negro parents in Hempstead, Long Island; Montclair, New Jersey; and Orange, New Jersey.

But it is in New York City, home of thirteen NAACP branches, that Zuber has achieved his most brilliant success.

In the fall of 1961, Mrs. Shirley Rector refused to send her fifteen-year-old son, Sheldon, to school. Her complaint was that Sheldon, as do practically all the Negro students from Harlem, had a choice between Columbus High School and Benjamin Franklin High School; she felt that the concentration of Negro high school students in these two schools constituted a kind of segregated schooling. Mrs. Rector flatly told the school board that she would not send her son to school and the board responded by filing suit against her charging that she was flouting the truancy law. Mrs. Rector retained Attorney Percy Sutton, who is also president of the Harlem branch of the NAACP. Sutton, in turn, called Paul Zuber into the case.

With Sutton's knowledge, Zuber took the matter into Federal Court and questioned the legality of the school board's action in concentrating Negro students in two high schools rather than following a program of open enrollment. Early in February of 1962, Zuber was invited to a private conference with Dr. John Theobald, New York City School Superintendent. Following the conference, Dr. Theobald announced that, as of the fall of 1962, New York City will practice open enrollment at the high school level. The practical meaning of this is that Negro pupils will be able to attend the better high schools in New York City.

There can be little doubt, now, that the school desegregation fight is shifting from the South to the North, where segregated housing makes for *de facto* school segregation and where the predominantly Negro schools have become citadels of bad conduct, crime, poorly prepared teachers, and racial frustrations. It is also beyond doubt that, for whatever reasons, the NAACP has failed to take command in the area of school desegregation—the area Roy Wilkins has called the key to the entire segregation issue —and that it has failed to do so even in the North where there is no fear whatsoever of white violence and economic reprisals.

I asked Percy Sutton why the Harlem NAACP did not take on the precedent-making Rector case.

"I have no comment as to 'why'," he said. "But I do want to talk about Paul Zuber. I have the deepest respect and personal admiration for Paul. He is one of the boldest, most imaginative men in the area of race relations today. All I can say about the NAACP is this: our branch is not interested in organizational glory and pride; we want the job done. Zuber has a name, a reputation, when it comes to school desegregation in the North. I know Paul, I respect him; I called him into the Rector case because we knew he could, and would, do a job. He has done just that. God bless him and long may he live."

How does thirty-five-year-old Paul Zuber live at all? That, as we used to say down in Georgia, is the real puzzlement. Paul Zuber took his college degree from Brown University in 1947 after doing a two-year hitch in the army. For the next several years Zuber worked for the New York City board of health and studied law at Brooklyn Law School. Zuber took his law degree in 1957 and on the afternoon of the day he was admitted to the bar he filed a law suit in behalf of two New York parents who wished to challenge segregation in the City's schools. He continued in the employ of the board of health for another year, however, but was forced to resign because of conflict of interest charges that arose when he accepted the case of nine New York Negro parents who filed an additional suit challenging segregation in the school system.

It was at this juncture that he was called into the New Rochelle school case, and school desegregation cases have taken all of his time since then.

Paul Zuber has a wife and a four-year-old daughter. From September, 1960, when he took over the New Rochelle case, until March 1, 1962, the date of this writing, Zuber's gross income has been slightly less than ten thousand dollars. Out of this he has had to pay his traveling expenses and several legal fees in behalf of clients. These are the principal facts about Zuber's income:

● He received $4,300 for the New Rochelle case which lasted from September, 1960, until late summer of 1961. This money came from the NAACP Legal Defense and Education Fund.

● Two private groups, one in New York City and one in New Rochelle, gave testimonial dinners for Zuber. He was given a five-hundred-dollar award at each dinner.

● Following the New Rochelle case Zuber settled down to private practice and received several cases having nothing to do with civil rights and which carried good retainers. Then, early in the fall of 1961, Zuber was called into the Chicago school case. He had to drop the private cases, return the retainers, and devote all of his time to the Chicago case.

● To date, Zuber has received six hundred dollars from the Chicago case. Out of this he has had to pay traveling expenses to Chicago (four times) and living expenses while there.

● Zuber's retainer as well as the money to get the Newark, New Jersey, school case underway is, as of this writing, tied up in a wrangle between the NAACP national office and the Newark chapter of the NAACP. To date Zuber has received nothing.

● Zuber has received two hundred dollars as a retainer in the Englewood, New Jersey, school case.

● Zuber has received one hundred and fifty dollars as a retainer and, I suspect, full payment for the Sheldon Rector case that opened all New York high schools to Negro pupils.

Two citations offer some comparison between what Zuber earns and the income of others involved in the same kind of fight:

● Some NAACP lawyers earn as much as ten thousand dollars a year in salary and, of course, the organization pays all expenses involved.

● The white lawyer who argued the New Rochelle case for the City received $7,500 for that chore alone, whereas Zuber followed the case all the way through the various courts involved.

Zuber was forced to close his New York law office for financial reasons. He is quite candid about it: "Louis," he said to me, "I couldn't pay the rent. I had to close my office or be put out. And," he added with a big belly laugh, "how the hell would it look for the man who cracked school segregation in the North to be put out because he couldn't pay his rent?"

Zuber and his family live in Croton, New York, some thirty miles from New York City. Mrs. Zuber's people are there and Paul is able to cut his expenses to the bone.

These are the facts about Paul Zuber, the rebel who is the fair-haired boy of those seeking relief from school segregation in the North. Zuber is no saint, he knows very well what he is doing; he is suffering not only for a cause but for professional advancement. If he and his family can hold out long enough, and if he continues his winning ways against school boards, he will be amply rewarded. Even now there is a move afoot to set up a legal foundation dedicated to nothing but northern school desegregation. Should the move bear fruit, and I predict that it will, Zuber will be called in to head the organization.

This will, indeed, set off great troubling at Twenty West Fortieth Street. A few days after the Zuber victory in New York was announced, the NAACP national office released the names of some twenty-five cities in the non-South where school segregation is allegedly practiced. The essence of the announcement was that the NAACP was moving into the cities to attack this condition.[3] The consensus is that the NAACP is too late; that the local people involved will more than likely seek Zuber's aid, and that when the NAACP does take a case it will not move with vigor and immediacy. A case to support this view is Hempstead, Long Island. The NAACP, as of now, is handling that school case and its first move was to place a complaint before the Commissioner of Education for the State of New York. Alas, it was this same Commissioner of Education before whom the New Rochelle NAACP placed its case; he studied it for six months and said there was no discrimination. Then the New Rochelle parents called Paul Zuber. The rest is history, and the feeling is that history will repeat itself in Hempstead.

Zuber, to be honest about it, is not the most disciplined

[3]The list included Robins, Illinois, one of the two all-Negro towns in America!

lawyer in the world. The way he prepares his cases gives the methodical, painstaking NAACP lawyers ulcers. In several instances, including the New Rochelle case, Zuber was given a major assist, if not rescued, by the NAACP Legal Defense and Education Fund staff. They feared he might make a legal error and lose an important case and thus muddy the water. Even so there is a place in the Negro revolt for a man like Paul Zuber and the greatest sin may well be that private groups instead of the established leadership organizations have given him an opportunity to emerge.

I have dealt with these matters at length in order to certify the fact that there is a growing tendency among Negroes to seek solutions to their problems without recourse to the established leadership organizations. The NAACP seems to be the hardest hit by this development simply because it had primacy in the field; the NAACP gave ground to CORE and the SCLC, and from Roy Wilkins' argument that the key to civil rights advancement is school desegregation, one would expect the NAACP to make a major move in this direction. Now it appears that even the school desegregation efforts in the North are being made outside the NAACP. Even more curiously, NAACP chapters are hiring private lawyers to come into their local communities and file school desegregation suits.

The NAACP has been given a large share of the blame for the current Negro leadership muddle, both in this book and by Negroes in general. Some of the criticisms may be unfair, but they are a symptom of our deep emotional attachment to the NAACP. In spite of the rise of other Negro leaders and organizations, the NAACP still commands the loyalty of more Negroes than any of its rivals; it is still the richest, biggest, and most potentially effective organization in the civil liberties field.

The NAACP was our big brother in the darkest days of this century: It spoke for us when we dared not speak for ourselves; it acted for us when we had neither the courage nor the know-how to act for ourselves. It was the work of the NAACP that set the scene for the Negro revolt, and we criticize it because we don't wish it to become as Joshua, who led the oppressed children within sight of the Promised Land, but who was then crushed behind the gate to the city as the masses surged along the final stretch to freedom. Lester Davis, a member of the executive board of the Chicago NAACP, had this to say about the NAACP leadership "turning deaf ears to the demand from the membership for internal democracy and a militant, direct, mass action program to implement legal victories: . . .

"The choice seems obvious, but will be difficult. . . . Few leaders of any organization will readily agree to changes which can destroy their positions of power and influence. All change is radical, be it chemical or political or social. No matter how gradual the prelude, there must come a point in which what was yesterday, is something else today. [The] NAACP must change with time or be destroyed by it."[4]

As far as the other civil rights organizations are concerned, the crisis in Negro leadership is largely a matter of public confusion brought on by overlapping programs and a lack of cooperative planning. It is to the advantage of the nation's civil rights organizations to get together, share program plans and, if at all possible, stake out areas of operation. It was both embarrassing and inexcusable for James Meredith to have been caught up in this confusion over just which civil rights organization is doing what and for whom. The turmoil became such that Meredith found it necessary to take time out from his studies and announce that (1) the NAACP did not sponsor his entrance to the University of Mississippi; rather he did it himself and then called on the NAACP for aid; (2) that his legal expenses were being borne by the NAACP Legal Defense and Education Fund, not the NAACP, as many people thought. The important thing is for the Negro leadership organizations to issue a clear call that both Negroes and white people can understand; it is essential for Negroes to understand in order that the revolt not dissipate into anarchy; it is essential for white people to understand in order for them to realize that they must deal with responsible Negro leadership and institute change. If Negro leaders fail to resolve their crisis and confusion or if the white power structure fails to deal with responsible Negroes and bring about change, then, in the words of Dr. Gardner C. Taylor, "The leadership of Negroes, particularly in our large cities, will fall into the hands of extremists whose preachments of violence endanger everything America stands for."

13.

THE BLACK MUSLIMS

THE EXTREME FORM of the Negro's revolt against his plight can be seen in the rise of the Honorable Elijah Muhammad, whose followers are known as the Nation of Islam or the Black Muslims.[1] Oddly enough, I may well have been somewhat responsible for the group's growth. But this is the way of publicity in America; it is impossible to conduct a public discussion of a group's activity without moving some people to go out and join that group.

It all started—for me, that is—on a Saturday night back in 1958. I was walking through Harlem with a fellow writer and friend, Robert Maynard, and his wife, Elizabeth. Bob is Negro, Liz is white. We paused to listen to a Harlem street corner orator rave and rant about the "condition of my people." I was fairly new in New York at the time and was struck by the inverse racism in everything the speaker said. I knew full well that if some white speaker had taken to a street corner platform to say similar things about Negroes there would have been hell

[1] The term "Black Muslim" was coined by Dr. Eric Lincoln while he was preparing his Ph.D. dissertation on the followers of Muhammad. They do not use the term when speaking of themselves. They call themselves "Muslims." However, they do not object to the term employed by Lincoln.

to pay and I would gladly be among those who dished it out. Yet—and this is what struck me—there the man stood, on a street corner in mid-Harlem, an American flag waving conspicuously (the speaker explained that "this damn flag is here not because I respect it or believe in it but because this is the only way I can hold a public meeting and not be put in jail").

"Now gather round," the speaker said. "I want to tell you about the white man."

"Say on, brother," some sister yelled from the crowd.

"Did you ever—hear me now—did you ever know a white man to do anything right?"

The crowd roared with scornful laughter.

"Hell, no," a man screamed out. "Right ain't in them!"

"Tell them about it," a woman joined in.

"Now listen," the speaker said. "I want you to understand how the white man, particularly the Jew, keeps you in the economic locks. Am I right or wrong?"

"You right," the crowd shot back.

"Now, now, now," the speaker stammered for emphasis, "this is the way it is. You get up early every morning with roaches and rats running round your bed. Is that right?"

"That's right."

"You stumble over to your child's bed to make sure the rats ain't done bit his ears off. Is that right?"

"That's right."

"Then you make it through falling plaster to a leaky water closet to wash your face."

"Yes, sir . . . that's it, that's it."

"You finally get the sleep out of your eyes and put on some clothes that are just about worn out but you ain't finished paying for them yet."

"Say on, brother. The white man ought to be killed!"

"Then, then, then—hear me now—then you go down in the subway and make it down to the garment district to meet the man. Am I right or wrong?"

"You right!"

"And this is where the economic lock come in; you go downtown to work for Mr. Eisenberg."

"Yeah!"

"You work all day, eight hours a day, five days a week for forty-four dollars."

"That's right."

"And while you making forty-four dollars, Mr. Eisenberg is watching you sweat and grunt and he makes forty-four hundred dollars. Am I right or wrong?"

"You right; great God, you right!"

"Say on."

"Tell it like it is."

"Oh, don't worry, brother, I'm going to tell it just like it is; I'm going to bring it right down front so everybody can smell it!

"Now—and watch this—you work all day for Mr. Eisenberg, you come back up here to Harlem and buy your clothes from Mr. Gosenberg."

"Yeah."

"You buy your jewelry from Mr. Goldberg."

"Yes."

"You pay rent to Mr. Fineberg."

"Yes."

"You get borrowed money from a finance company headed by Mr. Weinberg."

"Yes, tell it."

"Now what you don't know is that Mr. Eisenberg and Mr. Gosenberg and Mr. Fineberg and Mr. Goldberg and Mr. Weinberg is all cousins. They got you working for nothing, and then they take back the little nothing you make before you can get home with it. That's how they got you in the economic locks!"

And with this the crowd breaks with wild, pained laughter.

I did not grow up around all this, and I was shocked by it. My shock was translated into anger when one of the Negro men in the crowd came over and insulted Bob for being with a white woman. He told us to move on.

I wanted to stay and have it out, but Bob, by then used to such things, said no.

I went home that night and filed a feature story entitled "Harlem, Saturday Night" to the Afro-American newspaper. I was their United Nations correspondent at the time but I felt I had a better story in Harlem than I had down on the East River.

I never forgot what I saw and felt that night. And when, over a year later, I joined Mike Wallace's TV news staff, I asked and received permission to do a TV documentary on Harlem's street corner speakers. After a few hours of moving around in Harlem I discovered that the street corner speakers represented several African nationalist organizations. These organizations were composed of Negroes who deny everything American, think of themselves as Africans, and who view themselves as the real champions for African freedom in the United States. The more I probed these nationalists organizations, the more I heard about a group called the "Muslims." At first, like most Americans, I took the Muslims to be none other than followers of the Islamic faith in America. The evidence, however, began to indicate that they were a good deal more than that. I went digging for the Muslims and, after much secret negotiation and meetings in restaurants, I finally obtained information which resulted in a two-hour-long TV documentary called *The Hate That Hate Produced*.

The documentary opened with a recording made during a morality play given by the Black Muslims. The play, called *The Trial,* depicts the white man being tried by the remainder of the world for his crimes against black peoples. The prosecutor summed up his case with these words:

> I charge the white man with being the greatest liar on earth. I charge the white man with being the greatest drunkard on earth. I charge the white man with being the greatest swine-eater on earth. Yet the Bible forbids it. I charge the white man with being the greatest gambler on

earth. I charge the white man, ladies and gentlemen of the jury, with being the greatest murderer on earth. I charge the white man with being the greatest peace-breaker on earth. I charge the white man with being the greatest adulterer on earth. I charge the white man with being the greatest robber on earth. I charge the white man with being the greatest deceiver on earth. I charge the white man with being the greatest trouble-maker on earth. So therefore, ladies and gentlemen of the jury, I ask you, bring back a verdict of guilty as charged.

The jury brought in a verdict of guilty and the applause of the audience was so thunderous it drowned out the judge's voice as he sentenced the white man to death.

This play was staged before huge audiences all over the non-South, including two appearances at New York's Carnegie Hall, and it tells a good deal about the nature and purpose of the Black Muslims. The Muslims use a good deal of the paraphernalia of the traditional religion of Islam but they add a few innovations of their own. When Mike Wallace and I first broke the story of the Muslims they were denied by orthodox Moslems. However, the denial was retracted and since then the exact relationship between the followers of Muhammad and orthodox Islam has been a moot question.

The driving force in the Black Muslim movement—they now claim a membership of over a quarter of a million[2]—is one Elijah Muhammad, a sixty-year-old American Negro who was born Elijah Poole and spent his early life as a Baptist minister. Muhammad is a strikingly unimpressive man; he is small, five feet five, and speaks with a disturbing lisp. It is difficult to believe that he is the moving spirit behind a religion that is now being taught in fifty schools across the nation. Yet when Muhammad speaks the audience sits entranced for from four to five hours while he delivers a most amazing doctrine. And it is during the mass rallies where Mr. Muhammad speaks that the Muslims can best be studied.

[2]Experts on the Black Muslims say the membership does not exceed 100,000.

✓Their withdrawal from America is almost complete. They speak of themselves as a "nation," indicating that they are not of the American body politic; they do not vote nor do they participate in political affairs. The Muslim women keep their heads covered at all times; they wear the long, flowing, white skirts one associates with Islam. They have their own stores, supermarkets, barbershops, department stores and fish markets.

Minister Malcolm X, a brilliant man and an ex-convict, is Muhammad's chief lieutenant. Wherever Mr. Muhammad speaks, Minister Malcolm X sets the stage with an introduction. This is how Malcolm X introduced Mr. Muhammad during a recent Black Muslim rally in Washington, D.C.'s Uline Arena:

MINISTER X: Everyone who is here today realizes that we are now living in the fulfillment of prophecy. We have come to hear and to see the greatest and wisest and most fearless black man in America today. In the Church, we used to sing the song "Good News, the Chariot Is Coming." Is that right or wrong?

AUDIENCE: Right!

MINISTER X: But what we must bear in mind is that what's good news to one person is bad news to another. While you sit here today, knowing that you have come to hear good news, you must realize in advance that what might be good news for you might be bad news for somebody else. What's good news for the sheep might be bad news for the wolves.

The "good news" for the black man, according to Minister X, is that he is on the verge of recapturing his position as ruler of the universe. The "bad news" for the white man is that his wicked reign will soon be over.

Then Muhammad spoke. This was his central theme: ✓"The Christian religion has failed. Your leaders of that religion have failed. Now the government of America has failed you. You have no justice coming from no one. It is written that you are like sheep among wolves . . .

every wolf taking a bite at you. You want justice; you want freedom; you want equality . . . but get none. . . .

"The only thing for you to do is separate from the white man and have some land of your own."

Elijah Muhammad is aging, his health is bad and he bought a home in Arizona late in 1961 in order to live in a dry climate. Much of his work, and all his speaking engagements, are being carried on by Minister Malcolm X, whom many feel will one day be the leader of the movement. Malcolm X is a tall, lanky, light-brown-skinned man with an almost innate mastery of mass psychology. He served a prison term for robbery; now he is changed. He will not smoke, drink or even eat in a restaurant that houses a bar. He says the change came when he heard Mr. Muhammad speak and he lost his shame about being colored. During an extensive interview, Malcolm X gave me this outline of the Black Muslims' faith:

LOMAX: Mr. Elijah Muhammad teaches . . . that his faith . . . that the Islamic faith is for the black man and that the black man is good. He also uses the Old Testament instance of the serpent in Adam and Eve and the Garden of Eden, and he sets up the proposition that this is the great battle between good and evil, and he uses the word devils.

MINISTER X: Yes.

LOMAX: He uses it almost interchangeably and synonymous with the word snake. Well, what does he mean there?

MINISTER X: Well, number one, he teaches us that there never was a real serpent.

LOMAX: It was not a real serpent?

MINISTER X: . . . that went into the Garden.

LOMAX: What was it?

MINISTER X: But, as you know, the Bible was written in symbols and parables, and this serpent or snake is a symbol that's used to hide the real identity of the one whom that actually was.

LOMAX: Well, who was it?

MINISTER X: The white man.

LOMAX: I want to call your attention, Minister Malcolm, to one paragraph in this column [written by the Honorable Elijah Muhammad]. He said, and I quote him, "The only people born of Allah are the black nation, of whom the so-called American Negroes are descendants."

MINISTER X: Yes.

LOMAX: Now is this your standard teaching?

MINISTER X: Yes. He teaches us that the black man by nature is divine.

LOMAX: Now, does this mean that the white man by nature is evil?

MINISTER X: By nature, he is other than divine.

LOMAX: Well, now, does this mean he is evil? Can he do good?

MINISTER X: By nature he is evil.

LOMAX: He cannot do good?

MINISTER X: History is best qualified to reward all research and we don't have any historic example where we have found that they collectively as a people have done good.

LOMAX: Minister Malcolm, you know, in Chicago, and in Detroit, you have universities of Islam, do you not?

MINISTER X: Yes, sir, in Detroit and Chicago.

LOMAX: And you take your parishioners—you take children from the kindergarten ages and you train them right through high school, is that true?

MINISTER X: Yes, sir, from the age of four, I think, upward.

LOMAX: And you have a certified parochial school operating in Chicago.

MINISTER X: In Chicago . . .

LOMAX: And in Detroit . . .

MINISTER X: And in Detroit . . .

LOMAX: And kids come to your school in lieu of going to what we would call regular day school?

MINISTER X: Yes, sir, many.

LOMAX: What do you teach them there?

MINISTER X: We teach them the same things that they would be taught ordinarily in school, minus the Little Black Sambo story and the things that were taught to you and me when we were coming up to breed that inferiority complex in us.

LOMAX: Do you teach them what you have just said to me—that the white man is the symbol of evil?

MINISTER X: You can go to any little Muslim child and ask them where is hell and who is the devil, and he wouldn't tell you that hell is down in the ground or that the devil is something invisible that you can't see. He'll tell you that hell is right where he has been catching it and he'll tell you the one who is responsible for him having received this hell is the devil.

LOMAX: And he would say that the devil is the white man?

MINISTER X: Yes.

LOMAX: Can a white man join your temple?

MINISTER X: None has ever joined.

LOMAX: If one came up and attempted to join, would he be allowed to come in and be taught?

MINISTER X: No, sir.

LOMAX: Why not?

MINISTER X: Well, that's one of the reasons why most people think that Mr. Muhammad teaches hate, but if there is a rattlesnake in the field who has been biting your brothers and your sisters, then you go and tell them that that's a rattlesnake and all of the harm that's ever come to them has come to them from that particular source. Well, then, that rattler will think that the warner is teaching hate. He'll go back and tell the other snakes that this man is teaching hate . . . this man is teaching hate . . . but it's not hate . . . it's just that when you study people who have been harmed and discover the source of their injury—the source of all their defects, and you begin to point out that source, it's not that you hate the source, but your love for your people is so intense—so great—that you must let them know what is wrong with them, what is the cause of their ills. And this is one of the basic factors, I believe, involved, when the propaganda is put out that Mr. Muhammad teaches hate. He teaches black people to love each other, and our love for each other is so strong, we don't have any room left in our hearts.

It is clear, then, that we are witnessing the first home-grown American Negro religion. In essence, Muhammad is saying this: God and black are one, therefore all blacks are divine; the opposite of black is evil, therefore all white men are evil. Then he extends his argument: The world's black men are divine, therefore unified. The weakest link in the black brotherhood is the so-called American Negro, who is all mixed up with the white man. The return of black men to power, then, is waiting upon the American Negro to come out from among the white men and be separated—not segregated. To accomplish this Muhammad demands "some states" where the Negro can set up his own nation. (A group of us offered Muhammad Mississippi; he turned it down.)

Strangely enough Muhammad's demand for a "separate state" gets symbolic support from many non-Muslims because of incidents like the James Meredith encounter with Mississippi lawlessness. Many Negroes feel—and as a direct result of the Meredith case—that white people will never really yield, that we will spend the remainder of our lives waging a major war over a morsel. This results in a strange kind of spiritual withdrawal from the American community, a deepening faith that since we have little hope of being "of" the general American mainstream there is little or no reason why we should be "in" it, to complete the Biblical analogy. This is particularly true among the Negro masses—and they are those who come to hear Muhammad speak—who have never had a real "we" feeling about America.

But Muhammad's demands for a separate state, like his Islamic trappings, are not to be taken too seriously. Most people are convinced that he doesn't really mean this; and we are convinced that most of his followers are not culturally able to execute the alliance with traditional

Islam that the spokesmen for the movement would have one believe. These—the separate state and the Islamic trappings—are not the arresting things. There are matters raised by Muhammad, however, that demand, and have received, serious attention from sober Negroes:

First, Muhammad's indictment of Christianity has forced thoughtful Negro preachers into an almost impossible position. I have talked this over with scores of Negro clergymen, and, almost to a man, they agree that Muhammad has deeply shaken the Negro Christian community. Muhammad's recital of how the Christian faith has failed the Negro—"By their fruits ye shall know them"— has sunk deeper into the hearts of the Negro masses than Negro clergymen will admit publicly. But, and as a direct result of what Muhammad has said, Negro clergymen are scurrying around for new Sunday school picture cards, religious literature that pictures God and Christ, if not black, at least resembling a Negro. I know of one Negro minister, a Harvard graduate at that, who has delivered several sermons on the question of Christ's physical appearance. "And his hair was like lamb's wool." This, the minister says, is the only physical description of Jesus. Then he tells his middle-class Negro congregation that his, the minister's hair, looks more like lamb's wool than do Norman Vincent Peale's forelocks.

And although they are bitter ideological enemies, there is only a thin line between Muhammad and Martin Luther King. King, of course, will have none of Muhammad's blanket indictment of the white man; nor will King abide black supremacy notions. But both King and Muhammad are saying that the purpose of a religion is to explain life for the people who adopt or create it and that the function of a gospel is to speak to the frustrations of a people. Muhammad's gospel as a whole will not be accepted by the Negro. But—and this is the important thing—no gospel that fails to answer Muhammad's criticism of Christianity will be accepted either.

In the process of indicting Christianity and criticizing Negro leaders who seek "integration," Muhammad, largely through the spellbinding work of Malcolm X, has caused thousands of the Negro masses to become race-conscious in a way they never were before. It is the rise of Muhammad that has caused Jackie Robinson to realize that Negro leadership organizations are not reaching the Negro masses. William Berry, executive secretary of the Chicago Urban League, readily confesses: "Hell, these Muslims make more sense to the Negro on the street than I do!"

It is quite a pageant to see hundreds of Negro women, formerly Baptists, Methodists and what have you, marching into Washington's Uline Arena, draped in white, their heads covered, to hear Elijah speak. Their withdrawal is fairly complete. They have no more faith in the white man or in the American dream. They don't condemn the white man for they feel he is incapable of doing good. Their chant, like that of the early Jew, is, "How can we sing the Lord's song in a strange land?"

And police brutality, particularly in New York, has helped the Black Muslim movement. Two years ago, several policemen, all of them white, shot their way into a Muslim home on Long Island. They were under the mistaken impression that a fugitive was hiding there. The policemen terrorized one man, several children and two pregnant women. The Muslims retaliated with milk bottles, sticks and stones. Of course, they were all arrested for assaulting policemen. But an all-white jury set them free. Then there is the case of Johnson Hinton, a Muslim who happened to be on a Harlem street when a fight broke out. White policemen waded in swinging their clubs. Hinton fell to the ground, his head split open. He was hospitalized and five hundred Muslim men threw a cordon around the hospital and all but started a race riot. A steel plate was put in Hinton's head, and he recovered. He was acquitted of any wrongdoing. Then came the lawsuit. The jury awarded Hinton $75,000; then, rather than go through endless appeals, the City settled for $70,000.

It is no accident that the Black Muslims do a land-office recruiting job in the nation's prisons. These jails are jammed with Negroes who, even though guilty, have known the bitter taste of police brutality and short-shrift justice. To them, the Muslims present a deadly argument and the prisoners have responded by the hundreds. Just recently the Black Muslims went to court and won the right to practice their faith inside New York State prisons; in California prisons the Muslims presented such a challenge that state officials had to make special arrangements to accommodate them and their faith.

✓And it is just here, in their work with Negro criminals, that the Muslims have won the respect of Negro and white social workers. Their rehabilitation program is nothing short of miraculous. They start out by convincing the ex-convict that he fell into crime because he was ashamed of being black, that the white man had so psychologically conditioned him that he was unable to respect himself. Then they convince the one-time prisoner that being black is a blessing, not a curse, and that in keeping with that blessing he, the ex-convict, must clean himself up and live a life of decency and respect. As a result:

✓You never see a Muslim without a clean shirt and tie and coat.

You never see a Muslim drink.

You never see a Muslim smoke.

You never see a Muslim dance.

You never see a Muslim use dope.

You never see a Muslim woman with a non-Muslim man.

You never see a Muslim man with a woman other than his wife.

You never see a Muslim without some means of income.

You never see a Muslim who will not stop and come to the aid of any black woman he sees in trouble.

You seldom see a Muslim lapse back into crime. (A close friend of mine is a lawyer with Muslim clients and he tells me that he has known of only four Muslims who have returned to crime in the past five years. This is remarkable when one remembers that some six hundred convicts in prison join the Black Muslims each year. The Muslim leaders arrange parole for their converts and take them in hand. Parole officers and police have told me that the Black Muslims are the best rehabilitation agency at work among Negro criminals today.)

The crucial issue is that these criminals are rehabilitated along with the other members of the group (most of the Muslims are not ex-convicts) in a faith that denies and condemns everything American. They do it by simply reciting the facts about life for the black man in America. And it is this recital that caused James Baldwin to remark that others among us have the faith but the Muslims have the facts.

Because they have the facts, and none of us can dispute them, the Black Muslims have forced every Negro spokesman in America to assume a position more extreme than that he would have assumed had the Muslims not been among us. Not that the position is false; rather that Negro spokesmen, for all their fist-pounding, are cautious fellows. But once Malcolm X makes his speech there is neither room nor reason for this kind of caution, and the Negro spokesman who speaks less of the truth than Malcolm speaks simply cannot get a hearing among his own people.

The Black Muslims, like the sit-ins and the freedom rides, are part of the Negro revolt. They are not aimed in the same direction, but they stem from the same unrest: a rejection of segregation and all that it carries with it and a firm belief that the current Negro leadership organizations are not employing the proper methods to end that evil.

The Black Muslims are now accepted. Nobody bothers them much any more; they are part of the Negro community, their leaders sit on committees when community matters are being discussed. No sane man, black or white, dares plan a mass program in Harlem without including Malcolm X. For if it comes to a showdown, Malcolm can muster more people than Adam Powell, A. Philip Randolph, Martin Luther King and Roy Wilkins all put together.

The Black Muslims represent an extreme reaction to the problem of being a Negro in America today. Instead of working to improve conditions within the framework of American society, as do other Negro leadership organizations, the Black Muslims react by turning their backs on that society entirely. Their one positive aspect is that they work to make Negroes proud of being Negro.

As of now I do not feel the Black Muslims present a real threat to American society—they let off most of their steam harmlessly in their meetings and conventions, and the rituals and trappings of the faith take up much of their attention. But the Black Muslims do present a threat for the future. Should the white supremacists seem to be gaining the upper hand, if little or no progress seems to be made by the nonviolent means of CORE and the SCLC or the legalistic means of the NAACP, then the Black Muslims may grow from a curiosity on the American scene into a potent and dangerous force.

14.

THE WHITE LIBERAL

"OFAY," the adjective many Negroes use to describe white people, is pig Latin. There is considerable disagreement as to just what Negroes have in mind when they refer to white people as "ofays" but, as jazz critic Nat Hentoff suggests, there is good reason to suspect that the term is rooted in the Negro's view of the white man as his "foe." The phrase is general in "hip" circles, among musicians and theater people, and I did not run across it until I had long since completed school and begun to move around among "way-out" Negroes and white people, both of whom used the phrase.

All of which is by way of saying there are two ways of viewing the Negro revolt: If one feels—as does Black Muslim leader Malcolm X, for example—that the Negro revolt is essentially a war between the races, a struggle that must end in victory for one race, defeat for the other, then the white man is most certainly our foe. If, on the other hand, one views the Negro revolt as social evolution, a process of change growing out of ethnic groups interacting with one another, then the white man is but one of the elements involved, just another link in the chain of cause and effect which must remain taut if social change is to be orderly and sure. Personally, I hold to the latter view.

I do not view the white man as my foe, although I know some of them are just that; so, for that matter and for the same reason, are some Negroes. The Negro revolt is a struggle between two segments of American opinion and action, with both Negroes and white people on either side. When it comes to freedom riders, for example, George Schuyler, a Negro newsman, is just as much my enemy as, say, William Buckley of the conservative *National Review.* By the same yardstick, TV personality Mike Wallace, a white man, is just as much my ally as is James Farmer, the executive director of CORE. As one views the American populace dividing along ideological rather than ethnic lines with respect to the Negro revolt there is a great temptation to invoke Spengler's prediction that, in time, the Western race problem would transmute into a class problem. Some of Spengler's prediction has already come to pass; more and more, these days, one finds Negroes and whites on both sides of the question.

The Negro cause has always been laced with white people. It will be recalled that the NAACP was founded by both whites and Negroes; so were the Urban League and CORE. The Southern Christian Leadership Conference is a Negro organization but the bulk of its financing is white. And from the outset the student movement has been interracial. This presence of white people in "Negro" organizations has long been a source of complaint. There are many Negroes, James Lawson of Harlem's African Nationalist Movement, for example, who believe in a unilateral approach to the Negro question. The Negro extremists are not alone in this view; many middle-class Negroes feel the same way but refuse to speak for the record for fear that they will be called antiwhite. The proponents of this view argue that whereas white people should be allowed to participate in Negro action causes they should not assume leadership roles. There are many reasons given to support this way of thinking.

I remember when NAACP leader Walter White married a white woman and one Negro said that if the day came that we had to declare war on the white man Walter would have to begin by shooting his wife. This is an extreme example but the point is common; many Negroes feel that the presence of white people in "Negro" organizations inevitably leads to "go-slowism." They cite both the NAACP and the Urban League as examples. They are refuted, however, by CORE, which has a larger contingent of white people and is by far the most militant Negro action group.

Many Negroes argue against the presence of white people in Negro organizations on the ground of racial pride. This is particularly true when white people rise to positions of leadership within Negro organizations. The argument invariably comes in these words: "The Jews would die before they would let a Negro rise to the leadership of one of their organizations; so why should we let Jews, or any white man for that matter, head our organization?"

This precise argument was rampant late in the fall of 1961 when it was announced that Jack Greenberg had been named to succeed Thurgood Marshall as head of the NAACP Legal Defense and Education Fund. There was nothing covert or anti-Semitic about these protests; but they were terribly pro-Negro. The *Amsterdam News,* a New York Negro weekly, carried a scathing criticism of the Greenberg appointment. "I like Jack . . . BUT," wrote Editor James Hicks. The "BUT" was that, in Hicks' view, a Negro should have gotten Thurgood's job. The general reaction was such that the delegates to the New York State Conference of NAACP branches attempted to pass a resolution critical of the Greenberg appointment. The resolution failed, of course, when the delegates were told—to the amazement of some of them—that the NAACP and the NAACP Legal Defense and Education Fund were different organizations and that, thus, the delegates had no right to be critical of the action of another organization.

Then there are those who argue that to let white people into our organizations is but to invite spies who go back and let the white power structure know what we are up to. It is difficult to take this argument seriously. Indeed, one of my criticisms of Negro leadership organizations is that their programs are too much of a secret; even we Negroes don't know what they are doing. Perhaps it would be a good thing if a few white spies did ease in and let us all in on what's going on! But two can play this game. More than once, in the Deep South, light-skinned Negroes have sneaked into meetings of the White Citizens Councils and brought their plans back to the Negro community.

In another instance, also in the South, the coin was flipped over. A local Negro organization found that its deliberations were know at city hall within hours after their meetings closed. They suspected two white liberals who were members of the organization. After much secret detective work the spy was isolated: a Negro lawyer who had political aspirations!

There are very real and, I think, justifiable reasons why white people are in Negro organizations and should stay there:

The first reason is historical. White liberals spoke for us when we were, for the most part, unable to speak for ourselves. They had power, we did not; they had learning, we did not; they were white, we were not, and thus they could speak without the total sense of fear that enveloped every militant Negro in the last days of the 1800's and the early days of this century.

The second reason is financial. In the early days white people had money, we did not. Only in the last decade have Negro contributions to the NAACP matched those of white people; only in the last five years have Negro contributions surpassed those of white people. As of this day, the bulk of the money behind the Urban League, CORE and the Southern Christian Leadership Conference comes from white people.

The third, and I think most important, reason is that the presence of white people in Negro organizations keeps the Negro revolt from turning into a race conflict. American Negroes are becoming increasingly antiwhite; I am convinced that the presence of white people in our organizations is the major deterrent to total antiwhitism. I will never forget the young white college students, boys and girls, who have resigned from exclusive Eastern colleges and enrolled at Negro schools in the South in order to participate in the student movements. These white students experience considerable difficulty. The white community draws away from them, and they are not totally welcome in Negro circles. Their social life is confined to the campus and their "dates," ofttimes Negroes, arrange to meet them at the gym, the social center or wherever the function is occurring. Above all, they have willingly subjected themselves to an inferior education in order to work for a cause in which they deeply believe.

Although these white students are exposing themselves to an inferior academic program, they are experiencing a moving and important education in racial understanding. Racial ignorance is a staggering part of the whole racial problem in America today. Negroes do not know white people, and white people do not know Negroes. Even most white liberals do not know Negroes, nor, indeed do Negroes know them. The presence of white students on Southern Negro college campuses will go a long way toward wiping out this blight, not only for the persons involved, but for their families and friends as well.

There is an interesting sidelight to the presence of white students on Negro campuses. These white students have transferred from Eastern universities where they were expected to do work much superior to that required by the low academic standards of many Negro colleges. As a result, the white students capture most of the academic honors on the Negro campus. This has had a sobering effect upon many Negro students, and they have begun to realize that scholarship is as important as freedom rides. Deans on three such campuses have told me that many of their Negro students have thus been inspired actually to apply themselves for the first time in their academic lives. One of these deans is now enjoying his role as referee in a close race between a white girl and a Negro boy for senior class honors.

There is an equally rewarding role for white liberals

in the area of public information. Only recently have white magazine editors realized that part of their role is to tell the American people the truth about race relations in our nation; radio and television are undergoing the same growing pains. As one who has worked in both media, particularly television, I can testify to the growing number of white liberals who, off camera, are determined to warn the American public that racism can destroy us. The "white" daily newspapers, particularly outside the South, have also made commendable strides in this direction. Most of them now have Negro reporters, many of whom have advanced to general reporters handling matters of general interest.

I once had lunch with a prominent Negro who bemoaned the fact that the *New York Times* did not have "a single Negro reporter on its staff." As he made his point, the Negro spokesman waved a copy of the *Times,* carrying a front-page dispatch from Albany, New York, concerning Governor Rockefeller's budget program. The article was by-lined "Layhmond Robinson." Until I told him, the Negro spokesman didn't know Layhmond was a Negro.

In this same area, however, the white liberal can become a thorn in our side. I am thinking particularly of those "liberal" daily newspapers which become blinded by their liberality and thus find it impossible to say something critical about an individual who happens to be a Negro when, indeed, something critical needs to be said. The greatest offense of this kind lies in the alliance between liberal publications and certain Negro leadership organizations. They have smothered honest Negro self-criticism almost to the point of a grave fault. I once wrote an article in which I said certain Negro leaders should not have supported the civil rights bill of 1958. The editor to whom the article was submitted became indignant; he not only rejected the piece, but wrote me a sizzling letter in which he said I was nothing short of a traitor to my race. Nor was that all he did. Several weeks later I had an interview with the head of one Negro leadership organization and he told me that a "certain friendly editor" had written him to be on the lookout for me, that I was a traitor to the liberal cause. The gravity of this situation becomes apparent when one remembers that Negro writers are pretty much relegated to "Negro" topics and that these assignments come from "liberal" white editors. This is why there has been a dearth of Negro self-criticism. And it is significant that once Negro self-criticism began to appear in responsible publications Negro action groups found the courage to break out on their own and adopt new methods.

An example of both this new courage and the plight of white liberals is the raging controversy between the NAACP and the nation's labor unions over the question of discrimination within the unions themselves. Unions have been among the largest contributors to the NAACP and have all but convinced the general public that the fault for employment discrimination lies with the employers. This, of course, is not the whole truth. Many of the trade unions will not admit Negroes; many unions, such as the International Ladies Garment Workers Union, refuse to upgrade Negroes to supervisory posts. Early in the fall of 1962 the NAACP launched a bold attack upon discrimination in these unions. Union leaders cried "foul" and accused the NAACP of attacking its real friends. In reality the NAACP had done nothing more than lay bare the commonly known fact that many of the Negro's close allies are part of the conspiracy against him. It is much too early to predict the outcome of the wrangle between the NAACP and the labor unions. One thing, however, is clear: the NAACP has the facts on its side; labor's threats to withdraw its support from the NAACP have fallen flat in the face of general Negro willingness to support the NAACP in such a crisis. More, the President of the United States summoned labor leaders to Washington and stood watching as they signed pledges to end discrimination within their ranks. As the NAACP seeks to carry this fight to the bitter end—and it will—the conflict will flare again; old wounds will open. But the labor union affair is further evidence that the days of hollow white liberalism are about over.

It is impossible to write of the white liberal without making some detailed comment upon the relationship between Jews and Negroes, particularly outside the South.

James Baldwin concludes one of his early essays, "The Harlem Ghetto," with a brilliant, if rasping, analysis of the Negro-Jew relationship. Says Baldwin: "Just as a society must have a scapegoat, so hatred must have a symbol. Georgia has the Negro and Harlem has the Jew."

Baldwin's analysis is valid far beyond the boundaries of Harlem; indeed, I suspect Jew hatred reaches its peak, as far as Negroes are concerned, in the garment district and along Tin Pan Alley. Of late it has spread to suburbia, and I suspect the rise of anti-Semitism among Negroes—and it is on the rise—is due to more than the presence of Jews as merchants and bill collectors in the bedeviled Negro ghettos.

The Negro's close relationship to the Jew, as Baldwin says, is ambivalent. Some individual Jews are our closest allies,[1] and I fully agree with Baldwin when he says that Negroes expect Jews to "know better" because they, too, have suffered. I am with him, too, when he describes Negro resentment over certain practices carried on by individual Jews in Harlem.

Jews are white people, but orthodox, or conformist, Jews are more than just white; they are a people with a tradition which, as both a theoretical and practical matter, offends Negroes. The point I am belaboring was certified by a study of Negro integration into suburbia conducted by the University of Chicago in 1959. The study concluded that Negroes were getting into suburbia but that they were finding it extremely difficult. Of all the ethnic suburban ghettos, the study concluded, the Jewish com-

---

[1] Arthur Spingarn, the national president of the NAACP, is Jewish; so is Jack Greenberg, head of the NAACP Legal Defense and Education Fund. There are several Jews on the boards of the NAACP, the Legal Defense Fund and the Urban League. Privately, such Jews as Harry Golden and Kivie Kaplan are among the Negroes' closest allies.

munities were the most adamant about keeping Negroes out.

Jewishness, not prejudice, is the explanation for this. Jews in these gilt-edge ghettos opposed integration not because they hated or discriminated against Negroes; rather they were seeking to realize that element in their tradition which calls for togetherness.

In 1961 I spoke before the Jewish Graduate Club of Columbia University. This issue arose, with the younger Jews siding with me that the Jewish power structure upheld segregation—not out of prejudice but out of traditional motivations. The older Jews, however, became furious with me; the creepiest feeling I have had in a long time ran down my back when one of the older Jews shook his finger at me and said, "We Jews have had to fight everybody. Now it looks like we must fight the black man. If so, we are ready!"

How do you satisfy a Jew's right to live among other Jews without abrogating my right to rent or buy the house next to his?

What modern Solomon can mediate the conflict that arises when I try to rent a store on Harlem's 125th Street from a Jewish landlord who wants another Jew to have the space?

What court is ready to hear the case when I accuse a Jewish garment district magnate of intentionally upgrading Jews and leaving me to push carts?

Are Jews to be accused of discrimination when—having been denied entree to certain other industries—they take over, say, the liquor-distributing industry in New York and in their desire to bring other Jews into the industry keep Negroes out?

Can a magazine editor who happens to be Jewish be criticized for hiring Jewish associates and thereby refusing to hire Negroes, or any gentile, for that matter? More, can that editor be properly called a "liberal" if he hires only his own people?

These are troubling questions which our nation has yet to resolve. They bedevil the Negro for two reasons:

First, in many areas of the non-South we find ourselves discriminated against in employment, not because we are Negroes but because we are gentiles. The same thing occurs when we go to seek housing and recreational outlets. (This latter is particularly true, for example, on Long Island, where one finds row after row of "clubs" which are Jewish.)

Secondly, the motivation that drives the Negro grows out of a set of values which emphasize the individual's worth, not his ethnic background. When we Negroes think racially it is because we have been herded together whether we, as individuals, belong together or not; the ambition of the Negro individual, then, is to get the hell out of the Negro ghetto, be it physical or mental, as soon as he can. The conformist Jew, on the other hand, is motivated in precisely the opposite direction.

During an NBC-TV broadcast Professor Solomon Liptzin of the City College of New York had this to say about being a Jew: "We are a people and were a people whose heart is in Israel, whose lungs are in America, and whose limbs extend all over the continents of the earth."

This, to the Negro mind, contradicts everything he understands democracy to be for, and it is depressing for anyone who views the American experience as a journey away from group consciousness and toward individualism. And when this is placed contiguous to the fact that America, as of now, has "in" groups and "out" groups, the result is chilling indeed. For groupness, particularly when augmented by power, is the mortal enemy of democracy.

The nonconformist Jew stands with me on this. I am thinking particularly of Jack Greenberg. "After all," Greenberg told me, "civil rights is not a *Negro* cause; it is a human cause, a serious problem in world society. True, our organization is designed primarily to aid Negroes in their push for equality, but the cause is *human,* not *Negro.*"

There is power as well as truth in what Jack said; and

this is why it is mandatory that Americans of all ethnic backgrounds submerge their group loyalties in favor of the broad human values that undergird the democratic concept. This, to be sure, will take time; no one expects it to occur overnight. What we Negroes do expect, however—and now—is an announcement of this basic goal for American democracy. And it is precisely here that the white liberal is irreplaceable; he better than any one else can help the white masses understand our plea; he is of them and, as such, knows their fears; the white liberal is with us, and, as such, knows our pain. The American Negro is committed to action; if the white liberal will use his powers and influence to ready his people for honest, orderly response, the child of change will be born with less pain, less hysteria and less loss of blood.

So many white liberals waste their influence; they join too many organizations and wind up being of little service to any of them; they give a little money to dozens of civil rights causes and thereby fail to give a meaningful amount to the few civil rights groups that are doing a job. Then there are the white liberals who develop guilt feelings about the race problem and thereby immobilize themselves; once this happens they are of little value to themselves or to us.

What the white liberal should avoid, at least so it seems to me, is becoming a "knee-jerk liberal," a man with the correct responses but with no real feelings. This is the kind of fellow who would cry out against Little Rock but would not have a Negro as a next-door neighbor; he contributes indiscriminately to civil rights organizations and feels his race relations duty has thus been accomplished; he reads and quotes with satisfaction news of racial progress in the South but would not think of hiring a Negro as an executive in his own firm; the knee-jerk liberal is full of sympathy for the Negro in general, but he knows nothing of our history and is not acquainted with a single Negro well enough to have him as a guest in his home.

I do not expect that all white people relinquish their main interests and become totally involved in the race question. What is expected, however, is that all Americans, Negro and white, become aware of and act positively toward this menace to our society. And as the issue unfolds it is increasingly necessary that a distinction be made between those who truly support the Negro and his cause and those "liberals" who fail us when the chips are down.

Mrs. Eleanor Roosevelt has been everybody's white liberal for almost a quarter of a century; she knows the race problem, its complexities and dangers; she knows Negroes, their strengths and weaknesses; she is of her fellow white men, yet she never fails to call bigotry by its true name. In a recent newspaper column, Mrs. Roosevelt, speaking as a white person, isolated the core of the Negro revolt. Her presentation is a clear example of how the white liberal can prepare the white masses for honest and orderly response to the Negro's action plea:

> The trend in all parts of the world . . . is to do away with second-class people and second-class citizenship, and we are affected in our country by this same world trend. We would be shocked if anyone told us that the position of the Negro in this country seemed in other parts of the world to have some attributes of colonialism. Yet, this is actually the way great areas of the world look upon certain situations in both our North and South.
>
> We are extremely fortunate that our Negro leaders have worked under the spell of the Gandhian philosophy. Martin Luther King presses forward, but he presses forward without the use of violence and with the constant hope that there will be love and understanding growing out of each new gain. Passive resistance is used to oppose what our colored citizens consider injustice and inequality, which they will no longer tolerate. . . .
>
> At one time some 700 people were said to be in jail in southern Georgia. Nowhere as far as we know, except in South Africa, has anything comparable occurred. It is easy to say that this situation must be approached with patience, but that necessitates forgetting how much patience

our colored citizens have had in the past. They feel the time has come for action and perhaps we had better recognize this, for real results in equality of opportunity and achievement are long overdue.

Needless to say, no Ofay could have written that.

15.

PAIN AND PROGRESS

PAIN AND PROGRESS are inseparable.

The severest pain brought on by the Negro revolt stems from the cleavages that have developed within the Negro group; not the disaffection toward the established Negro leadership class to which I have given so much attention in these pages, but the Negro institutions that served their time well but have now fallen into disfavor because they are inextricably tied to the *status quo*.

The Negro college, the Negro press, the Negro politician and the Negro church all have this flaw in common: they were born into a segregated world and set out to serve us with the view that our separate world would someday be equal. As a result, each of these, in a different way, has a stake in the *status quo*. And, needless to say, *status quo* is now anathema to most Negroes.

Ten years ago, in 1952, a Negro college president who was able to talk some white philanthropist into giving him, say, a hundred thousand dollars for a new library was a hero and a highly respected race leader. Now the Negro college president must spend much of his time explaining himself, saying why he still heads a "Negro" college, trying to tell a skeptical world about the future of the "Negro" college, attempting to soothe the restless Negro students, who are embarrassingly aware that they are receiving an inferior education while being surrounded by all the trappings of segregation.

"Intellectual Uncle Tom!" That's the phrase one hears throughout the South nowadays. It is uttered by college students and their supporters, and it is used in the open, at public meetings and rallies. This is the students' way of talking about the "failure" of Southern Negro intellectuals—schoolteachers, for the most part—to support the Negro revolt in clear, open terms.

This is excruciatingly painful. Felton Clark, James Colston, H. Councill Trenholm, Rufus B. Atwood, Benjamin E. Mays, Rufus Clement, Albert W. Dent, W. S. Davis, George W. Gore, Stephen Wright—these were the heroes of my late youth and early manhood. All of them are college presidents; we sat at their feet and learned from them; many of us returned home and taught on their faculties. These men stood between us and the raw nakedness of our educational plight; they watched over us while we slept in the dormitories at night; during the day they went before hard-core segregationist school boards and pleaded for money to build us a chemistry lab, or a library, or a dormitory, or a football stadium, or to hire a new language teacher. It was often necessary for these men to humble themselves in order to get funds to keep our campuses going. I know of one college president who was scheduled to meet with a group of white philanthropists at a segregated hotel. The hotel refused to let him enter the front door; without blinking an eyelash, the president, a Ph.D. from an Eastern university, went around to the back door and went up on the freight elevator. He returned by the same route, but his college was fifty thousand dollars richer. I have been told of another college executive who met with a group of potential donors at a white church. He made his presentation and asked if there were questions he could answer.

To the educator's amazement, one elderly white woman stood and said: "Professor, before we talk about the money you want, would you please sing a few verses of 'Swing Low, Sweet Chariot'?"

The president cleared his throat and sang; he also got a new library.

It is often said that Negro colleges are inferior. This, of course, is true. It is also true that they would have been worse had it not been for these well-educated, determined men who braved insults and contempt to raise the money to keep these schools going.

Many of these men are still heads of Negro colleges, but now they find themselves caught in a cross fire. Today their students are involved in sit-ins and freedom rides, and the white donors are both amazed and angered to discover that schools supported by their money spawn "agitators" and "troublemakers." The philanthropists and state boards of education turn on the college administrators and demand that they call a halt to the demonstrations; the students, on the other hand, expect their college executives to stand with them whatever the consequences. Some of the presidents, like Stephen Wright of Fisk University and James Colston of Knoxville College, turned in statesmanlike performances. They not only supported the students but worked with the white power structure in their towns to make the desegregation of local facilities peaceful and orderly. Drs. Colston and Wright head private schools, however, and faced less opposition and pressure from segregationists than presidents of state-supported colleges.

Dr. Rufus B. Atwood, president of Kentucky State College, expelled twelve students and ousted two teachers in the dust-up created by the sit-in demonstrations; Dr. H. Councill Trenholm, president of Alabama State College, bowed to Governor John Patterson and other state officials and made a public statement saying he would exert every effort to prevent further demonstrations by his students. Other state college presidents took refuge in a sort of academic isolation. Asked to state his position on the sit-ins, Dr. George W. Gore, president of Florida A. & M. College, said: "I'm interested in education and scholarship, not politics. You can't be all things to all men."

Dr. W. S. Davis, president of Tennessee A. & I. College,

said: "This whole age is a little dramatic and bold and fast-moving and we have to adjust to it."

The adjustment will not be easy and the chances are that the worst is yet to come. Despite the move toward integration, the American Negro, particularly in the South, is still segregated; most of them, for another five years at least, will attend segregated schools. This fact of life will give the Negro college presidents a reason for existence. But as far as their students are concerned many of the presidents will not be respected. Dr. Gore looked out of his office window onto his moss-laden Florida campus. "College presidents are probably in ill repute at the moment," he said slowly. "We probably have never been in so low estate as now."

The man who is perhaps in lowest estate because of his stand—or lack of a stand—on the segregation issue is Dr. Felton Grandison Clark, president of Louisiana's Southern University. Dr. Clark's father founded Southern; he has developed it into the world's largest Negro university (it is not the best, by far, however). The all-Negro, state-supported school hires over six hundred people and has an annual budget of seven million dollars. Felton Clark earns fifteen thousand dollars a year and reaps such fringe benefits as a house and off-campus living expenses.

Then, in 1960, came the time of troubling. Students from Southern staged sit-ins. The all-white school board gave Dr. Clark his orders: Either the students ended the demonstrations or he must expel them. Dr. Clark went before his students and walked in the shoes of Abraham Lincoln.

"Like Lincoln," he said, "who sought to preserve the Union, my dominant concern is to save Southern University." Then he went on to tell them what the all-white school board had said. The students listened and then voted to defy the board. They staged the demonstrations and Dr. Clark promptly expelled the eighteen leaders from the university.

That was the beginning. Since then Southern's troubles have mounted, the demonstrations and controversy continued and, late in 1961, the school was forced to close its doors for several weeks. The school has since reopened; an attempted boycott of classes has apparently fizzled and Southern has returned to a state of troubled normalcy. The peace cannot last too long, however; for peace with segregation is peace without honor. The question, then, is not whether the revolt will break out again, but when and what students and faculty people will set it off.

Meanwhile Felton Clark sits atop his troubled university; and in him one sees the pain that comes with progress. Felton Clark is a brilliant man, a good man, an honest man, a dedicated man. If he could but say what is in his heart he would tell us that he hates and despises segregation as much as, if not more than, the rest of us. Yet if he were to say this he would not only lose his job but the university would probably be closed.

There are those who say that Felton Clark and other embattled Negro college presidents should do just that: come out in favor of demonstrations and suffer the consequences. They would all be fired but—and this is one of the twists of the new age—they would be acclaimed as heroes by liberals and given posts on the campuses of Eastern universities. But what about the five thousand Negro students at Southern? Where would they go if the university was closed? What about the pride Southern alumni take in their excellent football teams and choirs? Who will subsidize the families of these Negro students as they send their children to private schools at higher costs? What about Felton Grandison Clark, the human being caught in an era of change?

Fifty-nine-year-old Felton Clark is a sophisticated and persuasive man. During a recent interview he walked to the edge of his campus and then turned to look back and survey all he mastered. His eyes fixed on the reporter, Felton Clark made a wide sweep with his arms and waved toward row after row of ultramodern, expensive buildings.

"*Si monumentum requiris, circumspice.* Look around and see my monument," Clark said. He was talking to a reporter but it was clear that his words were for all his critics to hear. Then he continued, in a more serious mood: "Anybody would be deeply concerned about misrepresentations of himself, particularly when he has knowingly dedicated his life to uplifting and upgrading others. However, he has to realize that this is the price to be paid for leadership, especially when many of the led are young, frequently unreasonable and immature in their total outlook, and where some of the others are not devoid of jealousy, and envy, and in some instances outright malice."

Pressed to state his position concerning the expelled students, Dr. Clark was both quick and blunt: "Every time the board meets I ask that these students be screened and readmitted. The board has refused, which is its right. I may not agree, but it is still the board's right."

Asked how he, as an individual, could carry out an order he does not agree with, Dr. Clark argues that every day, everywhere, underlings carry out orders with which they, as individuals, disagree. He would draw the line on a moral issue, however: "I am not going to do anything immoral or to the detriment of my people or the American people."

Dr. Clark and Negro college presidents like him are faced with a choice between two goods: integration and education for the Negro. Their dilemma is that they must choose one over the other. If they support integration, they are in trouble with state officials; if they don't, they are in trouble with the students. But Dr. Clark is adamant:

"Schools like ours are needed for Negro students who have insufficient preparation to attend schools like L.S.U. and the University of Florida [integrated schools]. . . . Research indicates that a story stays in the headlines for about nine days; when it blows away you still have a lot of ignorant Negroes who don't have a lot of money and need a college education and who can come into full status only through education."

Dr. Clark's assumption that the integration story will fade in nine days has already been proved false. Much of what Dr. Clark says, however, merits consideration. He and other college presidents like him are conducting a holding operation and they have a sense of mission about it. They also have a sense of personal pride about who they are and what they have done; and it is a good thing that they do, for how else could they stand between the wrath of the young Negro and the obduracy of the white powers? I do not envy these men. Only with reluctance do I sing their praise. Yet praiseworthy they are. They fashioned us into the rebels we are. Perhaps the time has come for the Negro revolutionaries to pause and be gracious toward the Negro educators, men who served their time and served it well.

The Negro politician is also racked by the pains of progress. In the early days of this century, the Negro politician, particularly if elected to office, held a position of great stature and respect. Now, alas, he is just another politician, a ghetto politician at that. Although all the Negro politicians make speeches calling for justice and equality, they are not in the front ranks of the Negro revolt for they owe their existence to segregation. Men like Congressman Adam Clayton Powell will be undone by the Negro's growing demand that he be freed from the ghetto. Powell, to be sure, is for integration, but it is certain that he does not want to see his district integrated right out from under him, and his constituents dispersed.[1] Indeed, one of the arguments one hears as new, expensive apartments go up in Harlem is that there is a sinister plot afoot to reclaim Harlem "for the white man," that white people are building these expensive apartment buildings in the full knowledge that low-salaried Negroes cannot afford the rent and, thus, will be forced to move elsewhere.

This, of course, is the thorny issue raised by the revolt: Will the Negro become another "tribe," like the Jews and the Poles, in America, or is it his ambition to be absorbed

[1]At the time of the 1960 Congressional elections 88.5 percent of Powell's 301,574 constituents were Negro. Similarly, Congressman William L. Dawson's Illinois district is 92.1 percent Negro, and Robert Nix of Pennsylvania's district is 73.8 percent Negro. The remaining Negro member of the House is an exception: Charles Diggs's Michigan district is half Negro, half white.

and dispersed? For the Negro politician this boils down to whether he can maintain his power and get "Negro" patronage and "Negro" power at city hall. This is more than just a theoretical matter; in a few years Manhattan Island, as well as several other "central cities" in America, will be predominantly Negro. There is reason to believe that New York City may have a Negro mayor by 1975. Negro politicians feel strongly on this point.

"The Irish had their day in City Hall," one of them told me, "the Jews have theirs, the Catholics have theirs. Now it is time for the Negro to have his day."

This argument assumes that American politics will continue to mirror the emergence of the nation's various ethnic groups.

"Why the hell did they have to wait until we Negroes came into political power to get integrated?" another irate Negro politician said to me. "For generations they have been giving out a certain number of 'Jewish' jobs, a certain number of 'Catholic' jobs. Now, when we have enough power to demand a lot of 'Negro' jobs, everybody, including some Negroes, gets full of integration and says, 'Don't ask for jobs on the basis of race; appoint people on the basis of talent.' I say, appoint people of talent, but find talented Negroes for the appointments!"

My view of the Negro politician is shaped largely by Illinois Congressman William L. Dawson. For a short time I knew him well. I remember sitting in his office one day in 1957 and peppering him with all of the criticisms that were leveled against him: He was a "boss." He was a "ghetto politician." He didn't cry out loudly enough against the Eastlands in his own party. He was no better than the other politicians in Cook County, Illinois. I will never forget his sly smile as he limped toward the window, favoring his wooden leg.

"Hell," he snorted, pointing down to the black masses lined up to get into his office, "go ask them what they think of me."

I did. They thought he was Jesus come back for the second time. He saw to it that they cut through the red tape and got on relief; he saw to it that a few of their talented sons and daughters got jobs as secretaries and accountants; most of all, they idolized him because he was the man who walked into the office of the Mayor of Chicago and told him that his time was over. The very thought of a Negro having sufficient power to tell a mayor where to head in sent Chicago Negroes into ecstasy. One day Dawson will die; he will never be defeated.

I saw something of the same thing happen in Harlem in the early forties. Adam Powell was running for a second term. His main campaign gimmick was that he had taken to the floor of Congress and called the late Senator Bilbo of Mississippi a "cesspool." Late in the campaign, Powell's opponent, Grant Reynolds, got the point and he too called Bilbo a cesspool. By then, of course, it was too late; any man who called Bilbo a cesspool first was, indeed, a fit Congressman and Powell was re-elected by a staggering majority.

The Negro politician, like the Negro college president, has served his time. For the most part, he has served it well. Many white writers have made the point that none of the Negro politicians have proved to be distinguished public servants, that they have been, and are, hack politicians. I don't defend the Negro politician for being a hack, for, in American parlance, that is precisely what he set out to be. He made his way through the party machinery only because his fellow Negroes had sufficient political power to give him thrust. His role was exactly that of the other ghetto politicians who preceded him.

In time—and it has already begun to happen—Negro politicians will assume a new stance; they will be public servants, not Negroes. Dr. Robert Weaver, who may become the first Negro Cabinet member, is a hint of things to come. He is a well-educated man who has mastered his own field, housing; he had the wisdom to turn down several offers to run as a "Negro" candidate for office. And there are more like him waiting in the wings.

As far as the Negro individual in politics is concerned, the day has not quite dawned that a Negro candidate can get elected from a district that is not predominantly Negro. This day will come soon; I predict it will break over a suburban community of liberals, more than likely predominantly Jewish with a sprinkling of Negroes. When this day arrives, a giant step will have been taken toward the ultimate goal of the Negro revolt: that golden day when a Negro will stand or fall on his own merits, neither hindered nor helped by the fact that he is a Negro.

The American Negro Labor Council, founded and headed by the dynamic A. Philip Randolph, is another of the Negro organizations engaged in the process of putting itself out of business.

The Council is composed of some 10,000 Negro union members, some of whom are members of unions affiliated with the AFL-CIO, others of whom are members of independent internationals. The tie that binds these Negro unionists is that they are all Negro and that they are convinced that only by coming together in a separate Negro labor union organization can they fight discrimination in various locals as well as in the organizational structure of the AFL-CIO.

The Negro labor movement orbits around the being and oratory of fiery A. Philip Randolph, an old-time Socialist who shook Negro leadership to its foundations during the thirties and forties and who is now a vice president of the AFL-CIO. With headquarters located in New York's Harlem, the American Negro Labor Council has had more of an impact upon unionism than it has upon the Negro people in general; its best work has been achieved when it has dramatized the fact of discrimination in labor unions on the floor of the annual conventions of the AFL-CIO.

"Who appointed you to speak for the American Negro?" AFL-CIO president George Meany once thundered at Randolph. Meany soon got his answer as most of the Negro union members closed ranks around Randolph and forced Meany to retract the jibe as well as to reconsider a censure move that would have rebuked Randolph for double unionism and stirring up racial unrest.

"Most of the Negro labor leaders are captives of the trade-union bureaucracy," Randolph said. "They are dependent on the unions for their jobs, as are white staffers. Negro salaried staff members are even more timid and less aggressive. . . . I am independent of AFL-CIO leadership. I feel Negroes in other unions could be more articulate and I continuously carry on a program to educate both Negroes and whites at the local union level on the value of integrated trade unionism."

What Randolph seeks is an adamant stand by the AFL-CIO on the question of discrimination in unions. "I feel the AFL-CIO should give these biased locals ample notice and then expel them if they refuse to lower the color bar," Randolph told me.

What troubles union leaders such as George Meany is that Randolph finds it necessary to set up an organization outside the AFL-CIO to press for his goals. I asked L. Joseph Overton, national vice president of the ANLC, why it was necessary.

"We felt that since there is no such structure established by the labor movement to abolish discrimination, that it was necessary for us to build the type of machinery that could focus upon these ills in the house of labor," he said.

Yet when the issue of discrimination is raised the debate takes place within the AFL-CIO, and the reason for a separate organization remains unanswered.

Overton moved closer to the truth about the American Negro Labor Council when he said: "I say the Negro community is a different community from the white community. We have different needs and wants. That's why we need representation in the house of labor."

I asked him if this meant Negro representation. "Yes," Overton said. "Of all the members of the white leadership in the unions, you cannot find ten who have taken the time to visit any part of his black membership." He added: "I am elected by the membership of local 338. There are very few Negroes in my local. But I admit I have my post because of my work in the Negro community. The Negro community is responsible for me being where I am. When issues come up, we, as Negroes, are heard."

✓Thus the Negro labor organization is in the paradoxical position of providing Negroes with a platform from which they can work for integration and the elimination of all racial barriers and, at the same time, demand representation and a place in the sun on the basis of race.

I hasten to add that the motivations of A. Philip Randolph are not this narrow. Had they been he would have accomplished his aim when he was named one of the vice presidents of the AFL-CIO. Randolph is the grand old warrior, the brown brahmin of the American labor movement. The Negro revolt aside, things wouldn't be the same without Randolph around, his voice thundering out the sins of segregation. Some of the men around Randolph are less talented and therefore more *Negro* than he. Regardless of how much integration we realize in the next few years, Randolph will have a platform. But once he passes on, and when unionism lowers the color bars in the locals as well as in the organizational structure of the House of Labor, there will be little need for another A. Philip Randolph. This hurts, for there are scores of young Negro labor men standing in the wings waiting to take his place. But change is upon them, and if they are wise they will recast their ambitions and set out to become George Meanys and Walter Reuthers instead.

The Negro press—and this includes all forms of "Negro" communication—also pains as the Negro revolt continues. The problem of the Negro press arises from the fact that, like all other news media, it depends upon advertising for its existence. As I have already discussed, Negroes own very little business even in their own communities. As a result the Negro press must depend upon white businessmen for their advertising revenue. In the North, for example, the Negro press can afford to be very militant about integration and Southern police brutality, but it cannot expose sharp business practices and loan-shark dealings that keep the masses of Negroes in perpetual debt. I know of one Negro editor who has a fat folder full of evidence—pictures, affidavits, etc.—showing just how Negroes are swindled by some of his best advertisers. These articles will never be run. The businessmen know about the folder, however, and their ads will forever remain in the paper.

√On the whole, the Negro press has supported the Negro revolt. The lone exception is the highly respected, rock-ribbed Republican Atlanta *Daily World,* one of the two Negro daily newspapers in the nation. In its edition of Sunday, May 4, 1960, the *World* carried a double-column editorial asking, "Is This Type Of Action Necessary In This Case?" The thrust of the editorial was a criticism of the students who had organized an economic boycott of white merchants who refused to employ Negro persons in nonmenial jobs despite the fact that these businesses were located in the Negro community. The editorial was the climax to a long, quiet feud between the crusading students and the Atlanta *Daily World.* The students, with assistance from college faculty members in Atlanta, organized a weekly newspaper, the *Inquirer,* to offset the attitude of the *World.* The *Inquirer* has since won national notice for its crusading journalism and is singlehandedly responsible for the policy change that now allows Negro physicians to practice in formerly all-white hospitals. It is interesting to note that two days after the editorial critical of the boycott the *World* ran an editorial praising the student sit-ins at Savannah, Georgia, and Atlanta. The editorial said the sit-ins were "a wise course" of action and went on to thank the Savannah prosecutor for not "charging those students with every crime in the book as the Fulton County [Atlanta] prosecutor had done."

The case of the Atlanta *World* provided a moral: By failing to support the Negro revolt the Negro press may keep some white advertisers but it will lose its readers.

√The Negro press has received a big assist from the white press, which has shifted its race policy considerably during the past decade. After all, an advertiser can hardly afford to get angry with a Negro publication for approving the sit-ins and freedom rides when white publications, in essence, do the same thing. But when it comes to readership and advertising revenue, the white press is as interested in the Negro market as the Negro press is. To capture this market, as well as from conviction, the white press is becoming increasingly liberal. In New York, for example, the liberal New York *Post* can, and will, print any story concerning sins against the Negro faster and—because of superior manpower and wire services—better than the *Amsterdam News* can. This forces the Negro press to take an extreme view in order to maintain any semblance of uniqueness. And as a direct result of this hot competition for readership and support, the Negro press often moves to the edge of black nationalism.

It is impossible to discuss the Negro press without some reference to the phenomenal success of two Johnson Publication magazines, *Jet* and *Ebony*. Both magazines started out as status publications, dealing largely with the social and professional exploits of successful Negroes. As Dr. E. Franklin Frazier said of them, *Jet* and *Ebony* made a point of dealing with Negroes who engaged in conspicuous consumption.

Jet, a pocket-sized weekly, at first did not carry editorials and seldom dealt with "controversial" material. But as the Negro revolt got under way and Dr. Martin Luther King came to the fore, *Jet* joined the protest bandwagon and began running editorials that scathingly criticized racial abuse and discrimination. More, *Jet* plunged into the intramural dispute over Negro leadership. The July 6, 1961, issue devoted a cover story to "Who Speaks for the Negro?" and carried the picture of Roy Wilkins of the NAACP, James Farmer of CORE, Martin Luther King of the SCLC, and—surprise—Elijah Muhammad, leader of the Black Muslims. This was indeed a bold move for a publication most of whose readers refuse to admit that Elijah Muhammad, despite his large following, is a Negro leader to be dealt with and mentioned in the same breath with such as Roy Wilkins and Martin Luther King.

Once one opens the pages of *Ebony,* a monthly, he is

in for a sweet shock: There, in multicolored, full-page ads, one sees Negro models plugging the same products that are plugged by white models in *Life, Look* and the other "slicks." Johnson and his staff have been able to sell national advertisers on the basis of circulation and by submitting evidence that a twenty-billion-dollar-a-year Negro market exists. True, Negroes earn twenty billion dollars a year, but does this mean that they are a special market, potential buyers who are not reached through the "white" publications? This is a bitterly debated question in the advertising world today. My own view is that the Negro market does not exist as such; that, rather, we respond to a product we already know about when we discover that the makers of that product have invested time and money to make certain that they attract our attention.

The Negro press as a whole is walking a tightrope. To date they have been successful in reflecting the interests of their readers, but this success has been due largely to the assumption that there is a separate "Negro" audience with special interests that can be appealed to and exploited. This is true now, but there will come a time when the Negro revolt will make it less true. And it is against this day that the Negro individual who is a publisher must begin now to make his plans.

The Negro church is in something of the same fix. By nature and organization it is "Negro." Born, as it was, out of the refusal of white people to let Negroes worship in dignity in the "white" churches of the slavery era, the Negro church was not constructed against the day when Negroes would seek to remove all barriers. True, Sunday morning is the most segregated hour in American life; but the Negro churches are almost as responsible for this as the white churches are. And this very point is something both the Negro revolutionaries and their white opponents would do well to study. Even in the North, where Negroes are free to attend any church they wish, the Negro church continues to thrive. Some Negroes have joined white—

integrated, actually—congregations, but the Negro masses seem quite happy as they are. If current indications are any evidence, church integration is not something Negroes care about very much. Job integration, school integration, justice in the courts, open housing—these are the things that matter. These accomplished, Negroes tend to drift together for church and other social events.

Too, the Negro church has become a hotbed of Negro revolutionaries; our ministers give us a gospel of deliverance that we couldn't get in a "white" church. True, this gospel of deliverance chips away at the Negro church. This is but another of the pains of progress. Like the NAACP and CORE, the Negro church will enjoy its greatest and final success the day it destroys itself. This does not mean that the "Negro" church will die and the "white" church will survive; rather it foresees that one day America will become what it swears it already is, a truly democratic society. When that occurs we will be a nation with churches, schools, newspapers and politicians without an ethnic prefix. This, of course, is a long way off; but the day is not nearly so removed as it was when the inexplicable Rosa Parks sat down on a bus seat in Montgomery, Alabama.

The key factor in the future of all these people and organizations—the Negro politician, the Negro press, the Negro schoolteacher, the Negro church—is whether they will be able to make the shift from ethnic to general institutions. Under the able guidance of Dr. William J. Trent, Jr., executive director of the United Negro College Fund, many of the better private Negro colleges have already begun to work toward just such a shift. All of the Fund's member colleges have dropped the designation "Negro" from their charters and many of them have white students. There is no doubt that schools such as Spelman and Morehouse will attract white students once the air settles in Atlanta. Dr. Stephen Wright, the president of Fisk University in Nashville, Tennessee, put the argument this way:

"The nation needs more colleges and universities. Why talk of the Negro colleges closing down? Let's talk of the Negro colleges becoming good schools where all who want and are willing to work for an education can get it."

The Negro press and the Negro church will have a more difficult row to hoe. Unlike the Negro university, which can fade into a general market where demand exceeds supply, the Negro press—if it attempts to become a general news medium—moves into a market where new entries die like flies. The immediate future of the Negro press seems to be that of a community newspaper, and its future to be tied to that of the Negro church and Negro social clubs. After all, other ethnic groups in America have their newspapers, churches and clubs; the Negro will continue to do the same thing. The point to be underscored, however, is that these ethnic newspapers, churches and clubs are now supported by a shrinking number, generally of the older generation, which clings to the past. This, in time, will happen to the Negro church and the Negro press. For, as housing and job barriers fall, Negroes will drift from the ghetto into general American life, where they will rise to positions of prominence and leadership in the general American community, and as Americans rather than as Negroes.

Social history moves forward; far off though it may be, the hour of integration *is* approaching. With this progress there is, and will continue to be, pain. The only question to be resolved is whether these specifically Negro institutions and services will fall by the wayside as victims of progress, or whether they have the vitality to adapt to an ever-changing set of conditions.

PART III

The Way Ahead

16.

THE URBAN LEAGUE

IF THE AMERICAN NEGRO is going to realize his full role in the American experiment he must become a much more responsible fellow than he now is. For a long time we could justly blame the white man for our weaknesses and shortcomings; this day is about over. True, the residue of the dark days of the KKK are still with us, and it is reasonable to predict that no Negro scientific genius will come out of Mississippi in the next ten years or so; but, on the whole, this nation has moved forward on the race issue and we, as Negroes, must divide our time between fighting for our rights and helping the masses of our people to become first-class citizens of the Republic.

The Negro crime rate is too high; Negro relief chiselers are an abomination and an embarrassment; the unthought-out migration of Negroes into major cities of the North, Midwest and Far West is creating problems that need not exist in a civilized society.

The quiet joke among Negroes for the past five years, for example, has turned on the fact that the Urban League has opened up more job opportunities for Negroes in "white" industry than it can find Negroes to fill. And each year the League is out raising money—mostly from white people—to open more jobs which it does not have Negroes to fill.

There is a disturbing view held by many Negroes in high places that three hundred years of, first, slavery and, then, discrimination have destroyed the inner fiber of the American Negro masses; that, perhaps, they are spiritually incapable of becoming first-class citizens.

I once heard Dr. Benjamin E. Mays, president of Morehouse College in Atlanta, speak about a lion who had been caged. The lion paced back and forth in the cage for years; then one day somebody opened the door of the cage and the lion simply kept pacing back and forth.

During a recent trip South I conducted an informal seminar with several Negro college students, almost all of whom had been involved in sit-ins and freedom rides. Their apathy and preachments of futility were shocking. They simply don't know things have changed somewhat; they have no personal drive, no dreams beyond getting a degree from an inferior school and returning home to teach that which they do not know.

The same kind of apathy is to be found among Negro voters—nonvoters, actually. One reason why Negro leadership organizations think several times before launching highly publicized voter registration drives is that they know Negroes simply will not go to the polls and register. A failure, of course, would reflect on the leadership of the organization so they shy away from well-publicized voter campaigns. Harlem is a case in point. Almost half a million Negroes live in the district represented by Congressman Adam Clayton Powell. An estimated two hundred thousand of them are of voting age. Yet Powell returns to Congress every two years with about forty thousand votes. His opponents muster about ten thousand.

The usual Negro response to these matters is to say that the race, as a whole, should not be blamed for the misdeeds of some Negroes. This is a valid response. After all, why should, say, Duke Ellington be denied the right to buy a home because the Negro crime rate is high? Why should, say, James Gary, a close friend of mine and a Negro bellhop, be denied the right to advance in the hotel industry because an inordinate number of Negroes on relief cheat? Duke Ellington and Jim Gary have the *right* to buy homes and advance professionally. But, their *rights* aside, what of the Negro's *responsibilities*?

The Negro revolt begs the question of whether the Negro is ready to assume the new responsibilities and privileges his militant leaders are seeking. In a sense this is proper; after all, rights accrue to individuals, not races, and there can be no democratic justification of the denial of their rights and freedoms to some Negroes simply because all Negroes have not reached a given point in civic responsibility. No such strictures are placed against the individual white citizen and the Negro revolt demands that Negroes be given the same freedom from group responsibility. The question of Negro responsibility must be dealt with, however, and if someone could tie the question of Negro rights to that of Negro responsibility without offending individuals who are more than ready to assume the status of full citizenship, he would be executing a brilliant and meritorious maneuver. This is precisely what Whitney Young, the new executive secretary of the National Urban League, is attempting to do.

Forty-year-old Whitney Young staked his claim at the closing banquet of the 51st National Urban League Conference in September of 1961:

"We [the Urban League] will do an action research job —the sort of job that not merely identifies the extent of poor housing, unemployment and general social disorganization; but a research which concerns itself with community attitudes toward these social ills. Yesterday these attitudes generated resignation and despair. Today they are more likely to be expressed in resentment and hostility."

In a private interview, Young stated his philosophy to me in language much more understandable and to the point:

"Why in the hell should we sit back and let reactionary magazines and newspapers expose the sad truth about the Negro crime rate and other social breakdowns? Why let them expose it and then place their interpretation of what has happened to our people? I say we should tell the truth about our own community. We know about the crime rate—why lie about it? We know about family breakdown —why say it ain't so? We know about relief stealing—why say the white man is making the figures lie? Let's research and expose these things ourselves. That puts us in the driver's seat; we can say, 'Here is what has happened, here is why it happened, let's all pull together to do something about it.' "

As Young sees it, the family is "the primary rocket that thrusts the human being into social orbit." Thus, he concludes, "The Negro family as a unit must be strengthened. All too often, current society has battered and broken the Negro family and then placed blame on that family for what happened to it."

At first blush it appears that Whitney Young has taken a long, perhaps more honest, route only to arrive at the same conclusion others have reached: that discrimination is to blame for the Negro social lag. In a sense he has, but it is his program of correction that makes him different.

Young holds that the Negro family breaks down for two reasons: (1) the lack of a consistent breadwinner and (2) ignorance of, or apathy toward, community institutions designed to help the family in moments of crisis. Taking these in reverse order, Young has pledged the staff of the nation's sixty-two Urban Leagues to an active program of bringing Negro families and social-help agencies together. This is a far cry from trained social workers sitting in the League's office and waiting for some bewildered mother on Chicago's South Side to wander in and ask for help. It means the League will work with, say, the City Welfare Department; the League will find out who is in difficulty and why; the League will seek out that family and set up a rehabilitation program. As a further extension of this, the League is pledged to work with churches and other community gathering centers to inform the Negro masses that help is available and where they should go to get it.

As to finding jobs for Negroes, the League has long been

active on this front, but what Young has in mind is something quite new and exciting. He puts it this way:

"For nearly four hundred years the Negro has been consciously and deliberately excluded [from the American mainstream]. During this time he has been denied even the barest minimum in health, education, housing and cultural outlets. For him to catch up will require a few years of deliberate inclusion and special programming within the integrated framework to offset the scars which were inevitable under the kind of environment which America subjected him to. There is no way for the back wheels of a car to catch up with the front wheels even though they are going at the same rate of speed unless something special happens."

In effect, what Whitney Young proposes is this: that the Negro masses be certified as an underdeveloped people, and that they be given special, accelerated treatment in order for them to assume full responsibilities in American society. This is going to make a lot of Negroes mad for they will assume Young is saying they are inferior. The background of the Negro masses is inferior, for whatever reason, and Young is saying that to overcome this the current Negro generation must be moved forward en masse and at a swifter pace than the current white generation.

Whether Negroes like it or not, Harlem is the New World's Congo; it is a land occupied by black people but run by white people. If the white people left tomorrow morning the Negroes could not run their own town. It is not that the Negroes don't have the talent and ability, but that they have not been allowed to gain the technical and business experience necessary to keep a modern community going. Needless to say, then, if Negroes cannot run Harlem, few of them indeed are qualified to help run Wall Street. Young's thesis is that white business and industries must now take Negroes under their wings and train them, just as, for example, the British did Africans in Nigeria. But Young's is not the African argument; integration, not independence, is the goal. Thus Young is saying that, once trained, Negroes can move into American business and industrial life.

Young took his Master's degree in social work at the University of Minnesota in 1947. But while there, he took time out to join CORE and participated in student sit-ins that resulted in the integration of eating facilities near the university. It was fortunate indeed, then, that Whitney Young was dean of the Atlanta University School of Social Work from 1954 to 1961. For when the students in the university system began their Atlanta sit-ins they found in Whitney Young a powerful source of wisdom and guidance. So, for that matter, did Martin Luther King; during his most trying months, during the transfer from Montgomery to Atlanta, Whitney Young and Dr. Samuel Williams, a Morehouse College philosophy professor, were Dr. King's close friends and advisers. It is no detraction from Dr. King to say that Young and Williams provided him with insights and techniques which his theological background did not afford.

Most of all, Whitney Young took time out to write. There is something about writing that makes even a stupid man think; Young is not stupid and the more he wrote, the more his right little finger eased toward the question mark. By the time he took up his duties as executive director of the National Urban League, Young's articles had appeared in several major professional journals. Every writer, like every preacher, has but one theme; and beyond the social science jargon one finds Whitney Young repeatedly asking, "What is effective social leadership?" Sometimes his theme is changed and he ponders, "What is effective Negro leadership?" but in the search he comes back to his real obsession and states that effective Negro leadership and effective social leadership are the same thing.

This is the philosophy and program of the man who now guides the destiny of the nation's best-financed Negro organization. The League, as it is called, raised $3,163,992 during 1961 and spent $3,104,738. Four hundred thousand dollars of the budget went toward the operation of the national office alone. The 1962 budget calls for a three-hundred-thousand-dollar increase in the allotment to the national office; this will up the 1962 over-all budget to three and a half million dollars.

Over two million dollars of the League's annual budget comes from the United Funds and Community Chest; the remainder is raised from foundations and private gifts. Some of the League's sixty branches sell memberships, but these are a small part of the budget of the organization.

Young has more than three hundred paid staff members under his command. During the League's annual convention of 1962, Young challenged them to adopt his program for the days ahead. Said Young: "A famous painter was once asked to name his greatest work. He paused but a moment and then replied, 'My greatest painting? The next one.'" The League's greatest year of progress will be the next one, Young went on to say, and then made it clear that this would be the year during which the League would launch its all-out efforts to correct the cultural lag in the Negro community.

Whitney Young has not disclosed just what specific attacks he will make on the Negro crime rate. Negro crime, however, is involved in what Young calls "social disorganization" and is thus tied to his theory concerning the breakdown of family life. It is extremely difficult to deal with the issue of Negro crime; Negroes are deeply ashamed of it and many white people use it as a reason for practicing subtle discriminations against Negro individuals who are far removed from crime. More than once I have had New York cab drivers tell me they don't want to haul Negroes, not because they are prejudiced but because scores of cab drivers have been robbed and beaten—some killed—in New York's Negro communities. The cabbies are right; if I were a cab driver I would think twice before going into the Bedford-Stuyvesant area of Brooklyn at night myself. Indeed, many of the cab drivers who have been robbed are themselves Negroes. But—and this is where the matter becomes emotion-laden—what right has

a cab driver to refuse to haul, say, Harry Belafonte because Harry is colored and, presumably, wants to be taken
somewhere in the Negro community?

I have a close friend, a Negro, who attempted to buy a
forty-thousand-dollar home in an all-white suburban community. The white families on the block near the house
he sought met with him and frankly said they were not
prejudiced *but* the presence of Negroes in a community
meant the presence of crime. To a family, these white
suburbanites had Negro maids, housekeepers and yardmen. One wonders if it ever occurred to them that the
crime rate among Negroes who can afford a forty-
thousand-dollar home is apt to be a good deal lower than
among cooks, maids and yardmen?

But even among liberal whites the Negro crime rate is a
threat second only to the Russian menace, and Whitney
Young's proposed program of research and interpretation
will do much to destroy the myths that have grown up
around Negro crime.

Now let us turn to an honest examination of the true
Negro crime rate. All matters mentioned above considered,
the Negro crime rate is still too high. As to this I would
make these short observations:

1. There is a direct correlation between the Negro crime
rate and the inability of Negroes to get jobs. Most Negroes
would rather work than steal; by the same token they
would rather steal than starve.

2. "Frustration crimes"—dope addiction, sexual as-
saults, ofttimes murder—are rooted in the need to escape
from the ugly reality of life in the Negro ghetto. Even
more, they stem from a deep psychological troubling over
being Negro. White America does not realize it, but the
average Negro is actually ashamed of being Negro. The
entire American experience is organized to make him this
way: The *black sheep* is the wayward sheep; the *black lie*
is the evil lie; to be *blackballed* is to be kept out; a *black
hour* is a time of troubling. Now, all this, coupled with the
intentional failure to include the Negro's contribution to
America in the study of general history, makes life diffi-

cult and most unpromising for a young person who, at sixteen years of age, looks up to find himself black. From that moment on, he is in defiance of society. Crime is the next step.

3. Then there is this disturbing truth: Much of the "Negro crime" has to do with getting back at white people. I have talked with several Negro lawyers who say their clients repeatedly justify theft on the grounds that "the white man [from whom they have stolen] owes me something; after all, he worked my grandparents as slaves and did not pay them."

Another aspect of this is the Negro who commits a crime against a white person simply because that person is white. In mid-1961 there was a horrendous crime in Brooklyn. A white man was killed—stabbed to death—while entering a cathedral to pray. A crowd gathered as the police began to investigate. The police were still examining the body when a voice from the crowd said, "I did it. I just had to kill somebody."

That was the way the New York daily papers reported the story. They were correct up to one critical fact, which, I am certain, they omitted on purpose. What the Negro murderer really said was this: "I did it. I just had to kill a *white man.*"

If one were to visit American prisons and get the confidence of Negro inmates one could do quite a study of the relationship between racism and crime. I predict the findings would be shocking.

This, I gather, is what Whitney Young has in mind when he speaks of doing an "action research" job; this is what he means when he says, "We will certify the true facts about life in the Negro community and give them the proper interpretation."

The Negro crime rate is indeed an embarrassment, but I suspect the last cry will not be ours. Unless one is willing to argue that some men are by nature criminals, a position no sane scholar would take, then it can only be concluded that the high Negro crime rate is due, largely, to social conditions imposed on the Negro community.

This is not to say, however, that we as Negroes escape the responsibility of doing something about it. It does mean that we can approach the matter without a feeling of guilt, that we can certify the facts about Negro crime without shame, and then proceed to interpret these facts to the community in general and demand correction of the evils which have produced this deplorable state of affairs.

This, as far as the Negro crime rate is concerned, is what Whitney Young is all about. How many of the old-timers at the League he can carry along with him is yet to be seen. Whitney Young must first make the League once again a real force in Negro life, a major source of ammunition for those who are on the firing line as the Negro revolt continues.

Once upon a time the National Urban League was a factor in Negro life. Those were the days when the Negro migrant got off the bus and found an Urban League representative standing to greet him and tell him the way of things in the big city. Then, for some unexplained reason, the Urban League representative was no longer to be found at the depot. But the busses and trains kept on coming North, and West, and Midwest. Now the sons and daughters of these migrants are in trouble. Everybody tells them about their rights but seldom do they get a lecture on their responsibilities; even less often does anybody come around and help them learn how to be responsible.

Actually the League lost the respect of Negroes because it did not—indeed, it could not—attack segregation with the militancy and methods of other Negro leadership organizations. As a result the League became a job center, a place where two kinds of Negroes went in search of jobs: The Negro masses—at least those who knew about the League—went to the League's offices in search of jobs, usually as menials or factory workers; and "breakthrough" Negroes, those who were being let into certain job classifications for the first time, found that the League was their best ally and had usually opened the door for them.

This was good work, and such League staffers as Edwin Berry of Chicago did outstanding work, but it was overlooked and then forgotten as the shouts of the Negro revolt began to ring across the nation. Now Whitney Young seeks to restore the League to the front rank of Negro leadership organizations. Negro leadership is now a highly competitive, multimillion-dollar-a-year operation; Whitney will have to muster more than sociological theories if he is to make room for the League in the rank that includes CORE, the NAACP, SNICK and the SCLC. Young knows this and his first year in office seems to be a promise of things to come.

A clear example of what lies ahead if Whitney has his way occurred at the Harvard Club in New York in May of 1961. The National Urban League convened a Manpower Utilization Conference that drew top executives from fifty major United States corporations and ten Negro college presidents. The purpose of the conference was to urge these corporations to do special training and recruiting on Negro college campuses in the South. As a direct result of that meeting several major industries now have recruitment and placement programs on Negro college campuses for the first time.

Whitney Young glitters because he fully grasps the psychological quirks of the American black man. Black Muslim leader Malcolm X is the only Negro I have met in recent years who knows the soul of Negroes as well as Young does. This was demonstrated during the recent howl over relief chiseling. Abraham Ribicoff, Secretary of Health, Education, and Welfare, convened a number of experts to discuss the matter and they were about to invoke a rule calling for all able-bodied men on relief to engage in "busy work." Young moved in and said "No." Instead, he proposed, let the city or state hire these men and give them salaries rather than relief checks. Young's view prevailed, and the mental health of the unemployed —mostly Negroes—will be the better for it.

First-class citizenship also involves voting. To general surprise, Young has moved the Urban League into that arena also. During the summer of 1961 the Taconic Foundation of New York convened the several Negro leadership organizations and offered to underwrite a Negro voter registration campaign if the Negro leadership organigations would conduct the drive. The League was the first organization to adopt the proposal.

This is but a part of what Whitney has in mind for the League. He envisions close cooperation between the League and other Negro leadership organizations on the local level. Although he did not say it, implicit in Young's program is the intention that the League will work with white businessmen in the hope that they will see the rightness and wisdom of hiring Negroes. If these conference talks fail I am certain the League officials involved will communicate with action organizations such as CORE and the NAACP about the failure. This, I predict, will lead to picketing and demonstrations against the obdurate businessmen.

Whitney Young has staked out quite a claim for himself. If he begins to mine precious ore there will be those who will cause plagues and pestilences to be visited upon him.

"Regarding the future of the League and my own personal convictions," Young said, "we may as well realize that we are at war—at war against prejudice and discrimination, against apathy and indifference, against rationalization, greed, selfishness and ignorance. We will not hesitate to identify our enemies in this war—whether they be Negro or white—confident that by rendering this service to our communities our support will be increased, not diminished."

Urging the Negro masses to become first-class citizens is vital to the preservation and realization of our civilization; only when Negroes do accept their responsibilities along with their rights can the victories of the Negro revolt be enjoyed. Lucky for us all, then, that a man like Whitney Young, just fourteen years out of school, paused one day to think things through.

17.

THE AMERICAN NEGRO AND
HIS GOVERNMENT

DURING THE SIXTY-TWO YEARS of this century the Negro has shifted his reliance among the three branches of the federal government. Negroes had great faith in Congress following the enactment of the Fifteenth Amendment in 1869-70, but as Southerners gained power in both the Senate and the House this faith waned. Since the articulation of the "separate but equal" doctrine in the 1880's the Supreme Court has been the principal instrument through which Negro aspirations have been realized. As we have seen, Negro organizations, particularly the NAACP, have therefore placed much reliance on the courts. However, the implementation of these court decisions has always depended on the executive branch of the government. To date enforcement of Negroes' rights as spelled out in the Constitution and interpreted in the courts of law has varied widely with the Chief Executive in office. The record of this century's Presidents has on the whole been spotty.

Negroes felt they had a friend in the White House when Theodore Roosevelt became President in 1901. Roosevelt had Booker T. Washington to dinner less than a month after he entered the White House; two years later Roosevelt appointed a Negro as collector of duties at the Charleston, South Carolina, port. Negroes were overjoyed because of this appointment and many Negro papers began to speak of Roosevelt as "our President, the first we have had since Lincoln." (What was overlooked was that Roosevelt's predecessor, McKinley, had appointed more Negroes to federal posts than any President.) Then the famous Indianola, Mississippi, incident occured. A Negro woman had been postmistress at Indianola since the Harrison administration. Because of pressure from the local whites she resigned. Roosevelt refused to accept her resignation, and when she refused to serve, the post office was closed down.

Disillusion set in during Roosevelt's second term, however. The influx to urban areas created grave social problems that led to race riots. The crucial riot occurred in Brownsville, Texas, where a Negro regiment was charged with running wild and "shooting up the town." The details are still murky, but it appears that three companies of the all-Negro Twenty-Fifth Regiment became involved in a dispute with several white citizens; the dispute broke into a riot and several white people were shot, and one was killed. Only the firm hand of the white commander brought violence to an end. Roosevelt instituted an investigation and, on the basis of the report, dismissed the entire Negro battalion without honor. Negroes reacted with shock; even South Carolina's Negro-baiting Senator Ben Tillman objected to Roosevelt's heavy-handed ways and called the act "lynching by executive order."

Roosevelt's successor, William Howard Taft, showed no disposition to take the kind of firm, direct action Negroes felt was needed to stem the rising tide of lynchings and floggings. As a result, Negroes were faced with a painful choice in the election of 1912: Theodore Roosevelt ran again for the Presidency as the Progressive candidate and further displeased Negroes by his refusal to seat most of the Negro convention delegates and his failure to include a statement denouncing discrimination in his platform. Thus, though deeply skeptical, Negroes turned to the

Democratic party, which had been their enemy since slavery.

✓Negro leaders were particularly attracted to Democratic candidate Woodrow Wilson because of two campaign statements. Said Wilson: "[I wish to see] justice done to the colored people in every matter; and not mere grudging justice, but justice executed with liberality and good feeling." Then he added: "I want to assure them that should I become President of the United States they may count upon me for absolute fair dealing, for everything by which I could assist in advancing the interests of their race in the United States."

✓That is what Wilson said, but during the first years of his administration he did just the opposite.

The first Wilson Congress received the greatest number of anti-Negro bills ever introduced in any American Congress. No less than twenty bills were proposed that would segregate Negroes on public carriers in the District of Columbia, exclude them from commissions in the army and navy, and set up segregated accommodations for white and Negro federal employees. Other bills called for the exclusion of all immigrants of Negro descent. Most of the legislation failed to pass, but Wilson, by executive order, segregated most of the Negro federal employees as far as rest-room and eating facilities were concerned. This occurred as lynchings and mob violence against Negroes were on the increase. Then, in 1915, Booker T. Washington died. That left Negroes without a representative whom white leaders knew and respected. Some prominent Negroes, sparked by Monroe Trotter, went to the White House to protest Wilson's attitude. The delegation was dismissed because Wilson thought Trotter's language was "insulting."

✓But as relations between the Chief Executive and Negro leaders sank to a new low, the effects of World War I began to redress the balance. War, if American history is to believed, is the great integrator. When America declared war on Germany in April, 1917, Negroes thronged to register for the army but, for the most part, they were not received. However, the Selective Service Act was passed the following month and called for the enlistment of *all* able-bodied men.

On July 5, registration day, more than seven hundred thousand Negroes enlisted. Before the end of enlistments two and a quarter million Negroes had registered. Of the Negroes who registered, 31 percent were accepted for military duty. (Only 26 percent of the white registrants were accepted. The explanation for this is revealing: Whereas Negroes at first were not accepted, once they were allowed to enlist, white draft boards in the South discriminated against Negroes as far as exemptions were concerned; thus whites were exempted from army duty if at all possible while Negroes who had valid reason for exemptions were taken into service.)

The presence of Negroes in the army produced the kinds of problems that always result in Negro advancement. Where would they be trained? Where would they eat? Would they serve with white troops? Would Negroes be allowed to become officers? If so, would they preside over all-Negro units or would they have power over white soldiers also?

Negroes wanted to serve not only as enlisted men but as officers. The NAACP took the matter directly to General Leonard Wood, who promised that he would set up a segregated training camp for Negro officers if two hundred Negro men of "college grade" could be found. In May, 1917, a Central Committee of College Men was set up at Howard University in Washington, D.C. Within ten days it had the names of fifteen hundred college-trained Negroes who wanted to be officers in the army. The program gained the support of three hundred Senators and Congressmen and, despite opposition from some Negroes who did not want a segregated camp established, resulted in a training camp for Negro officers at Fort Des Moines, Iowa. Six hundred and thirty-nine Negroes were commissioned officers in the army at Des Moines; later, in the fields and on a nonsegregated basis, hundreds of other Negroes received commissions. Negroes, on the whole, served with distinction in Europe. Thus Negro leaders were armed with yet another reason to press for full equality. Their hand was strengthened even more by Negro civilians, who purchased more than a quarter of a billion dollars' worth of war bonds and stamps.

The decade after the war was marked by two major developments as far as the Negro relationship to his government was concerned:

Emboldened by their record as Americans during the war Negroes intensified their protest campaign and exerted increasing influence on the federal government to act. The NAACP official organ, *The Crisis,* carried an article which purported to speak for the Negro soldier. It said, in part: "We return. We return from fighting. We return fighting. Make way for Democracy! We saved it in France, and by the Great Jehovah, we will save it in the U.S.A. or know the reason why."

This was the spirit of the Negro militants of the twenties as they staged protest meetings and marches. Presidents Warren Harding and Calvin Coolidge, both Republicans, gave the Negro spokesmen a polite ear and made several impressive appointments but neither took strong action on behalf of the Negroes. This led to the second major development in the relationship of the Negro to his government in the decade following the close of the war: the Negroes' final disaffection with, and withdrawal from, the Republican party.

In 1928 the GOP sought to regain support in the white South. To do this the Republican high command ignored the Negro Republican leaders who had carried the party banner in the South since Reconstruction; they gave patronage to white Republican leaders and seated white Republican delegations at the National Convention. Negro Republicans denounced the scheme, Negro newspapers, most of which had been rock-ribbed Republican, joined in the denunciation and came out in support of Alfred Smith, the Democratic candidate and a Catholic. Smith lost but, as far as Negroes were concerned, so did the Republicans. At first it appeared that the Republicans had discovered a way to win the white South and thus forget the Negro vote. But it turned out that the Republicans had traded the Negro vote for white support, which was by no means permanent. Once the religious issue was removed, the white South resumed voting the Democratic ticket. Negroes remained in the Democratic column, partially out of anger, but mostly because by then, 1932, the depression was upon us and Negroes, low men on the economic totem pole, were attracted to the Democrats' welfare state program.

√Franklin Roosevelt and the New Deal completed the Democratic capture of the Negro voter. Like most other Americans, Negroes found Roosevelt a father image in the time of national trouble. The public works and relief programs of the New Deal were of particular aid to Negroes, who were hardest hit by unemployment. Two things enhanced FDR's prestige with Negro voters:

First, it was public knowledge that both the President and his wife had Negroes as personal friends. Mrs. Roosevelt was often seen in public with her Negro friends and one of them, Dr. Mary Bethune, was a frequent White House dinner guest.

Second, Roosevelt brought a number of "Negro specialists" to Washington as aids and advisers to major government departments. There was hardly a department that did not have a Negro in a top advisory spot. These Negroes were known as the "Black Cabinet." There were about twenty-five such "Black Cabineteers" during the last years of the Roosevelt administration. Among them were Ted Poston, now with the New York *Post;* Dr. Robert C. Weaver, now administrator of the Housing and Home Finance Agency; Dr. Anna Arnold Hedgeman, now a consultant with the Congregational Church; and an obscure Howard University professor, Ralph Bunche, who was first appointed to the Library of Congress and then to a State Department post.

However, our honeymoon with President Roosevelt had its rocky moments. Despite his liberal image Roosevelt got on too well with Southerners on Capitol Hill to please some of us; there were always rumors that he was playing both sides against the middle. Then there was the much more serious event of 1941 when Negro workers, led by A. Philip Randolph, threatened to march on Washington to protest discrimination in industries receiving government contracts. White liberals, including Mrs. Roosevelt, tried to stop the march but Randolph persisted in his plans. ✓President Roosevelt finally took action and issued an executive order which forbade discrimination in industries handling government contracts, and this led to the establishment of the Fair Employment Practices Committee.

As far as Negroes were concerned, Harry Truman made a better President than he had been a Senator. Despite his Missouri background Truman came through in the clutches and his 1948 executive order ending segregation in the armed forces was a major breakthrough. Truman was no Roosevelt, however; the Negro's New Deal ended the day Mrs. Roosevelt moved out of the White House.

Negroes remembered Dwight Eisenhower chiefly as the general who testified against Truman's move to end discrimination in the armed forces. True, Eisenhower spoke as an army man; his point was that white troops would resent integration and thus the effectiveness of the army would be impaired. Even so, his testimony was too close to the urgings of the white South for comfort and only 21 percent of the Negro voters supported the General in the election of 1952. Negroes along with liberals had placed their hopes in Adlai Stevenson, and with his defeat we expected little in the way of civil rights leadership from the President.

✓In the meantime our eyes were fixed on the Supreme Court, and at last, after four years of anxious waiting, the momentous school desegregation decision of 1954 was announced. All we asked of the Chief Executive, then, was that he enforce the Court's decree.

Eisenhower rose to the occasion in implementing the desegregation decision in Little Rock. And we were thankful that he didn't speak against us as we went about integrating Southern schools. A change in the Negro's attitude toward Eisenhower became apparent in 1956 when 40 percent of the Negro voters supported his bid for a second term. This was indeed a reward when one remembers that Mr. Eisenhower's 1956 opponent was the same Adlai Stevenson whom Negroes overwhelmingly supported in 1952. But Eisenhower was forced to share his civil rights glory with Congress and the Democrats; after sixty years of inaction, the Congress untracked itself in 1958 and passed a civil rights bill.

Whatever the accomplishments of various administrations in the field of race relations, progress did not come fast enough, or go far enough. This was one of the factors behind the birth of the Negro revolt in 1958, when the Negro masses took matters into their own hands. By the 1960 Presidential elections, the revolt had produced a large and powerful pressure group. Both parties recognized this and wooed the Negro voter: the Republicans seeking to increase their growing Negro support, and the Democrats striving to recover lost ground. The crucial move came in the last days of the campaign: Martin Luther King was arrested with fifty-two other Negroes during a sit-in demonstration in Atlanta. He alone was held in jail and sentenced, on a technicality, to four months' hard labor. John F. Kennedy interrupted his campaign for the Presidency to call Mrs. King to express his concern; the next morning Robert Kennedy called to remonstrate with the judge who had sentenced King. The following day, King was set free.

In *The Making of the President,* 1960 Theodore H. White underlines the critical importance of the Democratic candidate's intervention in the King case:

One cannot identify in the narrowness of American voting of 1960 any one particular episode or decision as being more important than any other in the final tallies: yet when one reflects that Illinois was carried by only 9,000 votes and that 250,000 Negroes are estimated to have voted for Kennedy; that Michigan was carried by 67,000 votes and that an estimated 250,000 Negroes voted for Kennedy; that South Carolina was carried by 10,000 votes and that an estimated 40,000 Negroes there voted for Kennedy, the candidate's instinctive decision must be ranked among the most crucial of the last few weeks.

In spite of this auspicious beginning, signs of disaffection on the part of Negroes and liberals began to multiply as President Kennedy's first term of office stretched toward the halfway mark:

● The President sent NAACP Executive Secretary Roy Wilkins warm greetings on the occasion of his thirtieth anniversary as a civil rights leader; Wilkins responded by criticizing the President for his failure to propose and vigorously support civil rights legislation as well as for his failure to sign the much-awaited order banning segregation in federally aided housing.

● Liberals in Congress, Republicans as well as Democrats, were obviously disappointed with the President's civil rights program and had taken to needling him in public. As witnesses came before the Special House Education and Labor Committee to testify in favor of an equal employment bill, Republican Representative Harold Godell of New York flashed a wry smile and urged them to "let your views be known at 1600 Pennsylvania Avenue."

● A liberal Senate coalition of Democrats and Republicans had established a timetable by which they would periodically tag civil rights riders onto administration bills in the hope that this battle of attrition would wear the President down and force him to submit civil rights legislation of his own.

● Although the President surprised critics by asking for civil rights legislation in his 1962 State of the Union Message, the press, almost without exception, openly charged that the President wouldn't make an all-out drive for it, and that he had made this vocal gesture only to silence his liberal critics.

● Even after the message Joseph Rauh of the Americans for Democratic Action (ADA) issued his report card on the Kennedy civil rights stance and found the President wanting; Kennedy got a "plus" when compared with Eisenhower, but a "minus" when compared with his own campaign promises.

The Leadership Conference on Civil Rights, a general committee of the leaders of all civil rights organizations and headed by Roy Wilkins, issued a call for a "march" on Washington.

"We plan to have a demonstration of representative leaders from cities throughout the nation to show that we don't agree with the Kennedy administration's civil rights position," Wilkins told a New York press conference.

The prospect of such men as Wilkins, Arnold Aronson, and Martin Luther King demonstrating before the White House was not pleasant.

Then the *New York Times* reproved the President for his failure to sign the order ending discrimination in federally aided housing. The *Times* editorial, the second such in ten days, warned the President against linking his civil rights program to public consensus and flatly suggested that if the President "accepted the doctrine of government by Gallup Poll, it marks a weakening in the concept of strong moral leadership by the President, about which the President spoke so movingly during the campaign."

As far as civil rights were concerned, John F. Kennedy's first year in office seemed to be a magnificent bust.

As the chorus of criticism rose, an unpublicized meeting took place at the White House early in January, 1962; the topic: civil rights. In attendance, along with their aides, were the President; Attorney General Robert Kennedy; Burke Marshall, the Assistant Attorney General for Civil Rights; Dr. Robert C. Weaver, administrator of the Housing and Home Finance Agency, and Louis E. Martin, the key Negro official of the Democratic National Committee. The meeting, to quote one of those in attendance, lasted "the whole damn morning," and then adjourned, *sine die,* the conferees having unanimously agreed to move in the direction they had been heading for the past year, but with more deliberate speed.

Having interviewed some of those present at that meeting as well as other members of the administration, I am convinced that the President's civil rights critics—including myself—were wrong. We were wrong partly out of ignorance of what the civil rights program really was (the administration having been unduly wary about letting outsiders, including reporters, know just what was going on), and partly out of ignorance of the President's style and method of operation. The President is a purely political man. This is not a disparagement; rather is it a description of one of the most classical political talents ever to occupy the White House. This fact goes a long way toward illuminating the President's civil rights program, which is tied to the rise of the Negro voter.

Shortly after his election President Kennedy let it be known that he considered the vote, particularly in the South, the key to Negro advancement.[1] For the President, this was a logical conclusion; being as political as he is, Mr. Kennedy felt certain that elected officials—county, state and federal—would be less abusive toward Negroes once effective numbers of them began parading to the polls. John F. Kennedy is not naïve; he knows that Negroes in the Deep South are systematically kept away from the polls by various legal devices and by fear. Therefore the President announced that he had instructed the Attorney General to institute suits to remove these impediments at the ballot box—to repeal the Black Codes adopted after Reconstruction.

After painstaking investigation and endless hours of legal research directed by the Attorney General, the Justice Department went into Federal District Courts and filed fourteen cases charging racial discrimination by various county registrars. These were not simple cases involving one or two Negroes who wanted to vote; rather were they pacesetters, cases that will strike down registration procedures in several counties in at least three states and admit thousands of Negroes to the polls.

[1] See Appendix VI.

The Justice Department realized that even when ballot box obstructions were removed Negroes who voted would face economic and, perhaps, physical reprisals. To prevent just this, as well as to aid Negroes who were already facing reprisals because they attempted to vote, the Justice Department successfully prosecuted two suits that won protection for Negroes who register and vote. More, these decisions upheld the government's right to seek swift action in behalf of Negroes facing such reprisals.

These are known facts, part of the Attorney General's 1961 civil rights report that was so roundly criticized by liberals. As administration activity in the area of Negro voting rights this is quite an achievement, but—for liberals, that is—it paled beside the administration's failure to support certain civil rights legislation and take executive action. What few people knew was that the administration's activity in the area of voting rights during the first year of the Kennedy era was but a warm-up, the readying of one end of a pincer movement designed to change the political complexion of the South, and the beginning of an unprecedented alliance between government and private money to achieve a civil rights gain.

During the early months of the Kennedy administration civil rights leaders were informed that the administration would be pleased if, in addition to sponsoring freedom rides and sit-ins, the various civil rights organizations joined together and undertook a major Negro voter registration program in the Deep South. The administration had announced its determination to clear the Negro's path to the ballot box. Would the various Negro leadership organizations work together and round up the Negroes eligible to vote?

The persons who discussed the administration's desire for a Negro voter registration drive were moneyed white liberals, sympathetic to the Kennedy view, with no official connection with the government. They concluded their feeler by assuring Negro leaders that if all the organizations would pull together for such a registration drive the money to finance the movement could be found. More,

Mr. Kennedy's friends argued, voter registration is the one area where substantial Negro gains could be made with strong government support.

The reasoning behind this was cold as steel and just as hard:

● Voter registration is the area where the Justice Department has the most power; it can move swiftly and, if need be, on its own motion.

● Voter registration is the one civil rights item white supremacists cannot afford to oppose publicly. The right to vote is so basic that even extreme segregationists shy away from a showdown on the issue. They will openly say they don't want their children going to school with Negroes but few of them, in this day and age, will admit they don't want Negroes to vote.

● A study of civil rights abuses shows that Negroes have the most difficulty in areas where their numerical strength poses a political threat. If these Negroes voted they could change things by electing decent city and county officials. This, in the administration view, would be the first step toward general civil rights progress.

● A major increase in the number of Southern Negro voters would not only change local attitudes but would also change the complexion of Congress; Southern reactionaries would either mend their ways or be voted out of office. Then, and only then, could the administration get its liberal legislation, including civil rights, through Congress.

The civil rights leaders with whom this program was discussed were Roy Wilkins of the NAACP, James Farmer of CORE, Martin Luther King of the SCLC, Whitney Young of the Urban League, Edward King of the Student Non Violent Coordinating Committee and Leslie Dunbar, the executive director of the Southern Regional Council. There was considerable reluctance on the part of some Negro leaders to accept the program; there was a very real fear that the move was an attempt to syphon off support for such demonstrations as sit-ins and freedom rides. This fear was enhanced when Attorney General

Robert Kennedy called for a "cooling-off period" during the 1960 freedom rides. This fear was overcome when the friends of the President pointed out that the voter registration program would not draw support away from civil rights demonstrations; that, in fact, it would aid those demonstrations by making it possible for civil rights organizations to divert the money now being used for voter registration to such mass protest projects.

Once this issue was clear, the program ran into trouble because the various organizations involved couldn't agree on just who would do what, who would get how much, and how they would arrange to stay out of each other's hair. The Urban League was the first organization to agree to the plan; then came CORE, the SCLC, the student organization and, after considerable delay, the NAACP. Once the Negro leadership organizations agreed, they found themselves the recipients of a quarter-of-a-million-dollar grant from the Taconic Foundation[2] in New York City. That was in the late fall of 1961.

The mechanics of the grant and the joint registration drive are complex. In essence, they boil down to this: The Southern Regional Council[3] will act as monitors of the

[2]The Taconic Foundation is a philanthropic agency incorporated in the State of Delaware but with offices in New York City. It gives grants to individuals and organizations for scientific, civic, literary, and artistic purposes. The two-year-old foundation is headed by Stephen R. Currier. Mrs. Jane Lee Eddy is the Executive Secretary. New York lawyer Lloyd Garrison, a longtime liberal and a member of the New York City Board of Education, is legal counsel for the Foundation and is the man who functioned as catalyst for all who are involved in the pincers movement. Foundation officials refused to say just where their money comes from.

[3]The Southern Regional Council and its predecessor, the Commission on Interracial Cooperation, have been active in the area of race relations since 1919. The Commission was founded by a group of the South's leading churchmen. Its main purpose is to encourage mutual understanding between the South's peoples through the exchange of ideas based on accurate research. The Council consists of a board of eighty Southerners, drawn from the major religious faiths, both races, and the thirteen states of the region. Financial support for the Council comes from church groups, foundations, trade unions, business firms and several individuals. The current president is author James M. Dabbs of South Carolina, and Leslie W. Dunbar is the executive director. Though based in Atlanta, the Council employs an interracial staff.

project, but the grant will go to the Voter Education Program, a new foundation set up for this purpose, which will also administer the project. Negro lawyer Wiley Branton of Pine Bluff, Arkansas (the man who made headlines as lawyer for the Little Rock Negro students), will move to Atlanta to head the drive. The various civil rights organizations will apply to the Voter Education Program for funds; the Voter Education Program will, in turn, endow offices in the various civil rights organizations for the specific purpose of voter education.

In the spring of 1962 the stage was set for John F. Kennedy to fight the civil rights battle of his preference on grounds of his own choosing. While the administration has appeared as a friend of the court in behalf of freedom riders and the sit-ins, the administration began to focus its own civil rights efforts in a different direction.

The administration is impressed by the fact that the Negro masses are now becoming involved in the civil rights struggle, and it would like to see this same kind of grass-roots movement involved with voter registration. If the President has his way—and this is the genius of the pincer movement—the Negro masses in the South will move to the polls under the combined leadership of the established civil rights organizations, while the voter registration movement will be financed by white liberals friendly to the Kennedy view (Kennedy also hopes that Negroes will see the wisdom of his plan and raise funds to augment the grant from the Taconic Foundation). Should Negroes encounter trouble as they attempt to register, the Justice Department will close in with the other end of the pincer and not only clear the path to the voting booth but provide protection for Negroes who register and vote.

The second-act climax of the Kennedy voting drama will come as Negroes parade to the polls and vote against not only those officials who have been abusive toward them but some of those who have given the Kennedy administration's whole program a rough time on Capitol Hill.

If one may continue the fantasy, the third-act curtain will come at the end of a busy day on Capitol Hill in

Washington. Two Southern Senators meet just outside the Senate chamber. They speak:

MISSISSIPPI SENATOR: By God, niggers are voting in my state.

ALABAMA SENATOR: Hell, they are voting in mine too; and furthermore, they ain't niggers, they are colored citizens.

The funny thing about this is that it is not an exaggeration. This is precisely what the Kennedy administration is up to.

Kennedy's registration pincer movement is a bold and imaginative plan, for such an alliance between the government and private money is a new thing. But it is only after one examines the studies made by the administration of Negro voting potential in the Deep South that the full political meaning of the plan becomes clear:

● Negroes comprise 40 percent of the voting potential in seven of Alabama's nine Congressional districts.

● Four of Mississippi's six Congressional districts are 50 percent Negro. In the other two districts, Negroes comprise 32 percent of the population in one, 23 percent in the other.

● South Carolina has six Congressional districts; Negroes account for more than 40 percent of the adult population in two of them, they represent 35 percent of the potential voting stock in two others, and more than 20 percent of the adult population in the remaining two.

● Negroes hold 33 percent of the potential voting stock in six of Georgia's ten Congressional districts; they are at least 25 percent of the adult population in all eight of Louisiana's Congressional districts.

When these Congressional district figures are broken down to city and county levels, the balance, in favor of Negroes, is even more impressive:

● Mississippi has eighty-two counties; the Negro population exceeds that of the whites in eighteen of these counties; five counties are about evenly balanced. These figures represent adults of voting age. The over-all population figures show that Mississippi has 1,257,000 white people as compared with 916,000 Negroes. The political implication of the Negro voting potential becomes clear when it is realized that only 298,000 votes were cast in Mississippi during the 1960 elections.

● Macon County, Alabama, is a classic case of Negro voter potential. It contains eleven thousand Negroes (the county includes Tuskegee Institute) as compared with four thousand white persons, all over twenty-one years of age. Yet, as of 1962, only one thousand Negroes were registered voters as against three thousand white voters. Lowndes County in the same state has made an even worse showing. There are five thousand Negroes of voting age in that county compared with only three thousand white persons; yet there are 2,240 registered white voters and not a single Negro voter.

√So, throughout the Deep South, the story runs. And it is the theory of the Kennedy administration that once these Negroes gain the franchise they can change things at home as well as in Washington.

The Kennedy voting scheme looks good on paper, but will it work?

"It's already working," Burke Marshall told me. "We have been working closely with the Negroes in Macon County [Alabama] and Fayette and Haywood counties [Tennessee], and changes are already in the making. We have gone into court to see to it that the Negroes in these counties are allowed to register and vote without reprisals. We won and they are voting."

I reminded Burke Marshall that Negroes in the Deep South hesitate to run the risk of voting when the choice is between two equally undesirable white candidates.

"We expect our voter registration efforts not only to produce better white candidates for Negroes to choose from," Marshall replied, "but we fully expect to have Negro candidates emerge, particularly in Macon County."

Attorney General Robert Kennedy was even more emphatic about Negro voter registration.

✓"We will advance civil rights legislation in due time," he told me, "but right now we are quite determined about the elimination of literacy tests and poll taxes as prerequisites for voting. We have already moved through the courts to strike down literacy tests in Louisiana and we are now preparing a case that will raise the same question in Mississippi. Our position is known, and we plan to go all out on Capital Hill for legislation in this area."

Other Presidential advisers told me the same thing and one of them showed me a list of Southern Congressmen who had to be "moved"—that is to say, horse traded with—to get such measures as a standard literacy test and the removal of the poll tax through Congress. The administration hopes to get the legislation passed in 1962; they are certain they can have it enacted by the time Mr. Kennedy runs for re-election in 1964. I came away from Washington convinced that the Brothers Kennedy meant just what they said. One week later, the administration placed all of its power and pressure behind a measure to strike down both literacy tests and the poll tax.

✓Thus the Kennedy administration may well usher in a new era in the Negro's relationship to his government. The President's voting plan recalls the evil days just after Radical Reconstruction; but perhaps this is where a new beginning should be made. After all, that is where things went wrong. Once the Negro lost the franchise, he lost his personal security and individual dignity; now the thing has come full circle. Only time can say if all this will work out, but the administration is fully convinced that it will. Two things, however, are immediately certain:

Negro leadership organizations are now committed to the voter registration drive. If they fail to produce large numbers of Negroes at the voter registration offices of the Deep South they will suffer an almost irreparable loss of prestige and national influence.

Second, the Kennedy administration has made an irretrievable commitment to provide access and protection for Negroes at the polls. If it fails to deliver, liberal faith in the Kennedys will be shattered and the nation's image will suffer before the burgeoning nonwhite nations of the world.

What the administration fears most at this juncture— and I think they are correct—is that the Negro leadership organizations, either because of bickering among themselves or lack of contact with the Negro masses, will fail to produce large numbers of potential Negro voters. This eventuality has already been foreseen. The grant made to the Southern Regional Council is not limited to the established Negro leadership organizations. Any group interested in voter registration may apply, and I predict that if it appears that the established organizations are not producing, a number of local movements—such as the Montgomery and Albany movements—will come into being with the aid of grants from the SRC and for the specific purpose of carrying out Negro voter registration programs.

The Kennedy pincer movement projects—and I think rightly so—the way minority problems must be resolved in a free society. The government may provide the initiative and offer every assistance, but the main burden must rest with the people who stand to benefit. This is the challenge Kennedy has flung at Negro leadership: that it move in the area of voter registration where the government has the most power to help them, and that gains made at the ballot box be translated into general civil rights improvement. Needless to say, the Kennedys will translate all this into Democratic votes.

Two incidents of late 1962 gave insights for those who are attempting to understand the Kennedy approach to civil rights:

Once the courts ordered James Meredith's admission to the University of Mississippi, the Kennedy administration was determined that he would matriculate, even if it took federal troops and bloodshed to do it. It took just that, and more. Now that Meredith is enrolled one can hardly be critical of the administration's role in the affair. Yet the criticisms abound. First of all, there are many who feel the President acted too late and with too much concern for those who stood clearly in the way of justice. Only time will tell how many Negro votes Kennedy lost—at least for a while—on the night he made the speech announcing that federal troops had been ordered into Mississippi to take Meredith to school. What galled us was the image of our President bending over backwards to oil ruffled feathers in Mississippi. We flinched and grew angry as the President droned on, calling the names of the great heroes from Mississippi who served the nation well. For many of us—and I am among them—there was an unforgivable gap in the President's speech: he failed to call the roll of the Negroes who had served, and died for, the nation, and he failed to make it plain to Mississippians that they were in the wrong, legally and morally. But now that Meredith is enrolled, one hopes the dust will settle, and, of course, the administration will add the University of Mississippi incident to its list of civil rights achievements to be considered by the Negro voter in 1964.

The Presidential order ending discrimination in federally aided housing came late in the fall of 1962. It, too, smacked of being too little and too late. During the 1960 elections Kennedy had attacked President Eisenhower on just this point. "By a stroke of his pen," Kennedy said, "Mr. Eisenhower can end discrimination in federally aided housing." Kennedy then pledged himself to make that stroke of the pen if elected. It took him two years, and the final version of the housing order was considerably less than most of us expected. Several drafts of the proposed order had been seen by Negro leaders, and the consensus was that we would get an order with the widest possible scope. We got no such thing; yet we got more than any other President had given us. And this is just the point: the Kennedy administration always manages to fall short of our expectations though, at the same time, it clearly outdistances all previous administrations.

The Kennedy approach to civil rights leaves many liberals cold; it does not have the warm emotional appeal of Mrs. Roosevelt or, for that matter, Adlai E. Stevenson, particularly during Stevenson's first campaign for the Presidency. They cannot envision victory for people who do not first learn to fight and do for themselves. John F. Kennedy is not much of a hand for doing things for people; he is quite adept, however, in providing people with the tools to do things for themselves.

Robert Kennedy offered a key to the administration's views on civil rights when he observed that the Irish were once despised and persecuted; now one of them, and a Catholic, is President. "In thirty years," Robert Kennedy said, "a Negro can also be President."

But to do this, the Attorney General implied, the Negro must do as the Irish did: they must organize, work together and become a political power force in American life. And the realities of American life are with, not against, the Kennedy stance.

The Supreme Court has been in the vanguard so far as civil liberties are concerned for quite a while now, with the other branches of government trailing well behind. Perhaps it is time to let the Court catch its breath while the executive and legislative branches consolidate our gains. Kennedy is the first President in history whom one can call a true liberal. Despite initial misgivings Kennedy's liberalism is now being felt, even though in a chillingly political way. Furthermore, as Thurgood Marshall once said, "Anyone who thinks that once Negroes get the vote they will all go to a civil rights heaven is badly mistaken." No, the vote is not the whole of civil rights; but it is a large segment. And if Kennedy does no more than secure Negroes access and protection at the polls he will have done more for civil rights than any other President in history.

18.

THE INTERNATIONAL CONTEXT
OF THE REVOLT

ONLY A SENSE OF PURPOSE, a dedication beyond his desire for civil rights, can sustain the American Negro in the days just ahead. As overt signs of segregation crumble in the border states and those of the not too Deep South, the intransigent white power structure in the deepest South will become even more obdurate and resort to violence. Even the most determined liberals, Negro and white, will begin to wonder if integration in and of itself is worth the price this nation will have to pay in Mississippi, certain sections of Alabama and southern Georgia. Personally, I am convinced that only martial law can bring about token integration in these areas. The cost of providing Negroes with the unhampered and unpunishable right to vote will be high indeed, and the desegregation of public facilities in these areas will bring on such raw ugliness that we all will be forced to stop and ponder whether we are fighting a battle that can end only in a Pyrrhic victory. Then there is the very real possibility that the Negro masses in these enclaves of white supremacy are so weary and defeated that they will hesitate to take advantage of the hard-won opportunities.

Yet the job must be done, the risks run, the price paid

because we, as a people, and America, as a nation, have no alternative if we are to survive and prevail. The American race problem is no longer a private matter among the citizens of this country. If one doubts this let him sit in the gallery of the United Nations during a heated exchange between this country and Russia. Always, as recently occurred during the debate on the admission of Red China, the Russians are able to wash our face with the race question while the Afro-Asians suppress sardonic smiles. In the instance just mentioned, Ambassador Adlai Stevenson had opposed the admission of Red China to the UN because, among other reasons, of the treatment of Chinese people within that ruthless Communist state. Ambassador Zorin of the Soviet Union arose and calmly replied that if the way citizens of a country are treated is a basis for membership in the UN, then the United States should be voted out of that body because of her treatment of Negroes. We get our faces washed by the race issue because the implementation of segregation transgresses everything we say we stand for; thus our enemies beat our brains out by simply measuring us by our standards, not theirs!

Our enemies are not the only ones who embarrass us by raising the question of the Negro in America. Early in July of 1961, an obscure Oriental diplomat to the United Nations made a speech before the summer conference of Elementary School Principals of the National Educational Association. He began by observing that Western writing was too involved with the physical aspects of sex and then went on to this passage of social criticism:

"One may well argue that over the years race relations in the United States of America have been peaceful and harmonious, but this peace and harmony has been only the absence of overt tension rather than the presence of justice which your great country stands for. The 'Freedom Riders' journeying to the South are looked upon in Asia and Africa as the champions for the Negro's holy war for freedom. It is obvious that their struggle is not purely a racial one; it has profound political implications. The traditional battleground of fighters for civil rights in this country for many years has been the courts of law. But court victories are only limited victories, since Congress has consistently refused to endorse them by passing law enforcement legislation. Therefore to fight in the courts is considered ineffectual, and more important, it is also to limit the Negroes' goal to the integration of specific institutions rather than to the political revolution that would transform the institutions. . . .

"Among other things the United States of America symbolizes human freedom and human equality, but this image has been greatly tarnished by reports of violent racial conflicts in the Deep South. Understandably these happenings have tremendous repercussions abroad, especially in nonwhite countries of Asia and Africa, and they create tensions *which are in many ways more explosive than political or cold war tensions.*" (Italics mine.)

Four months after Ambassador U Thant of Burma delivered that speech he was named Acting Secretary General of the United Nations.

Racial progress in America does more than help this nation make a good appearance before the world; it will, and does, strengthen our ability to deal with the disturbing phenomenon known as international racism. We are the cornerstone of the Western Alliance, and it is perhaps no more than a quirk of history that today's "have" nations —our allies—are the colonialist nations of the white world whereas the "have not" nations are their former subject, nonwhite colonies.

These Afro-Asian states form the majority voting stock in the United Nations. The Acting Secretary General is an Oriental; the current President of the General Assembly is an Arab; and one does not have to probe behind the scenes at the United Nations to discover that cold war politics and racism have coalesced to create an atmosphere in which the odds are against a white man becoming Secretary General of the organization. This nonwhite power bloc has shaken the United Nations to its foundation. This is why the UN could not act against India because of Goa;

this is why the Red China question must be rethought, and why the American people may as well prepare themselves for the admission of Red China to the UN; this is why there is so much talk, particularly in high European places, about the formation of an "Atlantic Alliance" that would by-pass the United Nations and deal with international issues; this is why we are unable to get our European allies to unify on a continuing "hard line" toward Moscow. For the truth is that many highly placed and powerful Europeans, including some Englishmen, are convinced that the next war will not be East versus West but, rather, white versus nonwhite. Those who hold this view see the day when Russia will be allied with Western Europe and America against Red China and the Afro-Asians.

Several African leaders are convinced that the leaders of "white" Western European countries are resigned to a race war; that France, Belgium, England, West Germany and Portugal are exerting every effort to get America to embrace that view. Africans have been concerned over this development for more than a year now, and several of them have suggested to me that the American Negro holds a key hand in the shaping of American and world attitudes. Their argument is—and I fully agree—that to the degree that the Negro wins his battle for total involvement in the American mainstream, the world will move just that much farther away from a race war.

International racism has become such a cause for concern in Europe that James Reston of the *New York Times* devoted an entire column to it on December 15, 1961. This is what Reston had to say:

> The British are genuinely worried about [Katanga], not primarily because they have commercial interests in the Katanga province of the Congo, but because they fear that the United States and the United Nations may help create a situation that will drive the white settlers from the Congo and start a tribal war that will get out of control and engulf the whole of Central Africa.
>
> Officials here are discreet about all this, but it is difficult not to infer from their statements that they think the United

States is taking positions which may be good politics in New York and Chicago, but reckless politics in an area which could easily slip back into tribal warfare and encourage the Communists to back the African Negroes against the Western whites.

Even when one talks about the Berlin question or the wider, long-range development of the cold war, the conversation in London and Paris turns to the question of race.

One official here put the problem in these terms: The white peoples have had a long period of supremacy and are now being challenged by the black and yellow races. This is natural and was probably inevitable. Just as you in America benefited by our industrial revolution, and Russia benefited by your scientific and technological revolution, so Asia and Africa in turn will benefit by both.

Our problem is to guide this development in the ways of freedom if we can, as the Roman Empire contained and influenced its competitors, but above all to unite so that we have the strength to withstand the pressure of races far more numerous than our own.

The white nations, he continued, have fought two civil wars in this century. They cannot withstand another. It would be the end of our civilization. This is one reason why, looking to the long-range future, some of us here in Britain think it is important to keep talking to the Russians, useless as it may seem.

A French official, quite unaware of this conversation, developed almost the same argument. With the population rising as it is in Asia and Africa, and China following the most belligerent policy in the world, he said, it may be that the great conflict at the end of the century will not be ideological but racial. We do not like this thought, but the duty of policy is to see not only the day-to-day problems but the longer problems rising in Africa and Asia. That is one reason why we are so doubtful of some of Washington's moves through the United Nations in Katanga and elsewhere.

This is strong stuff and it may be wrong, but it is being said, not by barroom philosophers, but by some of the most influential officials in the Western world.

This, it will be recalled is precisely what the Black Muslims are saying: that—they call it the war of Armageddon—rather soon now, Allah, the Black Man, will engage in war with the devil, the White Man, and that, of course, the Black Man will win. Thus, the Black Muslims continue, the American Negro had better come out from among white people lest he be destroyed with them. Racialism makes for strange bedfellows; the leaders of Western Europe and the Honorable Elijah Muhammad have arrived at identical conclusions through similar logic and both issue a call for racial "unity" for the strife that lies ahead.

It is both difficult and dangerous to assess all this; yet there is no merit in the timidity that ignores the obvious. I can only speak as one who has deep concern over the consequences that flow from the white man's refusal to take black men seriously. When colonial peoples clamor for freedom, they are ignored until blood flows; if the blood doesn't flow, white people assume that black people are docile, simple, childlike folk. The truth is black people are forced by the facts of modern life to play a cautious role against the day when they can muster the military might requisite to honest national expression in today's world. The hope of sane men, black and white, is that white men will voluntarily change their ways before black men can make them change. In my book *The Reluctant African* I expressed the hope that white men would learn to love before black men learned to hate. That was two years ago; everything I have seen since then causes me to lower my moral sights somewhat. Now my prayer is that white men will remove the reason to shoot before black men get something to shoot with.

Just as American Negroes have lost faith in the basic integrity of the white power structure because of unchanging situations in the South despite court orders, so have black men the world over lost faith in the power of talks and negotiation.

"Only the weak talk morality," one African diplomat told me. "The man or country who is strong gets justice because he is able to reward injustice with military destruction."

Thus when India marched into Goa the world reacted

along racial lines. Prime Minister Nehru took note of this division during a press conference. He observed that the West had condemned Indian action in Goa while most Asian and African countries "rejoiced" about it.

"I do not like this division of opinion—to put it very crudely, white and black," Nehru said. "I do not like it at all. It is a bad sign, but there it is. I have been distressed by this more than anything. We are developing a mentality of black against white, distrust of each other, dislike of each other, suspicion of each other."

The road ahead is mine-laden; in Mississippi and South Africa there are holocausts lying in wait. Should these disasters befall Western civilization, the race war envisioned by so many in Western Europe could well start. This, among other reasons, is why all Americans of goodwill should be allied with the Negro in his current revolt. Not only will victory for the Negro give the Negro his just deserts, but it will postpone, perhaps permanently, the day of an international race crisis.

Life is process; in the process of correcting our own society we save ourselves and activate the forces that will preserve our civilization. The crisis of modern man is spiritual; the surface conflicts—East versus West, white versus nonwhite—are but symptoms of a malady that afflicts all the world. That basic ailment is man's continuing inhumanity to man, the perpetual assault upon the dignity of some individuals by other, more powerful individuals. This is the toxin now flowing through the universal bloodstream. And the cure, like most antidotes, is a rearrangement of the elements found in the poison itself; that is to say, the political and economic power forces that were joined to produce inhuman treatment must now be rearranged to stop it, and then manipulated to bar such scourges as racialism and political domination from all lands occupied by civilized peoples.

EPILOGUE

WHATEVER ELSE the Negro is, he is American. Whatever he is to become—integrated, unintegrated, or disintegrated —he will become it in America. Only a minority of Negroes have ever succumbed to the temptation to seek greener pastures in another country or another ideology. Our lot is irrevocably cast, and whatever future awaits America awaits the Negro; whatever future awaits the Negro, awaits America.

And the Negroes' total commitment to America indicates that the prospect ahead seems bright. It is true that we are angry about our present plight, for we measure America by her potential rather than by her achievements: like a schoolboy genius with a consistent B average, America is too good not to be better. I have talked to scores of Negroes in the months of research involved in this book. What has impressed me is that although they were angry and often bitter, although they were discouraged at what could be done in a lifetime to rectify the effects of generations of oppression and servitude, not a single Negro doubted that we would one day get our full freedom. It has just never occurred to us that the Negro Revolt will not, in the end, succeed. This fundamental optimism is, I submit, a resounding statement of faith in the American dream.

Dr. Kenneth Clark goes to what I feel is the heart and truth of the matter when he says, "there is no point in

264

alk, regardless of how poetic it may be, about whether he Negro wants to integrate with America. He has no choice. He is involved, inextricably so, with America and he knows it. And the sensible Negro is the man who takes pride in this involvement and accepts it as a mandate to work for the change that is written in the way of things."

America is the latest outpost in man's journey away from provincialism. From here man will go forward, not backward, and he will be less encumbered by dividedness than he was when he spread from the old world to the new. The art of being a Negro consists in the realization of this central fact; the act of being a Negro in America consists in joining in every way the liberal forces who enjoy the challenge of tomorrow more than they do the comfortable provincialism of yesterday.

And so the hydrogen thing ticks. It may go off; then again it may not. I hope and pray it will not. But in either case man will survive; in either case provincialism is doomed. And if it is the lot of surviving man to probe the ashes of war in search of the will to carry on, he will know that America was once here. And if surviving man studies the evidence well, taking pains to blow away the dust of time, he will know that a disturbed, lonely, yet inspired, American black people once walked this way.

I. White and Negro Population by State, 1960 Census

STATE	WHITE	NEGRO	OTHER
Alabama	2,283,609	980,271	2,86
Alaska	174,546	6,771	44,85
Arizona	1,169,517	43,403	89,24
Arkansas	1,395,703	388,787	1,78
California	14,455,230	883,861	378,11
Colorado	1,700,700	39,992	13,25.
Connecticut	2,423,816	107,449	3,96
Delaware	384,327	60,688	1,27
D.C.	345,263	411,737	6,95
Florida	4,063,881	880,186	7,49
Georgia	2,817,223	1,122,596	3,29
Hawaii	202,230	4,943	425,5
Idaho	657,383	1,502	8,3
Illinois	9,010,252	1,037,470	33,43
Indiana	4,388,554	269,275	4,66
Iowa	2,728,709	25,354	3,47
Kansas	2,078,666	91,445	8,50
Kentucky	2,820,083	215,949	2,12
Louisiana	2,211,715	1,039,207	6,10
Maine	963,291	3,318	2,65
Maryland	2,573,919	518,410	8,36
Massachusetts	5,023,144	111,842	13,59
Michigan	7,085,865	717,581	19,74
Minnesota	3,371,603	22,263	19,99

STATE	WHITE	NEGRO	OTHER
Mississippi	1,257,546	915,743	4,852
Missouri	3,922,967	390,853	5,993
Montana	650,738	1,467	22,562
Nebraska	1,374,764	29,262	7,304
Nevada	263,443	13,484	8,351
New Hampshire	604,334	1,903	684
New Jersey	5,539,003	514,875	12,904
New Mexico	875,763	17,063	58,197
New York	15,287,071	1,417,511	77,722
North Carolina	3,399,285	1,116,021	40,849
North Dakota	619,538	777	12,131
Ohio	8,909,698	786,097	10,602
Oklahoma	2,107,900	153,084	67,300
Oregon	1,732,037	18,133	18,517
Pennsylvania	10,454,004	852,750	12,612
Rhode Island	838,712	18,332	2,444
South Carolina	1,551,022	829,291	2,281
South Dakota	653,098	1,114	26,302
Tennessee	2,977,753	586,876	2,460
Texas	8,374,831	1,187,125	17,721
Utah	873,828	4,148	12,651
Vermont	389,092	519	270
Virginia	3,142,443	816,258	8,248
Washington	2,751,675	48,738	52,801
West Virginia	1,770,133	89,378	910
Wisconsin	3,858,903	74,546	18,328
Wyoming	322,922	2,183	4,961
TOTAL, U. S.	158,831,732	18,871,831	1,619,612

Source: U.S. Bureau of Census

II. School Segregation-Desegregation Status, June 1961

STATE	SCHOOL DISTRICTS TOTAL	BI-RACIAL	DESEG.	ENROLLMENT WHITE	NEGRO	IN DESEGREGATED DISTRICTS WHITE	NEGRO	NEGROES IN SCHOOLS WITH WHITES NO.	%
Alabama	114	14	0	516,135**	271,134**	0	0	0	0
Arkansas	422	228	10	317,053†	105,130†	52,126	12,639	113	.107
Delaware	92	26	24	66,630	14,973	47,932	8,628	6,738	.45
Dist. of Columbia	1	1	1	24,697	96,751	24,697	96,751	81,392	84.1
Florida	67	67	1	807,512	212,280	133,336	27,502	28	.013
Georgia	198	196	0	626,377	295,255	0	0	0	0
Kentucky	211	172	130	593,494**	41,938**	445,000*	32,000*	16,329	38.9
Louisiana	67	67	1	422,181**	271,012**	37,490	51,113	1	.0004
Maryland	24	23	23	461,206	136,882	456,410	136,882	45,943	33.6
Mississippi	151	151	0	287,781**	278,640**	0	0	0	0
Missouri	1,889	214*	200	758,000*	84,000*	—	75,000*	35,000*	41.7
North Carolina	173	173	10	832,200	307,800	117,404	54,746	82	.026
Oklahoma	1,276	240	190	504,125	40,875	266,405	30,725	9,822	24.0
South Carolina	108	108	0	354,227	258,667	0	0	0	0
Tennessee	154	143	7	675,648*	152,352*	130,953	21,881	376	.247
Texas	1,531	720	132	1,840,987*	288,553*	800,000*	85,000*	3,500*	1.21
Virginia	130	128	11	668,500*	211,000*	177,731	52,286	208	.099
West Virginia	55	43	43	416,646	21,010	416,646	21,010	14,000*	66.6
Totals	6,663	2,813	783	10,173,399	3,088,261	3,106,130††	706,163	213,532	6.9

*Estimated.
**1959-60.
†1958-59.
††Missouri not included.

Courtesy of *Southern School News*

II. Expenditure for instruction per pupil in average daily attendance in white and Negro public elementary and secondary schools, United States and selected States, school years 1939-40 and 1953-54.

STATE	1939-40			1953-54		
	WHITE	NEGRO	NEGRO AS PERCENT OF WHITE	WHITE	NEGRO	NEGRO AS PERCENT OF WHITE
United States	$63.66			$177.52		
North Carolina	$34.27	$24.89	72.6	$132.46	$124.85	94.3
Georgia	42.34	15.98	37.7	(1)	(1)	(1)
Florida	51.80	23.09	44.6	175.92	160.61	91.3
Alabama	34.90	12.68	36.3	111.99	105.02	93.8
Mississippi	31.24	6.66	21.3	98.15	43.17	44.0
Arkansas	24.87	12.18	49.0	99.08	71.78	72.4
Louisiana	54.37	16.13	29.7	165.08	122.07	73.9

[1]Not available.

Note: The cost of instruction includes salaries, free text books, teaching supplies, school library books, and other instructional supplies and expenses. United States figures cover the 48 States and the District of Columbia.

Source: U.S. Department of Health, Education, and Welfare, Office of Education. Data for 1953-54 are from *Statistics of State School Systems, Organization, Staff, Pupils, and Finances, 1953-54.* (Biennial Survey of Education in the United States, 1952-54, ch. 2., p. 114, table 48.)

IV. Percent distribution of employed persons by major occupation group, color and sex, April 1940 and April 1960.

MAJOR OCCUPATION GROUP AND SEX	WHITE		NONWHITE	
	1940	1960	1940	1960
Total employed men	100.0	100.0	100.0	100.0
Professional, technical, and kindred workers	5.9	11.3	1.9	4.0
Managers, officials, and proprietors, except farm	10.6	14.6	1.6	2.7
Clerical and kindred workers	7.1	7.3	1.2	5.1
Sales workers	6.7	6.5	.9	1.9

MAJOR OCCUPATION GROUP AND SEX	WHITE		NONWHITE	
	1960	1940	1940	1960
Craftsmen, foremen, and kindred workers	15.5	20.0	4.4	9.0
Operatives and kindred workers	18.8	19.1	12.2	24.4
Laborers, except farm and mine	7.5	6.3	20.5	23.5
Service workers, except private household	5.8	5.7	12.4	14.6
Private household workers	.2	.1	2.9	.2
Farmers and farm managers	14.0	6.3	21.3	5.7
Farm laborers and foremen	6.8	3.0	19.9	8.9
Occupation not reported	1.0	—	.7	—
Total employed women	100.0	100.0	100.0	100.0
Professional, technical, and kindred workers	14.3	14.0	4.3	5.8
Managers, officials, and proprietors, except farm	4.3	5.1	.8	1.8
Clerical and kindred workers	24.6	32.6	1.0	8.9
Sales workers	8.0	8.8	.6	1.5
Craftsmen, foremen, and kindred workers	1.2	1.1	.2	.7
Operative and kindred workers	20.2	15.3	6.6	15.1
Laborers, except farm and mine	.9	.4	.9	.3
Service workers, except private household	11.3	13.8	10.5	22.8
Private household workers	10.8	5.9	58.0	36.9
Farmers and farm managers	1.2	.5	3.2	.7
Farm laborers and foremen	1.2	2.6	12.8	5.4
Occupation not reported	2.0	—	1.1	—

Source: U.S. Department of Commerce, Bureau of the Census, and U.S. Department of Labor, Bureau of Labor Statistics.

V. Median Income of White and Nonwhite Families, 1950-1960

	FAMILIES		
YEAR	WHITE	NONWHITE	NONWHITE AS PERCENT OF WHITE
1960	$5,835	$3,233	55
1959	5,643	2,917	52
1958	5,300	2,711	51
1957	5,166	2,764	54
1956	4,993	2,628	53
1955	4,605	2,549	55
1954	4,339	2,410	56
1953	4,392	2,461	56
1952	4,114	2,338	57
1951	3,859	2,032	53
1950	3,445	1,869	54

Source: Current Population Report, Consumer Income, Series P-60, No. 36 (and prior issues in this series), Bureau of the Census, U.S. Department of Commerce.

VI. The Nonwhite Population of Congressional Districts in Eight Southern States, as of January, 1962

STATE	DIST.	REP.	NONWHITE POP.	TOTAL POP.	NONWHITE AS PERCENT OF TOTAL
ALABAMA	1	Boykin (D)	171,117	441,490	38.6
	2	Grant (D	139,164	386,075	36.0
	3	Andrews (D)	122,311	310,947	39.3
	4	Roberts (D)	100,140	315,817	31.7
	5	Rains (D)	48,299	305,941	15.8
	6	Selden (D)	97,484	251,765	38.7
	7	Elliott (D)	23,491	236,216	9.9
	8	Jones (D)	61,296	383,625	16.0
	9	Huddleston (D)	219,829	634,864	34.6
ARKANSAS	1	Gathings (D)	116,985	360,183	32.5
	2	Mills (D)	21,803	182,314	12.0
	3	Trimble (D)	6,766	299,727	2.3
	4	Harris (D)	88,911	301,286	29.5
	5	Alford (D)	59,507	320,757	18.6
	6	Norrell (D)	96,597	322,005	30.0
GEORGIA	1	Hagan (D)	142,962	379,933	37.6
	2	Pilcher (D)	117,027	301,123	38.9

STATE	DIST.	REP.	NONWHITE POP.	TOTAL POP.	NONWHITE AS PERCENT OF TOTAL
	3	Forrester (D)	157,161	422,198	37.2
	4	Flynt (D)	99,329	323,489	30.7
	5	Davis, J.C. (D)	218,704	823,680	26.6
	6	Vinson (D)	136,481	330,235	41.3
	7	Davis, J.W. (D)	39,593	450,740	8.8
	8	Blitch (D)	79,608	291,185	27.3
	9	Landrum (D)	19,590	272,154	7.2
	10	Stephens (D)	115,438	348,379	33.1
LOUISIANA	1	Hebert (D)	145,470	449,491	32.4
	2	Boggs (D)	154,626	499,561	31.0
	3	Willis (D)	92,688	387,207	23.9
	4	Waggoner (D)	146,414	391,541	37.4
	5	Passman (D)	139,625	345,013	40.5
	6	Morrison (D)	189,982	536,029	35.4
	7	Thompson (D)	99,744	384,330	26.0
	8	McSween (D)	76,758	263,850	29.1
MISSISSIPPI	1	Abernethy (D)	117,663	364,963	32.2
	2	Whitten (D)	118,041	237,887	49.6
	3	Smith (D)	242,739	370,554	65.5
	4	Williams (D)	213,573	460,100	46.4
	5	Winstead (D)	121,540	295,072	41.2
	6	Colmer (D)	107,039	449,565	23.8
N. CAROLINA	1	Bonner (D)	110,996	253,511	43.8
	2	Fountain (D)	158,377	313,728	50.5
	3	Henderson (D)	113,072	382,124	29.6
	4	Cooley (D)	122,868	442,059	27.8
	5	Scott (D)	99,276	408,992	24.3
	6	Kornegay (D)	112,580	487,159	23.1
	7	Lennon (D)	161,992	455,630	35.6
	8	Kitchin (D)	88,703	396,369	22.4
	9	Alexander (D)	45,656	364,561	12.5
	10	Jonas (R)	81,217	452,732	17.9
	11	Whitener (D)	39,884	307,575	13.0
	12	Taylor (D)	22,249	291,715	7.6
S. CAROLINA	1	Rivers (D)	185,449	421,478	44.0
	2	Vacant	198,203	531,555	37.3
	3	Dorn (D)	78,409	318,809	24.6
	4	Ashmore (D)	94,604	444,230	21.3
	5	Hemphill (D)	91,169	272,220	33.5
	6	McMillan (D)	183,738	394,302	46.6

STATE	DIST.	REP.	NONWHITE POP.	TOTAL POP.	NONWHITE AS PERCENT OF TOTAL
VIRGINIA	1	Downing (D)	123,128	422,624	29.1
	2	Hardy (D)	139,644	494,292	28.3
	3	Gary (D)	107,856	418,081	25.8
	4	Abbitt (D)	169,052	352,157	48.0
	5	Tuck (D)	75,736	325,989	23.2
	6	Poff (R)	51,374	378,864	13.6
	7	Harrison (D)	25,772	312,890	8.2
	8	Smith (D)	87,174	357,461	24.4
	9	Jennings (D)	9,868	364,973	2.7
	10	Broyhill (R)	34,902	539,618	6.5

Courtesy of Democratic National Committee

THE FOLLOWING BOOKS and articles will be of particular interest and use to those who wish to do further reading in the areas covered by *The Negro Revolt:*

BOOKS

Allport, Gordon W. *The Nature of Prejudice.* Boston: Beacon, 1954.

Ashmore, Harry S. *The Other Side of Jordan.* New York: Norton, 1960.

Baldwin, James. *Nobody Knows My Name.* New York: Dial, 1961.

—————— *Notes of a Native Son.* Boston: Beacon, 1957.

Barnett, Richard, and Garai, Joseph. *Where the States Stand on Civil Rights.* New York: Sterling, 1962.

Franklin, John Hope. *From Slavery to Freedom.* New York: Knopf, 1956.

—————— *Reconstruction after the Civil War.* Chicago: University Press, 1962.

Frazier, E. Franklin. *Black Bourgeoisie.* Glencoe, Ill.: Free Press, 1959.

Gordon, Albert I. *Jews in Suburbia.* Boston: Beacon, 1959.

Greenberg, Jack. *Race Relations and American Law.* New York: Columbia University, 1959.

Handlin, Oscar. *Race and Nationality in American Life.* Boston: Little, Brown, 1957.

Herskovits, Melville J. *The Myth of the Negro Past.* New York: Harper & Brothers, 1941.

King, Martin Luther, Jr. *Stride Toward Freedom.* New York: Harper & Brothers, 1958.

Lincoln, C. Eric. *The Black Muslims in America.* Boston: Beacon, 1962.

Lomax, Louis E. *The Reluctant African.* New York: Harper & Brothers, 1960.

Myrdal, Gunnar. *An American Dilemma*. New York: Harper & Brothers, 1944.

Reddick, L. D. *Crusader Without Violence*. New York: Harper & Brothers, 1959.

Redding, J. Saunders. *On Being Negro in America*. New York: Bobbs-Merrill, 1951.

Rowan, Carl T. *Go South to Sorrow*. New York: Random House, 1957.

Thorpe, Earl E. *The Mind of the Negro*. Baton Rouge: Ortlieb Press, 1961.

White, Theodore H. *The Making of the President, 1960*. New York: Atheneum, 1961.

PERIODICALS

Abraham, Henry J. "School Desegregation in the South." *Current History*, August, 1961.

Baldwin, James. "The Dangerous Road Before Martin Luther King." *Harper's Magazine*, February, 1961.

Bennett, Lerone, Jr. Series on American Negro History. *Ebony*, July, September and November, 1961, and January, 1962.

Davidson, William. "Our Negro Aristocracy." *The Saturday Evening Post*, January 13, 1962.

DeVree, Charlotte. "The Young Negro Rebels." *Harper's Magazine*, October, 1961.

Dunbar, Ernest. "The Negro in America Today." *Look*, April 10, 1962.

Hentoff, Nat. "Race Prejudice in Jazz." *Harper's Magazine*, June, 1959.

Lomax, Louis E. "The Negro Revolt Against 'The Negro Leaders.'" *Harper's Magazine*, June, 1960.

———— "White and Black Views of the African." *The New Leader*, May 22, 1961.

———— "The Unpredictable Negro." *The New Leader*, June 5, 1961.

———— "Prelude to a New Africa Policy." *The New Republic*, September 4, 1961.

"One Tenth of a Nation." *The Reporter;* special section, March 31, 1960.

Rostow, Eugene. "The Freedom Riders of the Future." *The Reporter*, June 22, 1961.

Silberman, Charles E. "The City and the Negro." *Fortune*, March, 1962.